I'll *See* It WHEN
I *Believe* It

a path to ascension

Mary Beth Smith

I'll See It When I Believe It

Cover design by Mary Beth Smith.
Cover background and gears clipart: istockphoto.com; female silhouette icon: istockphoto.com, credit: Olena Kaidash.

MINDSTIR MEDIA

Published by MindStir Media, LLC
45 Lafayette Rd | Suite 181 | North Hampton, NH 03862 | USA
1.800.767.0531 | www.mindstirmedia.com
Printed in the United States of America.
ISBN-13: 978-1-962987-49-3

This book is dedicated to the three people who assisted me as Spirit and I created this beautiful book:

Marsh, you NEVER stop loving and encouraging me, no matter what.

Christine, my beautiful, kind, compassionate, intelligent sister who has taught me how much change a willing heart can create. BRING IT ON!

Kathleen, I am so proud of your willingness to learn and grow to become the incredibly wise woman that you are today. Your friendship means so much to me.

I humbly thank you all. This has been a true group effort. Most importantly—thank you, Spirit. Without you, none of this would exist.

Contents

Know this,

LOVE is an option

KINDNESS is an option

PEACE is an option

Choosing a different way of BEING

is an option

You will see it

WHEN you believe it

—God, Source, All That Is—

Are You Ready to Believe It?

So much of our spiritual journey shows up when we are finally ready to experience something new. Until that time nothing really changes. Once we open up our mind to something new and our heart to something new... something new shows up. *You'll see it when you believe it.* Many of us are soooooo asleep that we don't want to wake up to a new way of "being." What I mean when I say that we are asleep is... we are sleepwalking through our lives. We are not living our lives on purpose and with purpose. Because of this, the way we MAY need to be woken up is through hardship or pain. As long as everything is going fine and dandy, why would you want to change? We don't realize that it is only through change that our lives become so much more magical and sacred. This is why so much shake-up is happening on the planet. Spirit needs to gain our attention and they are excelling at it. Once they have our attention, we have an opportunity to wake up, shift and change to a new version of ourselves.

When we are willing to wake up or change in a kinder, softer way... then that will be our experience. *We will see it when we believe it.* For now—until that time, most are needing the trauma and drama in order to be willing to change. I speak from experience that when we experience the depth of despair, we are *finally* willing to look for something new or even be willing to try something new. When you feel or believe you have "lost everything," you are more willing to reprioritize your life. Notice if it is only then that you are willing to look at things differently and realize that—it may FEEL like you've lost everything, so that you come to realize that you have everything that you need within you right here, right now. I am not trying to make light of the devastation going on around us and in our own lives. I am assisting you in having a greater understanding of all that is unfolding. If you are not willing to let go of the old way of being, sometimes the old way of being will be let go of FOR YOU.

I have been told repeatedly by my team of Angels and Guides that what we believe, is what will show up for us. Now this needs to be what you believe with every fiber of your being. *I'll see it when I believe it.* If I believe that incredible things only happen to rich people, I will notice the proof of that showing up all around me as my bank account keeps dwindling. If I believe that lying, cheating, and corruption are the only ways to get ahead in the world, I will witness more and more people getting away with this type of behavior, or I will begin living my life in that way. Just look at how many people out there think that it is perfectly normal and acceptable to do dishonest things and that others aren't going to stop them. This is because so many people respect and even worship someone who does the least amount of work and gets the most amount of pay. Because of this and many other reasons, we are noticing that many are not showing up for work because we are bombarded with stories of all you need is an idea and then you can sit back and do nothing for the rest of your life. I ask you, how is this making our world a better place because you are here?

At first, this fascinated me, and then I saw how quickly this was turning into a wildfire. Parents are paying for everything and handling everything so that their children can have an easier life. Why would these kids ever want to be responsible and move out on their own if Mom and Dad will be responsible for every aspect of their lives? If we are encouraging our children to be less responsible... then that is what they can then become. *We'll see it when we believe it.*

I know I can throw out a lot of examples to support all the negativity showing up in the world, but I don't choose to stay there. Hopefully, you are noticing your mind going to so many young people who are making a difference in the world and being very responsible, maybe even your own children. See what I mean—*what you believe is what you will see.* If you believe the world is going to hell, then that will be your experience. This will even show up on your devices all day long supporting your own beliefs. If you believe that things are changing for the better, then that is what will be showing up on your devices AND in your life.

What narrative is showing up for you? Listen to the thoughts playing in your head. What are your thoughts saying? If you don't like what they are saying, only you can change them to what it is that you are ready to create. This is called thinking consciously. This is an aspect of living consciously. This is you consciously choosing a different way. We don't realize how stuck we are until something or someone shows up in our lives and shows us a different way of being. Is it a positive way of being, or a not-very-positive way of being? When you take the time to listen to your thoughts, you'll have a greater understanding of what you BELIEVE the most... what you FEEL the most.

How we break these narratives and beliefs can come in many different forms. You could be blessed with an Earth (GAIA) Angel such as myself showing up and planting seeds that will introduce another way of being. You could experience loss or devastation that stops your world long enough and shakes you up enough to get you out of your head and move you into your heart. You could witness or experience love and kindness and that could open up your mind and then your heart to assist you in becoming someone different… someone new.

Here being different is good. In fact, being different is very good. My whole life I had felt like an alien on this planet. The way people treated each other made no sense to me. The choices people made seemed crazy to me. Our priorities seemed so messed up. What Spirit taught me was that I was ahead of my time. The world was not ready for me yet. And then it was. I learned that there were so very many of us who felt like aliens— outcasts—when the truth was that the world simply wasn't ready for us yet. Suddenly, all that confusion and the difficulties I had experienced earlier in my life were worth it.

Now that we are waking up on the planet (not wanting to sleep through our moments anymore), people are looking for those of us who have spent our lifetime planting seeds, learning, and growing so that when humankind was ready, we would be available to assist. NOW is that time. Humankind is ready for a different way of existing—thriving. I truly believe that each and every one of us is here to be a teacher in some way—on some level. Our planet is a wonderful place to learn so much from, especially during this great shift that we are going through at this time.

We are shifting our consciousness, shifting our frequency or vibration, shifting what we believe; only then can we experience the shift of the ages. All that has come before, has happened to bring us to this moment. This is no small thing that is happening here as we move from the old Earth to our new Earth called Gaia.

I will continually ask you questions because a question opens a conversation, and we have so much to converse about. Please take in slowly the information I give you. Allow the light of these words to wash over you and become part of who you are. This cannot happen when you rush. We are human beings, not human doings. Be patient with yourself as you take in all of the information you are going to be given. Allow yourself to notice what resonates with you. Are you willing to allow it to change your life? Change who you believe yourself to be?

Are you ready to think a different way—believe a different way—"be" a different way? Then you are exactly where you need to be. We need each and every one of you to assist in this shift of the ages. It is vital that you have tolerance, for we are all going through this and we are all doing it in different ways. Allow others their own journey as others have allowed you to experience your own journey. We are ALL DIFFERENT. We are supposed to be different. Know that YOUR PIECE OF OUR ASCENSION IS IMPORTANT. MY PIECE OF THE ASCENSION IS IMPORTANT. Only when all of the pieces come together can we be whole. Only then will we be complete—whole—Holy!

You will see it—Be it—Experience it—when you believe it.

Be the Example

Know that when your frequency is consistently at a higher vibration, what your existence is… is indescribable. Yet, I will try to describe some aspects so you will notice and have a better understanding of what the heaven is going on here. Know and notice with this book, as has been the truth in my last two books, my sentence structure is a bit strange. My choice of words can feel off; this is because Spirit is asking you to hesitate and take these words in slowly. I would also like to mention that some chapters are more formal, while others are very fun and carefree. This is because the Guide or Spirit that is relaying the information to me for that chapter is a bit more formal, so their wording will be a bit more succinct and precise, while with the next chapter the Guide or Spirit coming through could be quite fun and carefree in frequency so their wording can be more joyful and simplistic. This all continually shifts depending on who showed up to share that chapter with me. Enjoy the journey my guides take you on, no matter who shows up and relays the information to you.

All is to assist you in taking in each concept you are being given. Savor how it feels. Allow your beliefs to change. Allow new possibilities in. Take it all in as deeply as possible, for this is a life-changing-forever book. Spirit would like to encourage you to take the time between each chapter (and if need be, during the chapter) to pause and allow all that you have just learned to not only sink in but to take root. Take the time to think about this truth in your own life. Again, this will help you to go further. The more time you spend integrating the information, the more your life will shift. Trust me—shifting is a good thing.

The words in this book are given to me (channeled through me) from Spirit in light code. These light codes will awaken aspects of you that have been asleep during this lifetime, but NO MORE. Your awakening is at hand. You may still experience "naps" at times, as in you may revert back to your old human way of existence for a short time. However, know that the uncomfortable way that this may make you feel will assist in waking you up from your nap until no naps are necessary.

The way that I have experienced the light code aspect of my books is that the book evolves as you evolve. What I mean by that is, as you live your life in a higher way, you have greater understandings of all that is unfolding in your life. So, depending on where you are in your ascension will depend on what you will hear and understand from a chapter. If you were to read this book again, the lessons and understandings would take you even further. This is because the light that you are, is getting brighter and stronger with every word that you are willing to allow to expand who you are and what you believe. How incredible is that?

Notice how your distractions will feel exactly like that—a distraction from what you came here to do, a distraction from who you came here to be. As you take notice of this and make the decision that YOUR ASCENSION IS YOUR PRIORITY, distractions will be less distracting. You will feel an energy within you that feels so POWERFUL, centered, and connected to truth, and that will be what you will choose to spend your time connecting to. This is your HIGHER SELF/SOUL. This is who you are on the other side, in the Heavenly Realm. This IS your Source connection.

The way you think will evolve and shift to much higher thoughts. The words that you speak will be filled with truth, compassion, and knowing. Your actions are those of an ascended being—how may I serve you? Your devotion is to assist the planet and all who reside on her, by existing in the highest way possible. Everything, everything, EVERYTHING is in alignment with the ascension of all.

I also want to take the time to thank the individuals (those people who stay stuck in negativity, doubt, and confusion) who play their part in duality and density so magnificently. These individuals will be the catalysts to assist many in waking up to no longer exist in such lower choices because of their example. Choices such as hate, righteousness, condemnation, and fear are the old ways of being. These old ways kept us stuck in fear, doubt, and lack, only to then be perpetuated out to the masses. All of that no longer exists in the lives of those who have CHOSEN a higher way of "being." This starts by feeling uncomfortable and eventually evolves to allowing the negativity to just fall away. This will be your new reality after much work and processing.

This does not mean that we do not see the lower-density existence playing out there on the world stage. We see what we see, however, it is no longer OUR experience of the world. We understand that all must walk through their lower density choices, until they no longer choose that. *They will see it when they believe it.* They are following in our old footsteps. For we too had to walk through our lower density choices before we chose a different way of existing—thriving. Why would we condemn another for what we went through ourselves?

All will go through their stages of evolution more quickly when they see our example of how to live differently, kindly, lovingly. Being different is a fantastic thing! Please allow yourself to feel such compassion for each and every one who is on their path of becoming more. More light, more love, more connectedness, more hope, more compassion. Be the answer to their questions. Be the example of love in all you think, speak, do, and ARE. This shift will happen through flow, NOT through force. *You will see it, when you believe it.*

How May I Serve You?

So much of what we are writing about in this book, I have touched on in my other books. Now that you have evolved even more, your understanding needs to evolve too. When our frequency reaches a certain level, a new gift, or you could even call it a "talent," shows up. For you are very talented. Depending on the way that Spirit communicates with you, depends on how this gift will show up.

Those of you who hear Spirit, you will most likely be told by getting a download. Those who get a feeling from Spirit will notice a distinct sensation. Those who see things will notice a frequency coming off what they need to notice, or they will see a picture of it in their mind. I am blessed with all three of these gifts, and I am so grateful. This gift or talent is used to assist us in noticing how we can be of service. What I noticed when this gift first arrived was a pause. The pause is BEYOND IMPORTANT! When you notice a pause, it is because Spirit or your Higher Self is trying to get your attention. *Stay with your pauses* until you understand what you are supposed to notice or learn from them. It could be the words someone is saying to you (they carry important information). It could be that you need to notice someone and acknowledge them (from there a dialog will happen that will shift one or both of you). It could be that you need to change what you are about to say (negative ways of speaking are no longer acceptable).

The pause is such a VITAL gift given to us. It changes the trajectory of an experience. When we notice a pause and we participate in whatever we are asked by Spirit to participate in, we move into an understanding that you and Spirit are one. You could say that Spirit becomes our consciousness. Every interaction can have multiple pauses in them. Each time we pause and allow an exchange to level up, WE level up. Yep, it's that HUGE.

From this space—from this way of living—you and Spirit become one. Their thoughts and wishes become your thoughts and wishes. Their knowing becomes your knowing. Their hopes and dreams become your hopes and dreams. This is a game-changer. Pause, pause, PAUSE. Notice and acknowledge the pause and it will escalate so quickly. Know that when this happens, there is no separation! I will go into greater depth about this in another chapter.

Time to get back on track with the gift of noticing how we can be of service. This is vital—essential—and oh so very important! When we have evolved enough on our path of ascension, all we want is to be of service. This is because we are understanding on a deeper level than ever before, that the person you are interacting with, their happiness is the whole planet's happiness. Their pain is the whole planet's pain. And so, you want to assist in another's happiness. You want to assist in alleviating another's pain. You want to assist in everything.

Here is where the beginning of the chapter comes in. You will be guided by Spirit or your Higher Self as to what is yours to assist with. If you hear Spirit, they will tell you something like, the person in the purple shirt could use some of your wisdom, or whatever it is you are told. You don't need to know what wisdom you need to share. In that moment you and Spirit are one. You will say exactly what that person needs to hear. You will be guided in ways far beyond your old understanding of being guided. You will be showing up as a higher version of yourself and you will make a difference and that person's life will shift when you do. Oh, I wish you could see how incredible this leveling up is.

I call it leveling up, but first, you have to show up. You have to be WILLING. I mean totally surrendering what that person might think of you. Totally surrendering the doubt that you have anything of value to say. Surrendering the times in the past when you weren't enough. All of that is gone. All of that is in the past. You have learned so much from your past. Now it's time to bring the knowledge you learned from those lessons and allow them to assist in creating this all-knowing and trusting moment, where Spirit asks you to step up and assist.

None of us are ready until we allow ourselves to be ready. None of us are willing until we realize that both you and the other person have absolutely nothing to lose, and everything to gain. Then your willingness steps up and says, I AM READY TO BE MORE. I am ready, willing, and able to step up and BE who I came here to BE! Why would we ever choose to be less, once we accept and understand what it means to be more? *You will see it when you believe it.*

I'm standing right beside you doing my happy dance when you realize what just happened. Take in the enormity of this moment. The *needs* of another are more important than the desire to be seen as "normal." The *needs* of the Planet and all who reside on her are now your needs. You realize that YOU MADE A DIFFERENCE—YOU TRULY *MAKE* A DIFFERENCE. YOU are the difference so many have been waiting for.

Are you WILLING to continue stepping up when you are needed? Are you willing to be the answer rather than the problem? Then sign up here _____! You matter. Your willingness matters. We all matter!

I would like to take a moment to help all of you to better understand that those of us who hear Spirit don't usually hear actual words and voices. Instead, we are given what they want us to know, almost like a download. We just know. And this knowing can feel all encompassing. There isn't usually an actual *voice*, just an absolute knowing. We know, what we know, that we know. If the person channeling is still full of spiritual ego, the message can be distorted somewhat, but that will shift as they move into more oneness and understanding that everyone matters, not just themselves. This is why channelers only hesitate a moment and yet we can relay so much information. We receive a download and then relay what we are given.

For those of you who connect to Spirit by "feeling" something, I want to address that now, before we close this chapter. You will feel a wave of energy come off of a person or object. This wave can even pull you in. Allow it—encourage it to pull you in. Once you are close enough, the words and actions will be wonderfully guided. You are guided.

Those of you who "see things" can notice a wavy energy like a heat wave; I personally asked to have the wavy energy turn into light so that I don't miss any of the magical interactions that are available to me. Sometimes a specific part of a person, place, or thing lights up. That guides me in knowing specifically what I am supposed to talk about when I approach this person. From there the wisdom and the words will be given to me.

These interactions that I am guided to are MINE. *My frequency* works well with *this person*, or maybe it's just the exact moment when this person is ready to open up to something different… something better. I'm not here to convert, I AM here to be supportive. I AM here to be the light. I AM here to be more. I AM here to serve.

I understand that we use a lot of duality words in this book—words like better or worse, good or bad, more or less. Duality is not part of our ascension, however, it is necessary to use such words when we need to get our point across such as in this book. So, understand that our duality words are not meant to create separation, but rather to create understanding. We thank you for your patience in this area.

You may also notice that a subject can be repeated in multiple chapters, however it is presented in a different way. This is because the subject matter is important for us to understand, and also different people will resonate with different approaches or ways of looking at something. For instance, one of the subjects I speak of repeatedly is being kind. If you notice that it bothers you that my "team" is talking about kindness again, you may want to look at why kindness seems to push your buttons. Notice that when you have a reaction to something, it is yours. That means that there is something about this subject that you may want to take the time to look at and resolve.

What are you noticing is yours, and what are you going to do about it?

My Stories

I am being asked by Spirit to give you a couple of stories of how I am able to notice when someone is lit up so that I may be of service to them and how this has unfolded for me. I have thousands of these stories, here are two of them.

My sister was visiting, and we were walking around a lake when, up ahead, I saw a young man in his late teens—early twenties. His smile was lit so bright, I mean I almost needed sunglasses to look at him. As he approached, I said, "I just wanted you to know how much I love your smile. Your smile radiates such joy that I feel happy just being in your presence. Thank you so much for sharing your smile with me." He was so startled at my words. You could tell that my words really affected him. He thanked me and walked on.

After a couple of minutes, we hear steps running up from behind us. I figured it was probably a jogger. It wasn't. It was this young man coming up to thank me for what I had said to him. In that moment I saw what other humans saw. This exceptional young man had very large protruding teeth. They are so large that he can't close his mouth enough to fully cover his teeth. Because of this, he has difficulty speaking in the way that most of us speak. He was smiling with every particle of his being as he thanked me again for what I had said to him. He seemed to want reassurance that I wasn't joking or teasing, but really meant what I had said. Once he was reassured, he asked if he could hug me. I said, "Of course." I sent so much healing love into that hug. Through that hug, I assisted in releasing some of the pain that had been inflicted on this sacred soul being held in my arms.

My beautiful sacred sister asked if she could have a hug too. He was very willing. Then my shy, quiet husband put out his arms and was given a special hug also. This young man told us where he worked and we went there often to see him and give him a hug. We let all his co-workers know how lucky they were to work with him. We touched a life so profoundly that day. I would like you to realize that if I hadn't been *WILLING* to step up and do what Spirit asked of me, so much would have been lost. To me that is unacceptable.

As a side note, all three of us were pretty quiet after this encounter. We were trying to take in as deeply as possible what had just happened. What I was shown and understood was that when I first saw this kid, I saw absolutely no defects. His smile was perfect and radiant. I was shown that in that moment I was seeing him through God's eyes. God sees his perfection and nothing else. See what I mean about you and Spirit being one? Another thing I noticed from this experience was that this special young man was a reminder that we can smile through anything.

During my sister's trip, we needed to go to the mall to get her phone fixed. Spirit is *very good* at creating situations (Christine's phone not working) so that we will show up where we are needed. While there, I saw a woman in the most beautiful white blouse I had ever seen. I had to say something—especially because her blouse was lit up. I approached and said, "Excuse me, I wanted to apologize for staring at you, but you are just so stunning. You have the most beautiful face and your blouse is amazing. You are the full package because I can see that you are beautiful inside, also." She thanked me and said that was really nice of me to say that. Christine and I walked away and found the phone store.

When we came out of the store, there was the beautiful woman I had complimented looking for me almost frantically. She wanted me to know how much my words had touched her. Today was her birthday. It was her first birthday since losing her mom. She was really feeling sorry for herself when I first approached her. However, because of the words I had given her, she said it felt like her mom was there with her for a moment. She asked if she could have a hug. I gave her "her mom's" birthday hug. I felt her mom's presence, and I knew that this moment was more important to this young woman than I could possibly comprehend.

As you can tell by my stories, when we are willing to allow Spirit to work through us, we are able to touch lives beyond human understanding. We truly understand the difference we can make when we are willing to step up and show up. We see the difference our life and our choices make. *You will see it when you believe it.* Are you ready to make a difference? I have made that choice already and it has made all the difference.

A Driven Life

Have you ever driven down a street and suddenly noticed there are no cars around you? If there are cars, they could be several blocks away or only coming from the side streets. Noticing this when it happens to you is important. Another example is when my lane is completely empty as far as I can see, while the lane next to me is bumper to bumper, along with the traffic going in the opposite direction. In that moment my hubby and I laugh. We can't help but laugh because we understand that this is a definite message from Spirit.

I am shown by Spirit that even though chaos is all around me, my way is clear. Clear of doubt, clear of lack, clear of opposition. Spirit is saying, "Move forward in your life filled with total trust and guidance, Mary Beth, because Spirit has cleared the way for you." Here I am given physical proof and it brings such joy and laughter to my heart. I have cleared away the fear and doubt for so long now and it's clear sailing on my path because of all that I have done leading up to this moment. Hallelujah! That does not mean that now I get to sit back and relax, living a life of ease and flow and doing nothing. While yes, my life is filled with ease and flow, it is also filled with being of service in whatever way Spirit asks me to show up.

Thirty minutes after my husband sent off book #2, *With a Promise of Ascension,* to the publisher, Spirit showed up asking if I was ready to start this book. I was shocked and then I remembered who I was working with and I was less shocked. Once I realized that it was time to step up again, I said, "What would you like me to do? How can I be of assistance!" First, I was thanked for a job well done on the book we had just completed together. I was asked to open myself up to a different energy with this next book. My hubby had gotten the title of this book two weeks earlier, so I knew it was coming. I just thought I would get more than thirty minutes before we started this next adventure. I spent the night sinking into what this new energy was going to feel like, and boy was it ever different.

I understood that we were going to hit the ground running. This book was going to come in quickly because the need for it is so great. This book is about once we are committed to our ascension—what that will do to our lives and what it could show up as. Ok, let's do it! When I received the first chapter I said, wow, this is going to be powerful, and here we are.

These are just a few examples of what having a guided life can look like and feel like when you trust. Spirit puts so many people on my path for me to assist and each interaction assists me also. Afterward, I have a deeper understanding and clarity—I have a stronger knowing of who Spirit wants me to show up as. I'll give you the answer rather than leave you guessing. They want me to show up as the one and only authentic Mary Beth. I get to be 100 percent me, 100 percent of the time. Of course, that means Spirit will be part of every moment. Spirit and I are flowing together within every aspect of my life and it's all perfect. I have confirmation of this by seeing that my lane is wide open on the road while others can be experiencing bumper-to-bumper chaos.

Now, when we see hardly a single car around us in the middle of the day in a city of 200,000 people… well, this is when I understand that my frequency is so elevated that I can neither see nor experience the lower-density existence in this moment. Yep, it all really does fall away. In that moment all I experience is higher vibrational beings. *You will see it when you believe it.*

I am so very grateful that more and more of you are joining me in this journey called ascension. Buckle yourself in for the ride of a lifetime, only to unbuckle later as you soar and fly beyond all restraints. This is the moment your Soul has been waiting for. No need to stay in the old navigational lines. Here we get to explore the life that we came here to live. A life filled with Wheeeee!

When you take the time to notice something like traffic disappearing, and you are grateful for it, more expansive experiences like this are part of your life. New realities pop up out of someplace special and you get to be the recipient of these very special gifts. Realities shifting can be so confusing at first, but oh so fun. Yippie!

It's Just a Matter of Time

Time manipulation and time shifting are real things. I slow down time all of the time. It started with my needing to be somewhere by a certain time and I was running late. I asked time to slow down, and it worked. I decided I wanted to take this further, so later I learned to be present with "time," and I begin to almost feel its heartbeat… its rhythm suspended as it moved into slow motion. It feels like there are extra beats between each tick of a clock. As I am being present with it in this moment, it almost feels like "time" is sleepy. It does a tick and then it stretches and yawns. Then another tick and I see "time" reaching for a blankie, and then another tick. Now it is snuggling in and there is another tick.

I love my different perspective on things. Telling you the story about time feeling sleepy gives you such a distinct picture and a greater understanding of what time slowing down can feel like and be experienced as. So often we are told things like… you can slow down time. And then the person saying that just deserts you. They are on to something else. It is my hope that I will go into greater detail so that your understanding will be more complete. This is to empower you to move forward in living a more expansive life.

Another reason I have learned to slow down time is if I am having a wonderful dinner with my daughter, or whatever the experience might be. I want to savor every moment, every word, every giggle. So, even though this started from a place of being late, it evolved into wanting my time with another to slow down because I am in my connected joy. I'm going to go see my sister in a couple of months and I am going to definitely use this technique a lot! So, slow down time to assist you in staying in your loving connection to another, any TIME you want.

How I am able to slow down time is I focus on how much I trust (believe) that this is an ability that I possess. I let go of all counterproductive chatter like—oh crap I'm going to be late, or I'll never make it in time. I don't focus on the clock. I focus on how much fun this is. Wheee, here we go changing our reality again. I notice amazingness and magic all around me and then it appears. Ask and you shall receive. Trust and it becomes your truth. Let go of all doubt and fear and just play with every bit of this. What have you got to lose? *You'll see it when you believe it.*

Let us shift to speeding up time. Yes, that is a possibility also. You may ask why would I want to speed time up? Well, there are tasks in your life that need to be done and they may not be what you enjoy doing. In those situations, you can speed up time. You do this by asking Spirit to assist you in allowing time to shift to a space where it moves swiftly and effortlessly—and then allow that to unfold for you. Later as you evolve in raising your frequency, you will find you choose to savor even the things you don't enjoy. This is because every moment is a gift. Every opportunity and even every obstacle is a gift.

Savoring our moments gives us an opportunity to take something that we can perceive as a burden and experience the blessings in it. For instance, getting my teeth cleaned at the dentist. Rather than speeding up time, I pause and notice the skill that my hygienist has. I notice how her training has really paid off. She is so gentle and patient. I notice all the effort she put into her career to bring her to this moment, and I am grateful. So, yes, we can speed up time, but eventually, you won't want to. Let's enjoy our journey. ALL of it!

It's time to move on to time shifting or morphing. Have you ever had lapses in time? You pause and say how did I get here? You remember starting the journey and then it is done. What happened to the middle? I don't know. I wish I knew, but I don't. I simply know that it is a thing because I have experienced it many times. I also have experienced being taken to the other side of the veils a lot and I come back with a very foggy brain. Why Spirit still believes I need to have the memory of what happened there, and what was said, to be only a faint memory, I don't understand… yet. Ok, now I do have a bit of an understanding, they just said that they need to keep me pure for the writing of these books. For now, I am to be in this place of not knowing so that I can walk you through this journey. OK, let's go for a walkabout.

There have been times when I start a conversation with a person and the next thing I know, they are saying goodbye. I ask Spirit what just happened. They inform me that what was said was not meant for me, only for the person who was given the words. I am totally ok with being the vessel that delivers a message that someone needs to hear. It just feels strange losing that block of time… and yet it wasn't lost at all.

Going into still point is incredible too. This is when the information or words that we are given goes so deep that it feels like we fell asleep. What the experience actually is, is that we are connecting to a very deep place within. One where our lower conscious self may not be ready to go, or understand, so our subconscious self steps in. Also, know that still point can happen in a very, very deep meditation. What happens is we are taken to our subconscious state… we are experiencing a soul connection that I would describe as receiving exceptional knowledge or even a major upgrade. We are able to take in this knowledge or upgrade, and it alters who we are and what we believe. Our human may have difficulty going this deep, but our Soul/Higher Self does not have such limitations. There are times you can go to a space where all is black, while other times it is filled with magnificent light, and you know that in this space you have access to all that is (also known as the Akashic records). It is the most incredible experience. There's no agenda at all here, just peace and knowing. Enjoy going into still point as often as you can, to assist yourself in quantum jumping your experience.

There have been many times that I have witnessed my husband's memory being wiped, only to later (when he is ready), have him experience small bits and pieces of the memory return to him. One example is thirty years ago when I wanted to understand why everyone was talking about Jesus, Jesus, Jesus and no one was even mentioning God. Some will say that this is because Jesus and God are one and the same. I agree that this is true, but it's also not true. I was so confused until Jesus showed up and tapped me on the shoulder in a parking lot. I had a wonderful life-realization conversation with Jesus in that parking lot (details of this story are in my first book *The Lie That I Am, A Journey Back to Spirit.*) No one could see Jesus. It just looked like I was talking to myself. My husband had no memory of any of this occurring (even though he was standing right next to me during this whole experience) until he stopped resisting that it could even happen. Then both clarity and bits of the memory were returned to him.

Another time in 1986–87, I received an activation on top of Diamond Head in Hawaii. No one there either saw or remembered what happened to me. It was not necessary to their story, only mine. I am told that I committed myself on Diamond Head to assisting in the shift of the ages. I began having greater clarity after that, though I knew not what it all meant, or what it was for… until I did. Again, my hubby had no memory of this occurring. This is why I would like all of you to be more patient with yourselves. There is much confusion as the human aspect of us gets used to a concept or idea and then the clarity will come in. The more you try to force anything, the longer it will evade you. When you let Spirit know that you desire to have miracles and synchronicities show up in your life, then they will show up. From there you will create flow, grace, and ease. Allow, allow, allow.

Allow your understanding of time and reality to shift, morph, and change. Play with all of this. Allow it to be part of your understanding of the universe and then watch for it to shift in such surprising ways. Ask Spirit and your Higher Self to show you new possibilities and then hang on for the ride of your life. Willingness is the key to ALL unfolding in new ways in your life. Are you ready? Are you willing? Go for it! *You will see it, when you believe it.*

Broaden Your Perspective

Broadening your perspective is another HUGE aspect of your ascension. The way that this started for me is that I was in conflict with another person. They were not even willing to hear what I had to say. I could feel myself becoming more and more frustrated. If they would just stop long enough for me to bring in the clarity, all would be well. But they weren't letting me, and I began to notice how frustrated and disconnected I was feeling. I noticed how I was in a space of force, not flow. How did all of this get so carried away? How could I have allowed this to happen?

Suddenly, I was floating above the conflict. I was shown that this is similar to the way God (Source) observes us beautifully confused and lost souls. We are observed from above with ABSOLUTELY NO ATTACHMENT to the outcome, for Source cares more about whether we are learning something new from the experience, rather than that we say and do everything perfectly in every moment. The attachment to an outcome is a human thing, not a spiritual thing. Spirit truly does allow us to be exactly who we are and do what we choose to do (this is our free will in action). As our frequency elevates and we ask and work on becoming a higher version of ourselves, that is when they step in and guide us.

At first, this will make absolutely no sense at all to us. And then it will. So, allow the seed to be planted so that when you have evolved and raised your frequency enough, the clarity can come in quickly and effortlessly. You WILL be able to stand back from a conflict or anything else that could cause fear, doubt, anxiety, pain, or even lack. You WILL be able to see so many layers of understanding once you no longer *need to be right*. There is suddenly an understanding of where another (the one you are experiencing conflict with) is coming from. It feels like a download given to you so you can understand—for instance, if they don't win this argument, all that they believe will unravel. Then who will they be?

Yes, these are the types of things that people are experiencing right now on the planet. They feel that all they are and all that they believe is under attack. The opposition wants to take everything away from them. Holy moly! No wonder why people aren't talking to one another. No wonder why people aren't listening to one another. To me, it looks like people are plugging their ears while yelling "La-la-la-la-la-la-la. I'm not listening, I'm not listening, you can't make me listen."

These people who have yet to awaken feel threatened. Their way of life is being threatened. That cannot be easy on them. However, this is about you. We can't change others; we can only change ourselves. So, stay in your space of observation, where you observe what is happening, yet you have no attachment to the outcome. Have compassion for all that these confused souls are going through, and yet know that their experience is their own experience. It is NOT yours. It can only become yours if you decide to take it on. If it's not yours, why would you take their issues on?

It doesn't assist them and it certainly doesn't serve you. Remember you are here to be of service. *You will see it when you believe it.*

As we observe an interaction from above and from a place of observation or broadened perspective, a very strange thing happens. We are so detached from needing the outcome to be a certain way, that if we look closely, we will notice that the participants don't even have faces. That is how detached we can be. Suddenly there is an understanding that this IS NOT PERSONAL. Some may say, "I don't want to be detached. I want to be fully engaged." Be careful what you ask for. Do you really want to be fully engaged in hate, fear, or conflict? As Spiritual beings, that answer would be NO. Hate, fear, and conflict can no longer be part of our existence. The only way we can exist in these frequencies is by observing them, but no longer can we participate in them. I hope that all of this will eventually make sense to you.

Now with almost every aspect of every conversation, I can take the experience to a place of a broadened perspective (observation) where I have so many insights and a broadened way of looking at ALL sides. I see possibilities where the lower-density human can see none. This is NOT a competition, it is simply an observation. We observe everything from this perspective. Some call this divine neutrality because we are coming from our divinity and we are neutral. Use the words that you connect with most: broadened perspective, observation, divine neutrality—the name matters not—the experience DOES!

An example I can give is our recent COVID experience. While many were going to a place of doubt and fear, I was given my broadened perspective. From there I could see the need to stop the insanity out there for a while so that we would go inside our hearts and minds so we could re-prioritize our lives. COVID affected 99 percent of the world's population. The devastation many experienced did not go unnoticed by Spirit. However, something needed to happen to get our attention to help shift us. I saw so much good that came from all of this. If you can only see the bad, you may want to take the time to look at that.

Are you willing to let go of the need to be right long enough to allow the way you look at things to change? Are you willing to look at things without judgment? Are you noticing your frequency dropping when you do go into judgment? That's fantastic. Celebrate that. Stop berating and getting frustrated when you make a boo-boo. See, even my words can't go to a place of harshness. It's now time to celebrate because we noticed the frequency shift. This shows us that something is no longer comfortable for us. It is no longer who we are, or who we want to be.

Learning what we don't want can be just as important or life-changing as learning what we do want. Allowing yourself or permitting yourself to see the bigger picture of "why, why, why," can change our thoughts, our beliefs, and our truths. Who wouldn't want to come from Spiritual truth rather than human truth? All it takes is allowing yourself to look at ALL from a broadened perspective. *You will see it when you believe it.*

A Pause is Everything

A Pause is an intervention from Spirit. Once you begin to notice these pauses, then you will see how guided your life truly is. Know that you have been experiencing pauses your entire life, you simply were not aware of their significance… until the moment that you "take notice" of them. For when you pause as you are about to say something and you take notice of what those words were, Spirit will provide you with a different set of words that you *can* choose instead. After you say these new words, you will eventually be given the broadened perspective of where your conversation was going to go verses where it ended up going. When this happens, you have a greater understanding of how the trajectory of the conversation was changed so that it would carry a higher vibration. What a sacred gift you have just been given.

The pause can also happen as you are about to do something. This can show up in several different ways, for instance, I can't move. As in, my feet are stuck where they are, letting me know that whatever I was about to do was not for the highest good of all, or that I was possibly going to be in danger. Another way the pause can show up to keep me from doing something is that I will slightly twist my ankle, which causes me to hesitate. Again, I notice what I was about to do and I make a different choice, and my ankle is fine. What about forgetting something and you have to turn around to get it? Notice who you ended up encountering because of this delay—or what you avoided because of the delay. Did you notice an accident or perhaps someone getting a ticket? Or, how about you dropping something—yep, that can create a pause also. Your car won't start, a door won't unlock, your phone rings as you're about to leave. All of these things and so many more assist in causing you to pause. Can you see how mundane this can be and yet very significant? Pause the way you would "normally" react to a situation and allow yourself to be a much higher version of who you are—who you are becoming.

As you train yourself to notice the pauses and then you train yourself to look at WHY a pause occurred—WOW. You now get to have the honor of Spirit intervening when you are about to do something that was not of the highest good for all concerned. You having a guided life has just been upgraded to you behaving more like Spirit would behave. You are behaving as an Ascended Being when you live in this way. You feel the benevolence in all that you are guided to do. This is such a game-changer.

Having pauses within your thoughts is another way that this shows up, which changes your thoughts to a higher way of thinking, which in turn changes the words you will say. This can also assist in changing your beliefs. This often happens when you notice as someone mentions a belief you share, or you can even think about a belief you have and it feels off. I would say that it feels downright awkward. This can feel startling because this same belief used to give you peace, and now it creates a pause and an awkward uncomfortableness. This is because it is no longer your truth. You have OUTGROWN that belief and are ready to be something different—something MORE.

Recently we were on an interstate exit ramp when I saw someone selling flowers on the side of the road. I felt a pause. As my husband continued driving, I asked Spirit what this pause was about. I was given a download of the man selling flowers. An older woman was in a hospital bed. So many loved ones around her. This man was trying to make more money so that he could help her. I asked Spirit if we should go back and buy some flowers. They said not today, but be prepared to do so another time… and we did.

Love your pauses, get excited about your pauses. Notice every pause that you can and your life will be transformed. The next leveling up is that you will begin to notice other people's pauses. Again, this can take you in different directions. Sometimes you will get to step in and teach a person about why they just experienced a pause. To help *them* take it further, please ask questions like… "Why do you think you paused? What were you about to say, do, or think and how did it shift?" That way, they can begin to notice what it feels like to pause, and how they can make a different choice in that moment of pausing. Know that we can give them the answer, they just won't learn as quickly because they didn't make the connection, and that's ok, too. I simply try to avoid taking away another person's opportunity to learn something in the highest way.

Here is one of my very favorites: I watch a person pause because I just witnessed Spirit placing a hand on their shoulder. In that flash of a second, I see that they have just been given a download. I watch confusion spread across their face like they were going to say something or do something and they have no idea why. Yet they also feel such a strong desire to do or say this new thing, but it makes no sense to them. Yet they do or say it anyway because Spirit guided them to do so. Now that I am aware of this existing, I experience it all the time. So, not only have I gotten an upgrade, but people all around me are getting an upgrade too. Double awesomeness!! *You will see it when you believe it.*

Pause, pause, PAUSE, and see where it takes you. This has been so very life-changing for me and I don't choose to ever go back to the old way of being. This goes so far beyond what I thought a guided life was before the—PAUSE.

Living as Consciousness

Consciousness is being that (whatever that is) on purpose. Consciousness is saying that (whatever that is) on purpose. Consciousness is doing that (whatever that is) on purpose. Consciousness is thinking that (whatever that is) on purpose.

Every aspect of your life that you are participating in—you are consciously choosing it. Before you were more conscious, you blurted out whatever came into your head. If it was offensive, you made excuses for it, saying something like, "Sometimes I don't think before I speak." *Somehow* you thought that made it ok. When you live consciously, you don't make those excuses anymore. You call yourself out with the understanding that wrong is wrong. Being that way is no longer acceptable nor is it your newly chosen way to live your life. Realize that this can create disharmony or confusion within you... until it doesn't. I would also like everyone to understand that once you say something, those words can never be unsaid. You can apologize and apologize, but they cannot be unheard. So please think before you speak. I promise you that when you begin speaking consciously, even your vocabulary changes. This is so incredible.

Consciousness is consciously choosing your words. Consciousness is consciously behaving in a certain way… a higher way. Consciousness is consciously thinking thoughts that create harmony and peace. Consciousness creates awareness. One of the ways that I witnessed consciousness showing up was in my family texts. We have a group text that includes many of my brothers, my sisters, and myself. At the time, we were texting all day and night because one of our brothers was going through his cancer experience. I would find myself reacting to something one of my siblings would say. I would write a response that was not very kind. Before I would send it, I would read what I had written. "Holy cow, where did that rage come from?" I would delete it all. I would re-write the text in a softer way. Again, I would read it and say, "Wow, that still sounds harsher than it needs to be." Sometimes it would take five to ten re-writes for me to get to a place of harmony and compassion.

When I consciously sent that text, I noticed that I felt peace in my heart. I had released layers of old negativity by *allowing* myself to go into my old negative way of being and then letting it go repeatedly. Until all that was left was a higher conscious way of expressing where we can choose to take this. The proof that living from this higher way was working, was in the responses I was getting from my family members when I came from love, compassion, and truth.

My siblings did one of two things. Often, they didn't respond. Spirit would tell me that they needed to take my words in more deeply so that they could see things differently. Also, some of them just don't want to change, so they would pretend those words were never written. The other response I got was total support and acknowledgment that what I said made so much sense and they couldn't agree more. Sometimes they would say, "Wow, I never thought of it that way." Starting with family can be challenging because there is so much history there. However, the rewards are immense.

When we understand the process of waking up and living consciously, we are way ahead of the game. That does not mean that it is easy. We have to walk through all our old "stuff," and there is a lot of "stuff." Old traumas and dramas won't carry the same frequency once we begin to look at them from a place of observation rather than, "They did that to me." Everything softens, everything is less intense and therefore you can see it from a different perspective of divine neutrality. From there, and ONLY from there, can you make a more conscious decision, or see it in a more conscious way. This is because you are consciously choosing to think about your trauma differently—consciously. You are willing to allow your relationships to exist from honesty rather than what you think will make them happy so that they will love you more. That is called unconsciousness or even manipulation. For you are choosing to manipulate someone into loving you. We see this a lot with dating, unfortunately.

It is very strange when we can even see making someone happy as being a manipulation. How crazy is that? It's true, though. If you are not being your authentic, highest self, and you are showing up as who you think they want you to be, it's a manipulation. Nope. That has *nothing* to do with higher consciousness. So, we stop and *evaluate* why we are doing this. Why am I saying that? Is that who I am? Is that who I want to be? The gift of a question is so very important.

The way I see and understand things usually comes from a three-year-old place of innocence. You can understand this better after reading the chapter about freezing at certain times in our lives. My three-year-old self embodies what I feel about ascension—curiosity, awe, silliness, joy, and simplicity. These aspects connect me to my Higher Self faster than anything else. I can see potential and possibilities in everything when I come from this totally open and innocent place. So, why would connecting to consciousness be any different? It isn't.

When I first began connecting to consciousness more consistently, it was A LOT of work. Choosing every thought, choosing the words I spoke, choosing the choices I made about anything and everything took time and patience… until it didn't. That is because after a long time of working on this, it simply became who I am. I began living from this place more and more consistently. I no longer needed to work on it. I no longer needed to focus on it. I was "IT." The way I saw this showing up in my life was that I saw blessings and gratitude in everything.

When we see blessings in everything, it moves beyond seeing blessings in our burdens. While yes, seeing blessings in our burdens is part of it, this goes far beyond that. We see the blessing that each person is, that we have the honor and privilege of encountering. We see such magnificence in all. We truly are seeing with new eyes. My sister was describing watching a movie recently that she had seen before and it was like a whole new movie to her. Yes—this is because she sees it in a new way—a conscious way.

My family thought I was ridiculous going to so many movies. But I would see and hear spiritual messages in them. I could notice the hand of God in them. Now here comes the fun part—the movies I saw this in, were all genres. I could see God in an action & adventure just as easily as I could in a romantic comedy. This is because I was existing from a place of consciousness. I experienced all, from a place of awe. I witnessed as an observer, by asking to see beyond the mundane. To EXPERIENCE beyond the old paradigm way of experiencing. This too is an aspect of consciousness.

There are so many who think that consciousness only exists in their meditations. It's time to take consciousness out of our heads, and into our hearts, and LIVE IT! BE IT. Be it, in all that we experience. Whether that is what we say, what we feel, what we think, what we do, what we experience—WHO WE ARE. When we live from this place of consciousness, we exist AS consciousness. *You will see it when you believe it.*

Over a decade ago, Spirit let me know that each and every thought is a prayer. Every thought we think creates a prayer—a way of telling Spirit what we want to create. Spirit is listening—Spirit is ALWAYS listening. For instance, if you say an actual prayer asking Spirit to help you by bringing you greater abundance, then you follow up from that prayer by reaffirming over 1000 times during your day how you have nothing, that is 1 prayer towards abundance and 1000 prayers towards poverty. And then you think that no one is listening when you experience greater poverty. Every single thought, action, and word is a request as to what you wish to create more of in your life. Be careful what you ask for… you may get it.

We notice how when a person says something that a year ago would have sent us into a rage, and now we go, "Boy, that's an interesting choice they are making." Our centeredness, our core is so very strong that nothing can throw us off. We know, what we know. We are, who we are. It is, what it is. You don't have to complicate this at all. Just consciously observe. Once you get to this point, you understand that none of this is a competition. Believe it or not, you get to the point where it's not personal, either. When you excel, all of humankind excels. This is called oneness.

Observation, I believe, is one of the quickest ways to connect to consciousness and then higher consciousness. When we observe, there is absolutely no agenda. We are simply witnessing the experiences around us.

No one is right or wrong—they simply are. Choices people are making are simply that—a choice. We don't *react*—we observe or witness. From this space, we have an understanding beyond our old understandings. There is no force at all here. If there were to be any force, then you would have dropped out of your consciousness and stepped into your old humanness or unconsciousness.

Here we exist as flow. When an issue shows up on our path, we are a curious child. Wow, what is this about? What do I get to learn here? Where did this come from? The gift of a question. This shows curiosity rather than stuckness. Questions are filled with wonder and awe. Can you see that? Can you feel that? Be curious about everything and from there you will learn what most lower-frequency humans cannot. There is so much more to our existence than we are aware of.

When we reside as "higher" consciousness, we go even further in our understanding. For instance, when a challenge shows up for us, we embrace it. We understand that we came here to experience this. The difference is… HOW we experience it. I was given the experience of cancer twice. The first time I lived from a place of reaction. The second time, I flowed and witnessed. I needed the two experiences so I could understand the difference. What a magnificent gift I was given.

With higher consciousness, we don't wish and hope for miracles—WE ARE THE MIRACLE. We no longer look out there for someone to "fix" us or "save" us, we look into our own toolbox and find the right tool for this situation. That tool could be going into observation, pausing, walking through the past without an agenda, softening, allowing, or whatever works for you. I am noticing that more and more often, in addition to seeing a movie in my head (as in a download from Spirit), I am the movie. I am the moment—witnessing all kinds of information. Notice that I said,

"I am THE moment" instead of, "I am IN the moment." Even this carries a different frequency. What I need to do is very clear, once I get out of my own way. Once I let go of the way it always worked before.

We need to be willing to let go of the old ways of doing something or even let go of who we believe we are. From there we allow in a higher way of being—of existing or thriving to appear. We need to even let go of the good stuff. How I used to do healings was wonderful. However, as I allowed it to morph into what was for the highest good in each individual situation, the better the results. I still start with basics, like, if we are dealing with the heart, this probably has to do with feelings or hurts from the past (hardening the heart). If we are looking at back issues, there is probably a lack of support in there somewhere (emotional support, financial support, familial support). When looking at feet or legs, it could have to do with a fear of taking the next step. This gives me a starting place and then I give my Higher Self free reign to take me to new possibilities.

So, when we exist as higher consciousness, the doubt of everything is lifted and we understand and know that the only limits that exist, are the limits that we believe. Miracles are a normal way of life. Choices we make can only be made if everyone wins. ALL has value and ALL is valued. *We will see it when we believe it.*

So much of this might not make sense, until it does. We are planting a seed for some of you so that later when this shows up in your life, you will understand. For others of you—these words are meant to help you take the understanding of your experiences further and further. Please, stop limiting yourself. When you act in the highest way, your experience will be the highest experience. Know that we are CONSTANTLY leveling up when we choose to level up. We are constantly changing when we embrace change. Be THE change.

Our soul came here to experience something that has never been experienced on this planet—ASCENSION. Please don't limit your own experience. Please don't limit your soul's experience.

I thought this chapter was complete and then Spirit said that they would like for me to address Christ Consciousness. This carries the same frequency as higher consciousness. However, for those of you who come from a Christian background, it is important for you to understand that Christ Consciousness is not Jesus. It is similar to living in the way Jesus lived. As in, knowing that miracles are a way of life and we are limitless. I don't know the quote nor do I need the exact quote, but Jesus said something like, "All that I do, you shall do and so much more." What I do know is that this is what Jesus says to me quite often.

Jesus' name is not Jesus Christ. He is Jesus the Christ. His name is Jesus and what he does—is live as Christ Consciousness. John the Baptist's name is John. What he is known as or for, is the baptism of people. So, Christ and Baptist can be thought of as their titles… what they came here to do. Who they are seen as. I don't say these things to upset people. I say them to help bring in clarity. So those of us with a Christian background, we get to shift from "what would Jesus do," to instead "live as Jesus lived."

Live without judgment, know that ALL are equal. That which you desire is yours—*when* it is for the good of all. Honesty is in everything that you do and are. Sharing is a way of life. Everything being fair creates balance. Justice while living from Christ Consciousness is—Just is. You can't even imagine a life without flow and harmony anymore.

It's ok to use Jesus as an example, but you came here to be YOU. These are different times we are living in. Therefore, how things are done will be different and yet the same. I know that I talk in riddles like that, but later in your evolution, everything is the same but different. Because you see all sides of everything. Your understanding is broadened to encompass all that is. So, you will live from an understanding of "it is, until it isn't." It's really quite fun and expansive!

Understand that, when we live our life consciously, we choose our words carefully. We behave with a higher intention. We think thoughts that assist in raising our frequency and the whole planet's frequency. When we step up and live our life from Christ Consciousness, it takes us so much further. When we are living consciously, we think as many thoughts as we can in a higher way. We consciously do kind deeds and say kinder words. Once we are able to do this more and more consistently, we move into Christ Consciousness, or higher consciousness. From this space, all is done from the very highest place.

ALL thoughts come from a place of love and kindness. Your thoughts are continually going to... how may I serve? How can I assist in the highest way for all concerned? Prejudice, envy, judgment, competition and intolerance cannot exist while living from a place of Christ Consciousness. You see all as an aspect of God/Source. ALL holds so much potential and you are so excited when that potential starts to show up in a higher way. This is done through encouragement and trust. Encourage both yourself and others. Trust that both yourself and others are doing the very best they can do, depending on where they came from, the choices they consciously make, who they choose to be, and most importantly, what they believe. Remember—*I will see it when I believe it.* We did not come here to be loved—we came here to BE LOVE. When we exist AS Love, all shifts in the highest way.

Are you choosing to live consciously or unconsciously? The choice is yours. How perfect is that!

Frozen in Time

There have been times when we were a victim and it goes far beyond having a rough day. The times I am speaking of are when we experienced the depths of pain, we lost all hope, and we fell into despair. When we felt there was *nothing* and *no one* that was going to rescue us. Some, like me, may have believed there was nothing to live for, but more pain, more anguish. These are the times that I am speaking of.

First of all, know that I hold you so tenderly in my arms and in my heart. I am so very sorry that you have ever had such a horrendous experience. I am so very sorry that you weren't able to experience all of the Angels, Guides and Ascended Masters that were there loving you during that time of pain. For THEY WERE THERE. Your soul chose those most difficult experiences to learn so much from. For as humans, we learn the most through adversity. That is until we have learned a different way—an ascended way. That is when everything changes.

Eventually, we learn through joy, peace, and observation. This is the ascended way. The hardship is gone and we experience such peace as we observe all through our divine neutrality. We know and truly understand that all is unfolding exactly as it is supposed to unfold. We have let go of the NEED that something MUST be a certain way. Righteous indignation is a thing of the past. All is love, and all is loved. This is where we are all headed, and there are many waiting for us to figure out our own way of getting there.

Until that time comes for each of us to live from a place of love, we need to figure out the multitude of tools we have been given which will assist in making our journey a bit easier. One of those tools is freezing in time. When we go through something so horrific and painful that a piece of us just can't go on. That piece of us stays frozen in that moment and just can't move beyond it. Eventually, there are many ways that we can move beyond it such as therapy, journaling so deeply that you work through the pain, and energy work. There are many spiritual practices that will assist also.

The things that will NOT assist in moving you beyond this pain are ignoring it, making pretend it never happened, or reliving the hate and pain until that is all you identify with or define yourself as. So, along with all that you get to work on and work through to access the ability to raise your vibration, you also get to heal the past. This is going to happen layer after layer. Please don't rush this process because each layer has valuable information for you to learn from. Remember—your soul came here to learn from all of this, so there is no sense in skimping.

Now we get to the part about an aspect or piece of us freezing in that moment in time. One of my first freezing moments was when I was 3 and I realized that my existence did not matter to my family. I was not enough. I can still see the ball I was rolling. I can still feel and describe the colors. You will notice that when you connect to a past horrific experience you can often describe things in great detail. This is a sign that an aspect of you may have frozen. For me, everything went into slow motion; I spent decades and decades reliving how much my existence didn't matter and I wasn't enough. I looked for proof of the fact that I didn't matter in every interaction I had until I was in my 40s.

Another experience where I froze in time, was when I was repeatedly sexually abused at age 7 and beyond. Again, things went into slow motion and I UNDERSTOOD that I was here to be abused. I saw how abusing others was a way of life for several in my family. They would laugh as they heard things pop or start to crack in my body. No one ever came to my rescue until I rescued myself. There were so many moments that I froze and it took a lot of therapy and working with spiritual healers and most importantly my team of Angels and Guides. None of this was easy, but it was oh so very important.

Because of all of the life experiences that I have gone through, I have a greater understanding of so many of my challenges and have therefore been able to go to the depths with others. I see this as a sacred gift now. Another thing that I learned from it, is that because of my freezing so many times as a child, I can connect to my innocence more easily and in a unique way because there is a rather large piece of me that remains a 3-year-old. This may also be because I know that I froze at least twice when I was 3. A piece of me is still 7 years old as I experienced being raped again and again. To add to this, that same 7-year-old (me) was told daily by her school teacher how stupid she was, and she (my 7-year-old self) believed her. Second grade was a very difficult year for me.

All of these pieces or aspects of me that froze in time are now able to assist me in knowing the innocence that resides within those aspects of me. The curiosity and purity of a child are mine anytime I want to connect to them, especially because of being frozen repeatedly as a child. I get to experience their magnificence in a way that others may not be able to. This is difficult for me to explain in words, but I have witnessed it in others a multitude of times. An old girlfriend of mine was frozen at age 8 because of her classmates making fun of her. Her relationships still resembled those of an 8-year-old. Even gifts she gave as an adult were often gifts an 8-year-old would like.

My husband almost died after having surgery at age 11. He went into a coma after complications took over, and when he finally came out of the coma, he was treated like a medical anomaly—a freak. He froze at age 11. Because of the emotional pain he experienced from this, he can experience social anxiety like an 11-year-old, so people's behavior tends to make no sense to him.

Spirit wanted me to explain this aspect of freezing because I have never really heard of anyone talking about this before. Spirit wants us to see the blessing in our burden, by understanding that having a part of us frozen as a child assisted so many of us in being able to see certain aspects of our lives through the eyes of a child. Believe it or not, this is a very good thing. To be able to see and understand things as a child, can connect us to curiosity, purity, and innocence. However, we also have to work through the pain to get there.

My nickname from Spirit is "But why?" because I see so much as a 3-year-old would, and I want to know why people do what they do. Why do they say what they say? This is a sacred gift to me. My girlfriend whom I spoke of earlier is very playful in her relationships because she experiences relationships as an 8-year-old would. What a precious gift that is for her. My hubby just does not care what other people think about him because he's too busy just living life as an 11-year-old. We have both learned that his 11-year-old is curious and wants to notice and learn about everything.

This is a gift to all who get to experience him. Please note that this does not mean all aspects of us freeze, only one or two aspects usually freeze. You get to figure out which ones they are. *You will see it when you believe it.*

Look at how much fun my 3-year-old is having
with my husband's 11-year-old.

Some of you have been blessed with not having experienced this freezing aspect. You had that rare gift called a happy childhood, or possibly a "normal" childhood. I celebrate that for you. However, for those of us who did experience this pain, I would love for you to find the blessing or the gift in freezing. Look at how you live from a child's perspective in "a certain aspect" of your life. Do you look at life with a sense of awe? Do you always want to know more, or even "but why?" How has this served you, now that you are an adult and can look at it from a different perspective? Does it help you understand why you are the way you are a little bit better?

Are you more curious or playful because of this frozen aspect happening to you? What are you wanting to do with this new information? How can you use this information to serve your evolution even more?

Enjoy connecting to these *sacred aspects* of yourself that endured so much so that you were able to connect to more simplicity, curiosity and innocence throughout your life. Look at how much more complex, or even boring, you may have become if you had not been given this experience. Isn't life complex enough? I am so grateful my husband doesn't take people too seriously because of his 11-year-old experience.

I'm grateful for the very unique perspective I have of life because of the multitude of frozen aspects from my own childhood. I am in awe of so much. I love bright colors. I love working with my Guides because they are always willing to teach me—BUT WHY! I love saying things like oopsie poopsie. I love noticing the little things in life like the perfection of a dandelion, or how the wind makes the leaves on the tree dance. This is what I mean by our ability to connect to the simplicity because of our frozen child. Not everyone has this. Are we willing to shift our old way of seeing our traumas and now notice something good that came out of them? Again—I am so very sorry that you ever went through something so horrific that a part of you froze. Learn from it, grow from it, so all you experienced was not for nothing.

Make note that it is not just an age that is frozen, but an understanding or definition of who you are, as in, I define myself as curious. My husband defines himself as awkward with people. My friend defines herself as being playful in her relationships. I will share another example with you… my oldest sister Christine's mother was diagnosed with cancer when Christine was 8 years old. She passed away two years later. Christine knew that it was her job to step up and assist in caring for her four younger brothers to help ease the burden on both her sick mother and her overwhelmed father. Christine froze during that time. She became a caregiver for the rest of her life until about eight years ago when she began her unique spiritual path of awakening.

Once Christine understood that everyone has things on their path that they are here to learn from, she realized it is no longer her job to fix everyone—to care for everyone. This does not mean that she does not care, for she cares deeply. She is present with whoever is on her path and assists in whatever way that she can. The difference is that she no longer *needs* to fix them or make them understand what she believes. She now knows and understands that they need to learn from those lessons. She no longer denies a person that opportunity to learn from those lessons by taking over and fixing everything for the people in her life that she loves and cares about. She now loves and allows, and if she is guided to... she assists.

Do you see how Christine being frozen in the *understanding* that she must step up and be a care provider was a burden, but also a blessing? She learned how to help EVERYONE and take care of EVERYONE. She has a very big and compassionate heart because of what she had to go through at such a young age. So being frozen helped her to transform easily into "How may I serve" later in her evolution.

I have so many questions about all I observe and I am grateful that my 3-year-old is continually asking "But why?" If I hadn't frozen at that age, I might not be *as curious* and asking questions all the time. That would have been a great loss for me. I feel I would have accepted whatever showed up rather than thinking there must be more to this. Now you can see the blessings that came from my trauma.

Look at how your being frozen in *time,* or a *concept* of you having frozen has served you. See how you look at and approach your life in a different way because of it. Now, see the blessing that came from this because it assisted you in some OTHER aspect of your life, which made you a very different person than who you would have been without it. This is so empowering if you allow it to be. Are you willing to allow it to be? *You will see it when you believe it.*

I hope that this assisted you in seeing something that you didn't understand in such a way before. You've got this! All is well.

Set Up for Success

What we came here to do and be in this lifetime (our time of ascension), we have successfully accomplished in a past lifetime. This is because God/Source has set us up to succeed, NOT fail. Really take those words in... That which you came here to do and be in this lifetime you already ACCOMPLISHED in a past life. As we progress, we notice that when we learn or experience something new, it can feel familiar. This is because our spiritual DNA knows this—remembers this. That part of us says, "I've got this." The very human part of you may say, "I haven't got this."

Which one you trust more shows you where you are on your journey and what it is that you may want to work on. In other words, which belief are you feeding? The one that believes, trusts, and knows, or the one that doesn't trust and doubts you and others, along with your own value? What a sacred gift this is. For when we connect to what we believe—we give ourselves permission to explore and take this information or belief further. We give ourselves permission to be limitless or limited, even if it's only in one aspect of our life; this is HUGE. As you will notice, there are a lot of "huge" aspects at play during our ascension. This is because our ascension is so HUGE.

We silly humans need to give ourselves permission in the beginning because of our lack of trust or even because of our limited background. I have so very many gifts and talents, and I love them ALL—they are magnificent. However, sharing those same gifts and talents with other people can be scary for me because of my background—my childhood. I don't doubt my abilities, I doubt that *others* are going to appreciate my abilities. I can also doubt that others are going to be kind to me. This is really important for me to understand so that I can shift that belief.

Once I can let go of my doubt about others, I can trust my abilities even more, so that I am limitless in this aspect of my life. I can also then work on giving myself permission to put myself out there knowing that some people are going to get what I am teaching and perhaps some won't. This is not my issue, this is theirs. This means that it's their problem *unless* I MAKE IT my problem. Only then can it also be my problem. I can choose to take on people's lies or issues if I want. This is something I did so well in my younger years as an empath, but no more.

With this clarification, let us get back to what we came here to DO and BE in this lifetime. I would love it if you could let go of your death grip on the NEED TO KNOW what you came here to do and be. When we get so wrapped up in the need to figure this out, we miss living our lives. We waste our precious moments. For what, I ask you? The best way that I know of to start to connect to what you came here to be and do is to start by *being kind.*

Be kind to yourself and others in any and every way that you can. This will start a connection and dialogue with your Higher Self/Soul. Once this becomes a way of life for you, you will notice more peace within you. From this peace, it is so much easier to comprehend what you do and why you do it. The gifts you will need to do the work you came here to do will show up effortlessly because of living from this place of peace and trust. This helps you to understand *you*. Now we are going to help you figure out what you came here to BE and DO. Notice what makes you different—unique. This usually has something to do with what you came here to do in this lifetime. Also, look at what comes easily to you.

To help you understand this, I'll use my own life example. I have always had a unique way of saying things and expressing myself. People have saved cards and letters I've sent them over the years because they felt seen and touched by my words because they are written as truth. This always seemed very bizarre to me since I had difficulty reading because I had learning disabilities, and yet I could write effortlessly from my heart. Writing came from my heart, from my soul. Reading came from my head. Already at a young age, I was living from my heart more than my head. Boy, am I grateful for that now, but back then it was so difficult. And now I am a writer. Back then my head and everybody else's head made little sense to me. Another gift I have always possessed is being a baby whisperer. I have an understanding of what a baby needs, and why. This helped me be successful as a daycare provider.

Being kind, and being nice, is where the journey can start for you. This starts us on the path of thinking of others rather than me, me, me. The next step is looking at what comes from you with such grace, ease and flow. This may be so basic that you don't even realize that it's a thing. Now… how can you take this thing that is a normal way of life for you and expand it? How can you use it to make a difference in your life, and the lives of others? How can you enhance it? Are you incredible at music? Do you have a gift for putting people at ease? Are you one of those people who sees the best in others? Does nature inspire you? Are you fantastic at making things—taking things apart? Are you amazing at seeing a different way of doing things? See, there are so many minute and enormous ways we are unique. What is it that resonates with you? I tend to see things from a different perspective, so that is one of my superpowers. I remember when my husband and I were first together, I would ask him what it is like to be so smart. He said, "I'm book smart, but you are people smart. What I wouldn't give to have what you have." I was so shocked by this—for the first time in my life I felt smart. My husband told me how in awe he was of my ability to put people at ease and bring laughter and joy in. Until that moment I never realized this was "special" or uniquely me. I now expand this out into every interaction because it's what I came here to do and to be. What a gift my husband had given me.

Explore and play with where you can take your own special way of doing something or looking at something. Look at it from a place of limitlessness. For a moment, allow yourself to exist in a place where money is not an issue, time is not an issue, nothing is an issue. All things are possible here. Just play—make pretend, and use your imagination. This will get you out of your head and into your heart and imagination. When we come from our heart and our innocence, we can be so much more creative. We can see possibilities that our logical mind won't allow. Get out of the limits you place on yourself and on others.

Realize that if God/Source is setting us up to succeed, why would WE set ourselves up for failure? ANYONE can say why something or someone will fail. It takes a higher way of being to set yourself or others up for success. Make note, this is not to come from a place of ego, but rather from a place of choosing to make a difference in the world. Choosing to assist for the highest good of all concerned. Only then does it shift the frequency for yourself and for everyone.

It is my belief and my understanding that God is setting us up for success during our shift of the ages. How this is done is by placing us in situations that we have been successful at in a past life. For instance, if you are here to make a difference politically, chances are, you were a politician who created great change in a past life. When you can connect to that, you will connect to the confident game-changer in you. You will know exactly what you will need to do, and why. Can you feel how powerful this is? Can you feel how powerful YOU are? Think about what it is in this lifetime that flows from you effortlessly. Now DO that, and BE that consistently, and you will feel your power assisting all humankind. *You will see it when you believe it.*

Know that these are different times and different circumstances than your past lives. This means you get to be creative and take your experiences further than ever before. You get to do things in a way that maybe has never been done before. Please don't take this to a place of putting pressure on yourself. That does NOT serve you. That does NOT serve US. Instead, take it to a place of curiosity, fun, and creativity.

When you play with this, do you notice that it raises your energy, or does it lower your energy? If it lowers your energy or frequency, then you missed the target—try again. If it raises your energy or frequency, stay with it; how can you take it further? Try writing it down. This helps us to use a different part of our brain. Keep writing and writing even if what you write makes no sense. Then Spirit can come through to give you greater clarity. We can learn a lot during our rambles in nature. Why wouldn't we also learn from our rambles in our minds or even on paper?

We came here to be successful, period. We came here to make a difference, period. We came here to learn and experience, period. What have you learned from your experiences? What have others learned because they were fortunate enough to experience you? Where are you a failure (in your opinion) and where are you a success? Keep asking questions so that you can take your understanding further.

I don't know about you, but just knowing that I was so successful in a past lifetime that I was encouraged to come here at this time to help Gaia (our new Earth) and all humankind in its greatest evolution—WOW! Everything I have experienced, everything I have endured, now seems so very worth it. Because of all I have experienced and endured, I have been God victorious in all I have accomplished to make a difference in our exalted evolution. Halleluiah! *You will see it when you believe it.*

A Changing of the Guides

We were all born with at least two Birth Angels, also called Guardian Angels. These Guardian Angels will stay with us throughout our entire lifetime. Our Birth Angels or Guardian Angels are the ones that keep us safe until it is our time to transition. There will be times when something or someone shows up just as something deadly is about to happen and you live to love another day. The person or situation that showed up tends to be either our Birth Angels, or a person sent by our Birth Angels.

I know that I have been asked to show up in a multitude of ways hundreds of times over the years. And yet, there are times I show up and still I have no idea why I was asked to be there. I am simply thanked by Spirit and have a knowing that something happened. Something shifted when I showed up. Was it a Guardian Angel asking me to intervene? I know that one of the times I was guided to show up, a person who had planned to commit suicide didn't do so. Spirit is telling me that it has actually happened many times. So, there you go. When you are asked to show up somewhere, please do so. You never know, you could end up saving someone's life, or even your own. When we show up in this manner, we are called Earth Angles (or Gaia Angels).

On a very cold, slippery night a year ago, I was asked to show up at a local store. I didn't need anything, but I did as I was asked. I got there a half hour before closing. I was the only one in the store except for the clerk. We chit-chatted and laughed for a while, and I went home. I had no idea at all why I needed to go there. Then a month ago, Spirit showed me the broadened perspective of what took place. The clerk had been stealing, and management was suspicious. She was about to steal when I showed up. I have no idea what I said to change her mind, but she did. Her family did not have to live through that shame. She did not have to live with the consequences of making such a poor life choice. All because my Gaia Angel aspect was called on to step up and make a difference.

Another aspect of your life path is that we have guides that assist us. Those guides can keep changing throughout our life. When I began channeling consistently in about 1996, my Spirit Guide's name was Charles. Charles was a hoot to be around. He had a wonderful sense of humor and made spirituality fun and playful (helping to bring forward my frozen 3-year-old). He gave me permission to be 100 percent me and that felt both wonderful and scary. If Spirit told me what to do, then I would trust my guidance. When I was on my own, I would be filled with more doubt. What value do I have? I'm a nobody—I'm not even vegetarian.

Yep, I was so confused and alone that I thought a person couldn't channel unless they knew how to meditate, were vegetarian, and had no nice possessions. Charles cleared all that up for me right away. Know that I didn't think this way because I was ignorant. It was because I couldn't read and I had no one helping me understand Spirituality. My heart was pure and I had a desire. Charles said that a pure heart wasn't necessary, but it sure helped. My hubby, Marsh, was not comfortable having Charles around, until he was.

What that means is it was strange how I was constantly saying things like, "Charles says you need to not give your opinion at work today. Just keep your head down and do your work." Or, "Charles told us we shouldn't go somewhere, or eat something." For a while, it was all day and night. It seemed like Charles had something to say about everything. I found myself talking out loud when there was no one physically there. Then Marsh saw how Charles kept us safe several times and how he was taking care of us. That was when he decided having Charles around was a very good thing.

About fifteen years later I noticed that the Spirits showing up were never Charles. I felt abandoned. What had I done wrong? How do I get Charles back? I was eventually told that our Spirit Guides switch in and out as our needs and God's needs change. I was getting into deeper and deeper transformational experiences. I needed guides that could assist me better with these new needs and desires. There are some people who work with a certain guide their entire life. However, it is more common to have our guides continually shift and change.

I have never been one who needed to know the identity of the Spirit coming through. I have worked with Mother Mary, Jesus, God, and Charles so much that I know what their frequency feels like. I also noticed that the Guides that show up in the beginning tend to be who we are familiar with. For instance, I was raised Catholic, so it would make sense that the Guides that would show up most often for me would be Mother Mary, Jesus, Joseph, and God. Later, as I let go of my limited beliefs, the Guides I was exposed to expanded to beings I had never heard of before. All of this made no difference to me as long as they showed up with wisdom and knowledge that assisted me and all humankind.

I have learned that on the other side, these "beings" don't have names. We humans are the ones needing labels (names) to identify one another. Out there in the Universe, one is identified by their frequency or energy. Perhaps this is why I don't enjoy labeling the "being" coming through. They are who they are. I am who I am. Labels create separation. Don't we have enough of that already? I simply enjoy the message and frequency of the "being" showing up. If they want to share their "human-type" name with me—fine. However, I don't NEED that validation. How about you?

Allow yourself to be open to your guides shifting and changing as you shift and change, along with your needs shifting and changing. Shift happens... and I am grateful. *We will see it when we believe it.*

Mary Beth's Different Perspective

Every step of my spiritual path has been beyond unique. The way I meditate is different in that my mind doesn't quiet down the way most people can experience. I once had a palm reader look at my hand as she was telling me that she had two Xs in the spiritual part of the hand (this is why she was so good as a palm reader)—my palm had at least seven Xs with two stars. Supposedly that is beyond amazing. But she kept saying, "You have lines everywhere, does your mind ever stop?" In that moment she gave me such a special gift. I now had confirmation as to why my mind was so busy. That gave me permission to allow it to just flow and see where it took me.

Eventually, I learned that if I said, "Thank you for sharing," I could stop my mind from chattering. My mind chatter is sacred to me. It is my own unique ideas and I don't want them to stop. They are so different from what other people's minds are saying out there. Then again, I don't listen to what other people are saying out there very often because I'm here to be something rather different. I really do have a different perspective on many aspects of life.

Let's look at healing. My chapter on freezing in this book will help you understand this better. At age 3, my mom and I were in the grocery store. A woman was standing in the frozen food aisle and I saw something in her body. She had a big black owie (a tumor) that I just knew intuitively, it had to come out. I went to reach into her body to take it out. I have no idea what would have happened if I had been ALLOWED to do that. The woman screamed and my mom was yelling at me as I was being pulled away and slapped. My mom ranted at me for such a long time. "You know better than to touch someone like that. I can't believe you would embarrass me like that. What do you think you were doing?"

Mom went on and on. When I was finally allowed to explain myself, I told Mom about the woman's big black owie that I saw. She told me that this was Satan's work. I was told I was evil and she can't take me anywhere. Like I said, it was a long rant. I froze in that moment of being shamed. What I learned just recently is that the healer in me is still 3 years old. So, the way I see and do healings can be very innocent and naive. For instance, I have always gotten rid of plaque in both my arteries and other people's arteries by placing Ms. Pacman in my/their veins in their wrists. I allow Ms. Pacman to go all through the arteries and veins eating up the plaque. Talk about a different perspective, hey?

Another woman I had worked with was dealing with some kind of blood poisoning, and we visualized bubbles going into the veins in her wrists. These bubbles absorbed any toxins in her blood. It pulled the aspect that was making her sick right out and when a bubble was full, I watched it float out of her body and up to the heavenly realm because God wanted it and thanked me for it. Both of these examples really do sound like a 3-year-old came up with them, but they worked, so that's all that matters to me.

This is me at 3 years old. Look at my innocence.

With the colon, I see what my 3-year-old calls mini volcanoes. We go up and visually place our finger on a mini volcano and say, "Boop" and then with gentle love, hold this volcano until it diminishes. Sometimes she even kisses them afterward. We do this all throughout the digestive system. Can you see how unique doing healings as a 3-year-old can be, compared to an adult? So maybe freezing at age 3 was a blessing instead of a curse. I do wonder what I could have done if I had ALLOWED MYSELF to continue doing visualizations and healings at age three even though Mom forbade it.

Another different perspective I have is how I see babies and children. Babies are still connected to the heavenly realm. They see and understand so much more than we realize. The problem is that they have no way to articulate what they know. Since we haven't figured out how to join them in their innocent understanding of what they see, know, and are experiencing, they learn to let that connection with the higher realm go and join us in becoming more human and less connected to the other side. What a bummer this feels like to me.

As a daycare provider for babies, it was my job to teach these babies how to function and I would even say, "survive" on the Earth plane. We did this in my daycare while still connecting to the wonder and awe of everything. I love lying down on my back and seeing what they see. Is this environment boring, or stimulating? Is it too stimulating? A baby's favorite thing is learning something new. Our children are as limited as we believe they are. My daughter wanted to learn to read at age 2. She was ready, but I wasn't. I made her wait until she was 3. I limited her because "I" wanted her to remain a child as long as she could. Silly me—she can remain a child and still read.

This is the magical space I created for me and my babies.

Being HONEST and CONSISTENT with our children is the greatest gift we can give them. One of the pet peeves I have still retained from before my spiritual awakening is how parents threaten and threaten and don't follow through. Never threaten anything that you are not going to follow through on. Your children are learning from you. What you teach your child when you threaten and don't follow through is… #1—you are a liar. Yep, you are a liar. #2—how to manipulate. Yes, to threaten is to manipulate. #3—your words and who you say you are can't be trusted. Holy cow, talk about a different perspective. Think before you talk. Think before you do things. Consciously raise your child—rather than unconsciously.

I feel like I have a unique or different perspective on practically any subject. Just yesterday on my walk through the neighborhood, I saw a fire hydrant. Spirit let me know that when you live in a home with a fire hydrant out front, you are making a promise or commitment to your neighbors. "Don't worry, I've got this amazing source of water right here if you ever need it. I'm here for you." I almost cried when I heard that. Of course, on a human level, people don't really think that, or say that. Yet, Spirit says on a certain level that is what you are agreeing to when you purchase a house with a fire hydrant out front. They say that it is an honor and a privilege to have a fire hydrant on your property.

The way I notice the frequency of words is unique also. For instance, there is no compassion in words such as "Deal with it." In fact, if you spend a moment with those words, you can actually feel how a person could feel abandonment when those words are spoken to them. Another phrase many people tend to use is "If you don't like it, then too bad." Some even add words like "we're doing it anyway." Again, do you feel the lack of compassion, the total lack of respect? Where is the kindness? How are you showing up when you use such words?

You can say… but they aren't listening to me. I ask you—are you listening to them? In that moment are you placing your own needs above another's? When these types of words are said surrounding a crisis situation,

I want you to ask yourself, is this your lifetime to make such a decision—or theirs?

Try instead to empower them by asking questions such as "Why do you feel so strongly about this," or "Why are you so convinced that this is the best choice." When you ask questions such as these, the other person feels heard and respected. They no longer need to be defensive because you aren't listening to them. You are empowering them by giving them an opportunity to talk out why they think, feel or believe something. A higher or "in"-lightened person does not choose to disempower another. All is done with respect. When everyone concerned feels heard and respected, then everyone wins and no one looses anything. This is a higher frequency way of existing. Does this sound like a different perspective to you?

Here's another different perspective: I talk to my Higher Self in the mirror. This shows me... proves to me that I AM my Higher Self by seeing the physical me talking to me AS my Higher Self. I connect to her so easily and effortlessly in this way and we have a different relationship or connection because of it. How I do this is I either sit on my sink counter in the bathroom or sit in front of a huge dressing mirror, and I talk to myself. I talk about my hopes and fears and I learn so much about where I am at and what is still bothering me, or affecting me.

As I connect deeper and deeper, the woman in the mirror transforms. She has this amazing wisdom. She shares that wisdom with me. I feel her compassion for what I perceive I am going through. She really, really wants the highest outcome for me. Ask your Higher Self in the mirror questions and allow THE TRUTH to come through. NOT what you *hope* the truth is, but the absolute TRUTH! This will also assist you in learning to channel more consistently. This is so beyond fantastic. I wish I did it more often, but like I said earlier, my mind is constantly going with new and different ideas.

There are so many different ways to look at things and understand things! This gives us permission to do things differently from everyone else. For instance, did you know that there are over a million different ways to ascend? Spirit encourages me constantly to do things in a different way. Approach things in a different way. See things in a different way. Can you give yourself that same permission? Lately, I haven't been able to read or watch anything spiritual. Spirit always wanted me to walk my own unique path in my own unique way. When I imitate others, I tend to fall short. So instead, I use others to inspire me and then I take their wisdom in a different direction—my own unique direction!

Are you brave enough to do that same thing? Use the words in this book to inspire you, but with the understanding that I am not you. I came here to be Mary Beth. You came here to be YOU. How do you know who you are if you just keep imitating others? I am not a doctor or medical professional. I just follow the guidance of a 3-year-old. How fun is that? I play, play, play with my spiritual learning. To work at them feels too heavy to me. Again and again, I notice that my perspective is very unique. That is why my YouTube channel is called *Mary Beth's Different Perspective* (@marybethsdifferentperspective)— and my book website is https://*marybethsdifferentperspective.com*. This is because the titles of my books are each going to be different; however, my different perspective is consistently present in every chapter.

Play with your own unique way of doing things and when you embrace it, it will show up more and more consistently in your life. *You will see it when you believe it.* Understand with every fiber of your "being" that you came here to be you. You came here to be unique. You came here to live from your own different perspective. And nothing less is acceptable if you truly want to excel at BEING YOU! No one else on the planet gets the honor and privilege of being you. Own IT. Do IT. BE IT!

My Background

(how I got here)

There is very little about my life that has been "normal" and that's ok. Because of that, I can be very resourceful, and think outside of the box. Spirit has asked me to give you a little background on my life. It's not a fun place for me to go sometimes. From age 8 to 22, I was constantly asking God to die. This was because being physically abused, mentally abused, and sexually abused was not uncommon for me. To add to this, the people who supposedly loved me, were the ones that were abusing me. Because of this, I thought love was a negative thing.

When I watched TV and saw that there were families that had a different experience about love than I did, it made me curious. However, it also assisted in making me feel even more sad about what my family experience was like. When I was 4 or 5, I was finally able to stop sleeping in a crib in my parent's room because enough of my older siblings had moved out that there was a space for me upstairs. I quickly learned to hide in my closet so no one looked at me and remembered that I hadn't been abused yet that day.

Inside that closet was heaven on earth. Mother Mary held me as I cried. Jesus told me jokes. All these spiritual beings gave me hope, and believe it or not... some normalcy. Yes, it was normal for me to talk to so many Spirit friends. As an adult, I realized that who showed up in my closet, was who I had been exposed to at school and church. I went to a Catholic school so it makes sense that Mother Mary and Jesus would be my best buddy pals. So already I was training with Spirit. It wasn't until I met Buddha in a Chinese restaurant that I became curious about him and he became part of my circle of friends. I met Quan Yin at a spiritual bookstore, and she fascinated me.

From this experience, I realize that in the beginning, I didn't let just anyone and everyone into my spiritual circle of friends. I limited who I allowed in by whom I had heard *friendly* stories about and later it included who I was drawn to. Now realize that this is my own story, and this all changed later on in my life as I changed. Back then these were my own limited beliefs. *I saw it because I believed it.* I have never met Moses that I know of, I never encouraged a relationship with him because he sounded bossy to me when I heard his story as a child. Spirit wanted me to survive my childhood so that I could live to do my part in our ascension, and a million other reasons. So, they limited who they exposed me to at first.

I scared easily as a child and young adult, so only Angels and Ascended Masters that I saw as friendly were allowed to be in my life to soften my experiences so that I would hopefully one day choose to live. So, do you see how I taught Spirit what made me feel safe and gave me moments of peace? They learned what could calm me down from my terror.

Unfortunately, as I moved into adolescence, I confused EVERYTHING. I felt I needed to let go of my "make pretend" friends in the closet and so I moved to a space in the attic. My Spirit friends weren't allowed there because I needed to grow up. Instead, I grew even sadder. I felt such overwhelming hopelessness there. I truly hated myself. The self-loathing was all-consuming. *I saw it because I believed it.* When we moved, I was 16 and I just felt so lost. I no longer had my torture chamber in the attic, where I had continually told myself what my mom taught me—I was worthless, I was ignorant, I was not special—so I returned to my closet, but it was different now in the new house. My Spirit friends weren't in this closet. I was alone—I had been abandoned. At least that's what I believed.

This gave me a reason to hate Jesus and Mother Mary for awhile. I believed that they no longer cared about me, they no longer showed up when I needed help. Thoughts of suicide kept getting stronger until at the age of 22 I had decided to end this pain that was my life.

As I wrote my suicide letter, Jesus showed up, and he asked me, "Do you really want to die?" I had to think about that. "If this was living—if this was going to be my life—then, YES." He asked me what it would take for me to stay. I said, "I've heard of this thing called happy—I would really like to experience that." Jesus said, "What if I told you that there is a man that is coming to you and he is going to love you no matter what?" I told him, "I don't know what those words mean. So far love has only meant hurt and pain." His response was, "That was not love."

From there I was taken to the Akashic records. I was shown my future with this man. I don't remember any of it. All I remember is when I came back to my life on this side of the veils, I knew with all that I AM that I was going to meet a man who was blond-haired, blue-eyed, 6 feet tall, and wore a navy blue uniform. This man was going to love me no matter what and we were going to get married. That is exactly what happened 2 ½ years later. There is a lot more to this story, but I need you to understand my background so you have a greater understanding of why I connect to Spirit the way I do.

Marsh and I less than a year after we met.

I had trust issues, and because of that, how Spirit was able to approach me and connect to me was my own unique way. For me to tell you—if you want to have a greater connection with Spirit, you need to do A, B, and then C—would be a disservice to you. My way of connecting with Spirit is unique to my path. For instance, I could not figure out how to meditate back then. My mind is constantly going. So, Spirit just shows up without me calling them in. I don't work with only one guide, I work with a team of hundreds of guides, I work with whoever shows up. All of this is because of the way they trained me and I trained them. I let Spirit know that I will only allow "beings" who are of the light to come through. This assisted me in knowing I would always be safe with them.

I had let Spirit know that I wanted them to come through for most of my adult life. I had been experiencing messages throughout my life, but none of it was consistent and I never knew when an intervention or a message was going to show up. Many times, I didn't know what to do when I did receive a message. I had noticed that when I relayed a message from Spirit to friends and family, they thought I was being bossy. They responded, "Who do you think you are? You don't know anything." Because of this, I learned to stop sharing what I was told.

Eventually, I learned to inform people that this message came from Spirit. Some began to take notice. The problem was that I didn't always know that it came from Spirit until I began channeling more consistently. In the beginning, it felt like this "knowing" came from me. I guess that it would be fair to say that I don't always notice the difference between Spirit and myself the way others do. I am Spirit and Spirit is me.

When I was 18, my father got me a clown costume for Christmas and my sister Christine enrolled me in clown classes for my birthday. Believe it or not, this was part of my spiritual training.

It's amazing the transformation a little makeup will do. Me at 18 years old.

One of the things I learned from clowning was how to approach a child. I would bend down to approach them at their level. And now because of that training, I try to bend to where others may be coming from so that they can have a greater understanding of their connection with Spirit. Doing magic taught me how to notice how magical my life was. I continue to see Spirit as a child does. None of my spirituality has to do with shoulds and have tos or I will go to hell. The mouth coil magic trick I did, where streamers are pulled from my mouth, showed me that I could have something extraordinary come out of my mouth, not just the mundane. I know that it may sound like I am stretching all of this to make it work. Spirit has shown me the truth of it, and it makes total sense to me. Because of how much I doubted myself, Spirit literally needed to approach me in magical ways.

One primary thing I learned from clowning was how to connect to people as someone other than myself. Unfortunately, at the time, it backfired. That is because I wasn't ready. No one wanted Mary Beth to come to their party, they wanted my clown character to show up. I again fell into the belief that I, Mary Beth, wasn't enough. Decades later as I allowed Spirit to show up through me, I understood the part I was to play in giving Spirit a voice.

Even once I began channeling more consistently, my friends would call wanting to talk to my team of guides, not to me. Again, this created more self-loathing and doubt because Mary Beth wasn't enough. For a long time now, all of that has changed because when anyone talks to me, they talk to Spirit. I no longer experience that division because I have done so much work on releasing my old doubts and self-loathing.

In fact, sometimes people just want to talk to me, and both Mary Beth and Spirit will show up again and again. What I learned from all of this is that Spirit and I are one and there is no separation. If someone is uncomfortable with that, then they don't remain in my life for very long. If they do remain in my life, but don't want to do the spiritual stuff, then our relationship is all boring surface stuff and we don't talk very often. I keep evolving and changing and so does what I am willing to allow into my life.

I am no longer desperate for love and attention from family members and people from my past. If they don't want to be part of my spiritually involved life, I will give them their space. When and if they are ready to have our relationship be something different, then I will be right here waiting. I no longer bend and contort myself into someone that they are comfortable with, but I am not. I have become too strong and powerfully connected to be anything less than the highest version of myself. *I see it because I believe it.*

I had my greatest desire come true in my late 20s—I became a mom. I absolutely loved being a mom. It gave me an opportunity to live that happy childhood that I had always dreamed of. Being a stay-at-home mom gave me so many opportunities to do things in a different way—show up in a different way. I explained everything that I could to my daughter, and she was a sponge—absorbing it all. Laughter, joy and silliness was my favorite part of the day.

Having the honor and privilege of helping her grow into the wise, compassionate and loving adult that she is, has been incredible. I empowered my child continually. Giving her choices so that she could learn from them and to help her realize that she always has choices. Making mistakes is part of life; embrace that. Yep—I love being her mom.

Spirit told me a long time ago that I was given Marsh as my husband because he allows me. He allows me to explore who I am, what works for me and what doesn't. He allows me to work, or stay home. He allows me to become and believe whatever feels right for me. He's not always comfortable with my choices and yet he still allows me my choices. Because of this, I am able to give myself permission to move beyond and explore so much.

My life has transformed from wanting to die, to wanting to live fully. Exploring new concepts and possibilities with Spirit is one of my absolutely favorite things to do. Living as an expression of love has shifted my life dramatically and I choose to never go back.

Training Spirit

I see something spiritual in every single thing because I am willing to see it. *I will see it when I believe it.* I can do this because my spirituality comes from a child's way of looking at life. This is again because my spirituality was frozen at a very young age, and I love to see things with wonder and awe. Know that you do not have to go through this type of trauma in order to experience this. All it takes is connecting to your innocence. Be filled with wonder as often as you can, and you will better understand what I am talking about.

If you are wondering why you can't connect to Spirit in the same way that someone else can, there are a couple of reasons. One of those reasons is because we are all different. I know that it sounds like a cop-out, but it's true. How we access Spirit is quite different because of what we agreed to before we came down here, what our beliefs *allow* us to believe and let in, and most importantly, how we train Spirit to show up. Obviously, we can't do much about what you agreed to before you were born. We can, however, work on our beliefs and also on how we train Spirit.

If you believe that you don't deserve to have Spirit communicate with you because of mistakes you have made or because you believe you are a nobody, or if you believe that it is wrong or evil to communicate with Spirit, then you may have some obstacles ahead of you. That doesn't mean that it's impossible, only that you are going to need to get rid of or clear your old limited beliefs. You see, the words you say and the thoughts that you think, create your reality. If you believe that you CAN'T do something, then it is like you are asking God to limit what you CAN do. You could even see it as a prayer. *God, please don't let me talk to you or the Angels and Ascended Masters because I am not worthy. Only prophets can do that and I am no prophet.* This is what your limited thoughts say to Spirit when you doubt yourself… limit yourself.

In just those couple of sentences, you really limited yourself and you even limited what God/Spirit is able to do to connect to you. If you have free will and you say, I can't do this and I'm not that, then God listens and *gives you your limited life.* Congratulations, now you don't have to step up and do amazing things or experience amazing things because of all the ways that you continually tell Spirit that you can't. The exception to this rule is if it is on your life path (it's what you chose before you incarnated). When something is on your life path, it's what you came here to do, be, or experience, and it's going to show up, ready or not.

I NEVER, EVER wanted to write a book. I liked my simple, flowing life. Yet, Spirit put a woman on my path who asked me why I was in the desert when I needed to be near water (I was on vacation in Arizona). Then she informed me that I was to write a book before the summer of 2020. I had been getting hints for years that Spirit wanted me to write a book filled with my transformational stories. I found that if I ignored the people that I encountered telling me I should write a book, I could move beyond this nonsense. But this woman was different. She said that time was running out and it was now or never. God needed me to step up and do what I came here to do. This woman is what is called an Earth/Gaia Angel, and also an intuitive.

I was terrified of writing my first book. Yet when I felt drawn to writing, Spirit showed me something like a movie of my past and I wrote about it. Sometimes they just took over and guided my writings. As I wrote, I was able to process my past. I was shown how to broaden my perspective or come from divine neutrality more consistently so I didn't latch onto the old victim way of experiencing my past. Again and again, I had to let go of my belief of what someone had done to me and realize how much I had done to myself by believing in the pain more than I believed in the healing. I had to let go of the belief that I couldn't write because I had learning disabilities. I let go of so much that I didn't even recognize myself by the end of my first book *The Lie That I Am, A Journey Back to Spirit*.

Once I was willing to start writing the book, I needed to train Spirit as to how I would like this process to unfold. I don't like to type because I'm painstakingly slow, and my flow is so disjointed because I need to focus on each keystroke. I considered talking into the computer or tablet and having it type the words for me, but while my loved ones began researching speech-to-text programs, I began writing with pen and paper. I loved it. Spirit says that when we physically write, it helps us process on a different level. In other words, it can be very therapeutic.

Here I am on my third book, and I'm still writing with pen and paper. So, both Spirit and I have learned how to make it work. If they dictate too fast, I write notes in the margin. Sometimes I'll have multiple Spirits come through, and it can get rather confusing when this happens. I let Spirit know that I'm going to take a break and get some food. When I come back, you need to decide who is going to be the spokesperson so that we can have more clarity. And that is exactly what happens when I return. Because of having so many different Guides coming through, you can better understand why each chapter has its own unique personality.

Another thing they like to do is to dictate the chapters to me at 2 A.M. I agree that I am clearer and I am able to let go of the agenda from the day because believe it or not—I have no plans for 2 A.M. So much magic happens between 2–4 A.M. There is less push and pull during that time and so we are pretty wide open and that assists us in experiencing a lot of opening and shifting.

I had blocked so much of my past, that Spirit taught me multiple ways to connect to past memories so that I could be as accurate as possible. They taught me how to see things from other people's points of view by teaching me a broadened perspective and also divine neutrality. The more I loved learning new things, the more I had new gifts and abilities show up. I was letting go of one "I can't" after another because of my willingness. We have no idea how much can shift and change if we are *willing*. That is the most important component in connecting to Spirit—our willingness. Desperation will close down the connection, so take note of that. *I see it because I believe it.*

Here is a strange way that Spirit started training me to really pay attention to the people I was interacting with. When I got into my car after having a sweet interaction at the store, Spirit would ask me what color were the eyes of the cashier who checked me out. I had no idea. What color was her hair, her shirt? Again, I didn't know. I could guess, but that's all that it would be.

From these questions, I was shown how I was not paying attention to anything except what my next words would be. I was being present, but not fully present and I needed to understand this. I was told not to worry about the words… they would come to me. Instead, notice all that is showing up around me. There is much that I am missing with each interaction. If I would like to learn how to notice the subtle shifts that were occurring around me, I must pay closer attention. Only then would I begin to notice all that is shifting into a new reality.

Because of this training Spirit was giving me, I began to notice more distinctly the "warble" that I see when I am supposed to speak to someone about whatever had a warble or vibration coming from it. I later trained Spirit that I would prefer something more noticeable than just a warble or vibration because if I got distracted, I could miss certain opportunities. This was when they changed things up and made adjustments so that what I was supposed to notice would light up or stand out in a more noticeable way.

Notice again and again how Spirit and I are working as a team. They let me know what they need from me, and I let them know how if we tweak it, it would work better for me. This is because my relationship with Spirit is different just like every other aspect of my life. I don't just accept whatever Spirit says. I question them and the information that they give me. NOT because I don't trust them, rather, I do it so that I can take the information I am given, further and *deeper*. This has transformed my relationship with Spirit beyond the norm, into the most extraordinary relationship. For instance, if I am given a mundane answer to a question, I ask them what that means, and I'm given more details. Then I ask, "but why," and I am given more. On and on Spirit and I go until I feel complete about receiving as much information as I can. This is what I mean when I say that I question *them*, not the information.

Approach Spirit with as much love and curiosity as you can. Once they know that you really are ready and willing to move your relationship with them in a different direction, they will begin by putting thoughts and ideas into your head; again, this feels like a download (this is the most common form of channeling). So many don't even realize that they are channeling because they don't hear a voice. The more that you trust this when it shows up, the faster that this will evolve. But know that you have to prove that you are willing and that you are going to follow through on whatever they ask of you. Know that there will be strange tests for you on this new path. Spirit will ask you to do something like open a window, and you need to step up and do it without hesitating to show or prove your willingness. Know that this is a huge step in your evolution of being a more spiritual being.

Talking out loud seems to intensify the connection in the beginning. *You will see it, when you believe it.* When you show up ready and willing to be of service rather than self-serving, your Angels and Guides will show up more consistently also. This does not mean that your Angels and Guides will not help you as an individual. They are going to assist you so much that you can't really remember your life before all of this guidance. However, once you begin assisting all of humankind—well, that's when everything changes for you. Your team shows up with more gifts and abilities. There are so many new people and experiences that show up. *You will see and experience all of this because you believe it.*

If you can approach your relationship with Spirit with the knowing that it's going to be totally different than anyone else's, that will help to set you up for greater success. Allow everything to unfold and flow in its own unique way. After all, isn't that what we are doing with our own ascension, finding our own unique way of connecting to all that is?

Here comes another part of my training. Quite often I will have a plan or idea and my physical body can NOT go in that direction. I sure do have fun *trying* to do something different just to see how far Spirit will take it. You see, I have also taught Spirit how much I enjoy a good laugh. Because of their follow-through, I am reminded in that moment how connected I am.

Just recently before an appointment I had in town, I had planned to go to a certain pharmacy that had wonderful cards that weren't too expensive. Valentine's Day was coming, and I love sending cards. Then I realized that I had a lot of extra time before my appointment and decided to check out the local Dollar Store for cards since I had quite a few to purchase, and so I did. Next, I went to my chiropractor, and when I came out, I headed for my car. Which was straight ahead. But Spirit had other plans for me. Every time I tried to go straight, they had me going to my left. I eventually realized that was the direction to the pharmacy I had initially planned to go to for cards.

After explaining to Spirit that I no longer needed to go there because I had already purchased my cards, I again tried to head towards my car. Again, my body went left. I was trying to convince Spirit right there in the parking lot, and they refused to listen. I let go of my own agenda and finally followed theirs. When I went into the pharmacy, they had a 75 percent off table that lit up. I went over to look at it. I saw nothing I wanted or needed. Then I noticed a sweet, precious woman looking at that same table. We had such a long and magical conversation, during which I watched her open up repeatedly to new ideas and possibilities. I understood on a very sacred level that she had been praying and asking something of God. I was the messenger that God put on her path that day to let her know that she was heard. Every word I said was guided. I witnessed her opening up more and more. When we were complete, she didn't want me to leave. She had learned so much in our short time together. I remember very little about our conversation because it was given to her by God, and I was simply the voice that God needed to relay His message.

This woman who I had met that day, later ended up asking about me at every business and shop in the area; eventually, she was able to track down my chiropractor and give him a thank you card for me. That's how important our conversation was to her. Every word that came out of my mouth for her was exactly what she needed to hear. I love it when Spirit uses me in this way. I am always so surprised at the wisdom that I am able to impart to these individuals that I encounter. And yet a part of me is not surprised at all. So, while I train Spirit as to what I feel comfortable with and what I enjoy, they train me by letting me know that the more I show up with a willing heart, the more they allow me to be of service in whatever way they need. SO WHEN I LIMIT WHAT I AM *WILLING* TO DO… I LIMIT WHAT I AM *ABLE* TO DO. I try not to limit myself anymore. *I see it because I believe it.*

I have learned that when I let Spirit know I'm going to be here at this time and then I plan to go over there, and lunch will be at this restaurant and then finally I will stop at this other place, I notice that each place I go into, I encounter people that seem to be almost waiting for me. I am able to relay messages from Spirit and everyone feels so very loved and blessed. I am so grateful for these magical days and moments. I love watching person after person being touched, opened up, or even transformed. In those moments I know that all my training has paid off, along with all the training I have given Spirit.

Spirit and I are a team and it flows so incredibly because we have both taken the time to get to know each other and to understand our needs and desires. I am living a life far beyond what I thought any human could experience. That is because I am a human becoming. I'm moving beyond human limitations and creating new possibilities. You too can do this if you are willing to let go of your limited beliefs and show up and tell Spirit what it is that you desire to create for your life and in your relationship with Spirit. It is beneficial to include what you are comfortable with. However, try not to limit yourself. Then sit back and watch your life and your experiences transform.

One of the many ways that you can do this is when something shows up, you can accept it, or reject it. I remember the first time I saw a person down on their luck and I said, "Bless them on their path." In a flash, I was given a download of their life. I had to pull over to cry. I was honored and uncomfortable at the same time. To me, this information was private, and I felt like I was invading their privacy. I noticed that I continued to experience this once in a while, but it was more filtered—less intense. Spirit felt my reaction and wanted to keep me comfortable, so they "lightened" my experience. Because they want me to continue to do this work, they try to work within the parameters that I have set (without realizing I was even setting any parameters).

So again, you can see how I am training them. Once I began channeling, I felt like the robot in the movie *Short Circuit*. I want more input, more input. Give me more information so I can understand on a deeper level. Getting a download about someone's life back then felt intrusive, but getting *some* information so I may assist them felt more respectful. Now I tend to just allow and allow. Because of this so much amazingness shows up in my life. And the self-imposed limitations fall away.

Decades ago, I was doing a mediation and Jesus showed up. As we greeted each other, he stepped into me. I was given every experience he had ever had, along with every thought he had ever had. When he stepped out of me, it was gone. In that moment, I had an understanding that this was normal on the other side. There on the other side of the veils we have nothing to hide from one another. From there I was able to get more comfortable with experiencing telepathy. At first, I was embarrassed that someone might learn this or that about me and not want to be a part of my life anymore. Now I realize it is part of our human experience to make mistakes and I am no longer embarrassed or uncomfortable by that. I am who I am. This philosophy and understanding has assisted in my ability to write about some rather uncomfortable things that have happened in my life.

The more I am willing to be wide open and do whatever is asked of me, the fewer limits I have and the more gifts that show up. Sometimes these new gifts feel like a thank you for all of my willingness. My latest gift is, as I am telling a story to assist in taking a person's understanding further, this person will say to me, "Oh, my gosh, I can see what you are saying. I'm right there watching exactly what you are talking about." This has happened multiple times so far. I encourage it and ask to have this become a way of life for me to be able to *transport* my listeners right into my story—what a sacred gift. In other words, I am training Spirit again.

I hope that all I have been teaching and explaining has assisted you in being able to take your own experiences further and further. Ask Spirit for help during every step of your journey. Let them know what you would like more of, and what you didn't enjoy or aren't ready for… yet. Train them so they understand in what ways you are willing to have them work through you. Let them know that you are ready to step up and serve in whatever way they need you to serve. Because then—*you will see it because you believe it.*

My life has been so very enriched by this willingness. The people I encounter and the things I get to experience are beyond words. Join me in changing our world by changing the way that you and Spirit work with each other, one experience at a time. This is when you will realize what a creator you are and what the saying, "Heaven on Earth (Gaia)" truly means. We are so very blessed.

And so it is.

Expand Beyond Limitations

Expansion is in EVERYTHING on your journey of Ascension. I feel like there are not enough pages in a book to cover all that expands during your transition.

Think about so many aspects of your everyday life. How can you take the mundane into your heart and bring it to a place of extraordinary? Look at how you greet a person. Is it the same for everyone you meet? Are you *willing* to see the individual and greet them by expressing what you feel *in* their presence and *from* their presence? One of my sisters used to say, "Awesome, awesome, awesome—yes, yes, yes." It felt fantastic the first 20 times she said it, but after a while, I noticed that she would say it about the weather, how she was doing that day, and how her kids were doing. It just didn't change and I went numb when she used those words.

Eventually, I noticed that by her using these words, she felt she was being optimistic, but it actually meant she did not want to share anything. If I ask her about the weather, I would hear—awesome, awesome, awesome— the conversation stops and I don't have a clue about the weather. I ask how she is doing—awesome, awesome, awesome. It stops the conversation, and

I hang up knowing nothing new about her life. I ask about her kids and I hear—awesome, awesome, awesome. I'm grateful they are doing well, but I don't learn how they are changing and growing. So, while she is trying to be upbeat, she is closing down our connection. Because of this, I noticed that "awesome" became just "ok" in my own head.

Once I was able to show her this and explain where it takes our relationship, she was *willing* to see and understand what I was experiencing from these interactions. Now when she says awesome, it can take me to that place of awesomeness because it is not over-used and thus mundane. So, try to catch yourself with your verbiage. What is your catchphrase? Are you over-using it? Does it even carry any truth when you use it anymore? I very seldom say, "Have a nice day." People are numb to those words. Those words no longer hold the meaning that they used to. The same is true with the words, "How are you" and "Fine." Both the question and the response are automatic—boring.

Are you brave enough to say something like, "I hope your day has been beyond fantastic so far." When I say something like that, I notice a pause. You know how much I love a pause. Next, a smile comes across their face and I know that they just *gave themselves permission* to feel fantastic. How long they retain that feeling is up to them, I was simply the catalyst of the feeling.

With your expansion, are you willing to send a heartfelt note to someone more often? When we take the time to write something down, that person can re-read the message you gave them again and again. So many people have saved my cards and letters over the years because the words I wrote came from my heart and they were felt by their own heart. Do you see how I could have just said heartfelt, but instead I took the time to *expand* my words and then *expand* the understanding of my words?

Limiting words and boring words don't assist in expansion—instead, they can put people to sleep. Remember this is a time of awakening.

In an earlier book, *With a Promise of Ascension*, I taught the difference between doing good and making a difference. Making a difference feels so limited now that I have fully stepped into "being of service." Of course, being of service does "make a difference" and it is "doing good," but it encompasses so much more. Every encounter I am given, I look at how I can serve this person. Because Spirit's presence is now part of who I am, I feel like I am being asked to step up to impart whatever wisdom they are in need of and this has repeatedly been the answer to a person's prayer. This is truly a humbling honor.

Because of my willingness to expand, unexpected words flow from me as I watch the transformation take place in another. The words I speak may not be what a person was *hoping* to hear, however, it will be the words that they *need* to hear. At first, there may be resistance from the person receiving the message. As a person opens and allows (but only if they are willing to receive the message), they are transformed—shifted into a new reality. In that moment they move into a different understanding of themselves and what they need to do. This usually has to do with letting go of something that no longer serves them. This can require a leap of faith, or letting go of a belief. *They will see it when they believe it.*

Expanding our thoughts creates new possibilities and new realities to show up. As long as I limit my thoughts there can be no growth. For instance, if I believe my hubby, Marsh, is not able to connect to Spirit in the same way that I connect with Spirit—I have just limited him. However, if I am *willing* to see the subtle shifts and changes that are occurring in him, I can allow those thoughts to change. As a side note—my hubby is not here to connect in the same way I do. He has his own individual journey to experience, so why would he do anything the way that I do it?

Our birth family can be such an enormous challenge in this area. Many in my family still see me as the unhappy pessimistic teenager I was. They aren't interested in seeing me in a different way. Bummaroo for them. Look at people with your new expanded eyes and go beyond the label you gave them when you experienced your first impression of them (or even your last impression of them). Be willing to see more potential and possibilities in them and for them. Stop the definitions you have of people, places and things as much as you can. If you must define something, use it to have a greater understanding. Once that is accomplished, try to let go of the definition so they, the person or thing, can become more expansive than a definition will allow them to be.

Back to our thoughts—take any thought you have and play with how you can expand it. I'm going to take something so boring and show you how I can shift it. My plans for today are—to write a little, eat, take a bath, go to the bank, and then go into town. My expanded thoughts for my plans for today are:

- Write what Spirit inspires me to put on paper. Stay open to new ways of looking at something as I write.
- Ask my body what it would like me to take in for lunch to help it in the highest way.
- While soaking in the tub, allow my thoughts to be filled with flow, letting go of all agendas. Anything my body no longer needs is released down the drain and is given to Mother Gaia for her highest good.

- Go to the bank and celebrate; today is payday! What do I want to do with my money? Who do I want to share it with?
- Allow something new to show up on my path. While in town today, I feel there is a new movie out that will inspire me—I look forward to seeing what it is and how it will assist me. I am curious whom Spirit will want me to approach and what Spirit will guide me to say to each of them.
- I wonder what incredible deals I will come across and if I will want to participate in those deals.
- I'm feeling extra lucky today; I may choose to buy a lottery ticket. I wonder if the jackpot will come to me, or go to someone else and I get to contribute to their dream.

Which plan for the day feels like there will be room for amazingness and expansion? Do you see how much I can expand and expand the mundane? This is so important. Break open the boxes that you have put your whole life into. Does each person have their own box? Are you willing to let them out of their box so that they can come out and play with you? Remember—connecting to our innocence is important to creating joy and simplicity in our ascension. Is your job in a box, too? Are you willing to let it change and expand to something more? What about your community? More boxes? Our home, our vehicle, where we put our money, how we spend our time? Are these each in a box, or are you playing with newness each day? Are you allowing anything and everything to become more expansive than you've ever ALLOWED it to be?

How about how you express your love to all of the people you care about? Is it, "Love ya, bye-bye?" When Marsh and I were dating, he gave me a peck and said, "Love ya." I stopped him and said, "Seriously—is that the best that you can do?" He paused and asked me what I meant. I explained that this moment of affection needs to hold me for the entire day. I don't think you are expressing your love for me in a very impressive way. He then kissed me like he really meant it. When he said, "I love you," he looked into my eyes and into my heart. That night he thanked me for teaching him how to be a better man.

This is a picture of Marsh and I on our first date.

From this story, we can now understand that we can teach others how to expand who they are and how they show up. That doesn't mean we "make" someone do something. Nope—not ok. We can ask, we can suggest, and we can be an example. Nothing should be forced. Remember, free will is at play here.

Showing respect shows up in many different forms. Here's a strange one. Many people in my life have changed the name that they would like me to use when addressing them. The shorter version of their name doesn't seem to fit them anymore. Many are choosing their "given name." A person's given name can carry a much different frequency, it carries who they came here to be, and/or who their parents wanted them to be—who they were "born" to be. Isn't that fascinating? Where do these words take you? Calling people by the name they are comfortable with is a sign of respect. We now choose to live from a more respectful place by showing up in this way.

I have been noticing a pattern lately, and I would like to take a moment to address it here because it has to do with expansion. When did it become ok, normal, and acceptable for older siblings to treat their younger siblings like they don't matter, like their existence is a joke or a bother? This isn't just when they are young, it can remain a way of life sometimes until the very end. So many missed opportunities to have a more substantial relationship can be lost. Are you willing to expand your relationship with your siblings into something beyond a kid who doesn't know anything? Are you willing to learn more about them? What brings them joy? Maybe allow your relationship to become a friendship? They are your siblings for a reason. Are you limiting what this relationship could be? As you look at how you can make a difference in the world, maybe ask yourself how you can make a difference in your own family. Just something to think about as you expand your beliefs into something more.

I know that this chapter just keeps going on, but I want to cover another aspect of expansion that is very, very different from all that I have been talking about. I would like to talk to you about expanding your physical body. No, this has nothing to do with weight gain. This has to do with consciousness expansion assisting your physical body and letting in more light. Let us move into learning something new. As you settle in for your quiet time or meditation, take several deep breaths. Notice your body. Connect to it. Ask permission to go deeper within your body. Now take the time to notice and then connect to the cells in your body. Get comfortable with this and then visualize them expanding larger and larger. Visualize the space in between your cells expanding.

I have been told by Spirit that the space in between your cells can be a super highway for light and energy to flow through. When we are contracted, it can be more difficult to have this higher vibrational light and energy flow with grace and ease. As we visualize this space in between the cells expanding and expanding, we create these super highways of light bringing in Christ Consciousness, healing, turning on our higher mind, and connecting to our Higher Self—our Soul. Talk about expansion!

As you begin your visualization, breathe innnn and ooout as you connect to your cells. As you continue your meditative breathing, thank your cells for all that they do for you. Really notice how beautiful your cells are and how much they help to create this beautiful, physical body of yours. Now allow your cells to expand and expand. Allow the space in between the cells to expand and get larger. It may be beneficial to push out with your hands in all directions to encourage this expansion. Once you truly connect to this, using your hands is not really necessary. As you continue to connect to your cells and the space in between your cells, keep expanding and expanding. Breathe it in and expand it out. Soon you won't be able to fit in the room you are in. Keep going—expand to the size of the building you are in. Go beyond that, and expand beyond the community you're in, your state, your country, the planet. Keep going as you breathe in all that you are and breathe out a more expansive version of yourself. Expand beyond our galaxy to the universe and the multi-universe. Expand until ALL THAT IS exists within you. Stay with this expansion. BE this expansion. Breathe this expanded experience into every particle of who you are.

Notice everything that you can. Realize that this is an aspect of oneness. If all that exists is within you, then you can have greater clarity of God/Source, the Heavenly Realm, the Ascended Masters, and the Universe. Ask if there are any messages for you here. Be patient as you wait for the messages to show up. Know that your connection to all that is in this moment is expanded beyond all past knowings. Allow all limitations to fall away... you are limitless! Notice your place in all of this. Just BE and ALLOW.

You can stay in this expanded state as long as you would like. Notice as much as you can. Hear all the wisdom that is being imparted to you. This is your time. This is YOUR EXPANSION of who you believe yourself to be. Allow these new understandings to be part of your experience. Allow, allow, allow.

As you *slowly* come back into your room, it would be beneficial to journal about your experience. When I do this, I find I am given even more messages and information that will assist me in taking all that I have just experienced even further. *You will see it when you believe it.*

Like I said in the beginning... expansion is in everything on your journey of ascension. Expand your wardrobe, your circle of friends, your relationships, your priorities, your choices. Be willing to look at all aspects of your life, and see how you can expand each and every one of them. In doing this, you may find that you are ready to get rid of many aspects that are no longer serving you. That is as it should be. Who you were when this spiritual journey began, and who you have become, are totally different people. Let us give everyone permission to become someone different by not limiting them. Allow everyone to expand and become more. Allow Gaia to expand and become more.

We are ALL meant to be MORE!

Take a Breath

I'm sure that all of you know how to center and focus on your breath as you meditate. If not, you may want to watch some videos, or take some classes because it is a very beneficial and sacred part of our connection to all that is. I always have to do things a little bit differently and breathing is no exception. I have had people say, "Breathe in love and breathe out peace," or "Breathe in _____ and breathe out _____." You fill in the blank. When I FIRST began meditating, I felt like I was breathing in a word and breathing out a word. That is all that I usually felt because it seemed like I could focus on the breath or I could focus on the emotion, but I tend to get flustered with multiple tasks UNTIL I let go of my agenda. I know that sounds ridiculous, but it CAN BE my truth.

Then I came across the teaching of breathing from my heart center. As I focused on my breath there, I noticed this very solid light. As I focused on the light, my breath did what it wanted to do. I tried to keep doing deep breaths and holding, then releasing and holding, and all that this entails, but the light was pulling me in. After doing this for a while, what I noticed was that with every breath this light became brighter and stronger. It felt like my breath kindled the flame.

Oh, how fun is this. So, I began experimenting. Can I breathe out the light and then breathe the light back in? Oh my gosh, I can do that. I began trying to see how much or how far I could breathe this light out. Can I assist in having it go further out with every breath I take? Yep, I can do that. Pretty soon I am having my breath go out to my neighborhood, and then my entire city. After a while, it covered my state. Keep going innnn and oooout. Now it covers the USA. Next, it's North America.

This is so wonderful! I'm sending out giggles with my light. My light is no longer coming back in, it's just expanding and expanding out until it covers the entire planet. I begin to get very emotional. The light feels deeper or thicker somehow. All I know is that I want to do more. Suddenly, I notice that as I breathe in, I'm breathing in something new. This new energy is giving me delicious tingles and I feel my tears pouring down. I notice my Angelic tones are intensifying.

So much love—so much intensity. Finally, I go into still point (where breathing or anything ceases to exist). I have no idea how long it is before I begin breathing again. I'm filled with sparkly light. I'm filled with so much love and gratitude. Once I can focus again, I ask Spirit what had just happened. And when can we do it again?

Spirit said, "That light you sent out to the entire planet was the light of your soul. As individuals felt your pure love, they sent love back to you. This created a soul connection with so many beings all over the planet. This was creating activations and healings again and again. Please keep showing up, Mary Beth, with your curiosity and your innocence. From this space, you can achieve so very much. We all want to thank you for your willingness to continually show up and touch lives and even souls." You are welcome. This was another win-win because I received so much in return.

I was able to accomplish something similar while my brother was going through his cancer experience a few years ago. When I would hear the song "You Raise Me Up" in my head, I would witness an aspect of me going out to the front yard. I would rise a hundred feet or so above the ground. And I would notice a basket over my left arm and I instinctively knew that I was to sprinkle this sparkly dust inside the basket. I went state by state, and then country by country doing this. I was singing "You Raise Me Up" and spreading love. This was so much fun, and through it all I felt so much LOVE going out to the world, while there was so, so much love coming back to me.

After doing this over a dozen times, I saw dolphins, whales, and sea turtles popping their heads out of the oceans and asking for my loving sparkly dust over the waters, too. I was happy to comply. Spirit has let me know for over 3 decades now that dolphins, whales, and sea turtles are very highly connected beings. They are assisting our planet in so many ways. This helps me to understand why my daughter is so connected to them. Almost every time she is in the ocean, sea turtles show up. I'm so very happy for her.

I have no idea what all this means, but it seems to calm things down on the planet. I just do what I am asked and I am honored to do so. I know I am sprinkling love, and that is all the explanation that I need. No competition, no agenda, simply love.

I was given another breathing experience about ten years ago, and I found it very beneficial. When I noticed tension in my body, I found that taking in a big breath and blowing it out very quickly and forcefully would cause a huge woosh of a sound coming from my mouth. This air that was released carried the tension I was holding within my body. I began to notice with each release that there was less noise and less tension. This is because so much tension, anxiety, or frustration is leaving with each exhale.

Soon I notice that when I do the forceful exhale, I am noticing no sound at all except a simple breath which is very normal. All the tension, anxiety, or frustration has been released or cleared out. I notice my verbiage is filled with more light again, along with my thoughts. What a beautiful and easy gift this is for us and it can be done anywhere at any time. *You will see it when you believe it.*

Here's a little quirk I noticed with this exercise. It is beneficial to turn your head away from other people when you do this exercise. A few people said they felt bombarded with intense energy when I exhaled toward them. This was another confirmation that what I felt was happening, was another's experience also. I am grateful.

Spirit is very chatty today. They would like me to describe another unusual thing that I get to do. I am able to birth enormous butterflies from all over my body. And no, no one else can see these butterflies except me—yet. I can do this anytime and anywhere. I will describe this process in as much detail as I can. Maybe it will inspire you to try this, also.

As I was meditating, I noticed something black appear below my chin. This black butterfly head was peeking over my chin. Once it realized I wasn't afraid and I wasn't going to freak out, it emerged fully from the heart center in my chest. Its wings were so large as they emerged from curving around each of my shoulders. I had never seen anything so beautiful. This first one was a beautiful shimmering blue. It looked me in the eyes for a moment. I thought I heard a thank you, a nod, and then it flew off. As I collected myself, I noticed another one emerge a few inches lower on my body. This one came more quickly. It was a shimmery emerald green. Again, it paused, nodded, and flew off. Next was a golden yellow.

These butterflies continued and continued. All different colors and sizes. Where they emerged from on my body was also so different. I even had a velvety scarlet one come from my armpit. I laughed and laughed. After doing this for what seemed like 100 times, I finally stopped it. Normally I don't stop something. I let it continue until it can't anymore.

I was told that I could do this continually all day and night if I wanted to. I will have access to this for the rest of my life. Wow, what a gift! Spirit explained how I am assisting so many in emerging out of their chrysalis and becoming their ascended selves, and here is the proof. Thank you for entrusting me with this incredible honor. I am truly grateful and blessed.

So, what color butterfly are you? Are you ready to come out of your chrysalis? Are you ready to participate in your new ascended life on Gaia? Whomever you are and whatever you decide, it is a sacred honor to meet you. I thank you for your participation in our ascension. Please say hi as you fly by on your way to your next adventure.

I may not have been very good at breathing in love and breathing out peace in the beginning. Fortunately, I have gotten much better over the years. The adventures I go on may not be the norm, but they certainly are exciting and frequency-raising. Come join me and my butterflies as you go deeper and higher in your ascension and your understanding of all that is. *You will see it and experience it when you believe it.*

What are You Willing to Allow?

How can we take allow, surrender, and giving ourselves permission, further? First, I need you to look at these different concepts and realize that they all carry a similar frequency and can sometimes be used to achieve the same outcome. Allowing is a very, very powerful technique used to release and shift. The question is, are you willing to allow it to be bigger and more powerful, or do you want to continue limiting it?

When you say words like, "I allow myself to be more," you can take a baby step or a quantum leap. Step out of the duality of the word "more." *ALLOW* it to encompass every aspect of your life. *Allow* your gifts and abilities to expand. *Allow* yourself to be more on both a human level and a spiritual level, until your human is your spiritual. When you start asking things like… was that me, or was that Spirit who suggested that? This is when you and Spirit (your soul, your Higher Self) are integrating until you are completely one and there is absolutely NO separation. The only reason that you are questioning this is because it "feels different," that is all.

It feels different because it is different. Everything about this IS DIFFERENT! YOU are becoming something *more* and something *different* with every breath you take. *Allow* this to be your experience. *Surrender* to this being your truth. *Give yourself permission* again and again to be something that you weren't yesterday. *Allow* Flow in. *Allow* curiosity and joy in. Allow and allow, surrender and surrender, give yourself permission and more permission.

Now let's let go of all that we used to tell ourselves. Things like, "I shouldn't have to give myself permission." If it works, it works, period. Stop putting guilt or blame, shoulds and shouldn'ts, on yourself or others. That's the old spiritual ego junk. That doesn't work here. *Allow* the spiritual ego belief of "we should never say this or do that." Sometimes those words or understandings are EXACTLY what you need to hear or understand. So, again let go of those parameters you gave yourself and everyone else. *Allow* what needs to happen—to happen. *Allow* your thoughts to be your thoughts without filters for a moment. Sometimes we need to give ourself *permission* so that we can break out of our old junk when nothing else seems to work. *Allow* that to be your truth, and then you can move on and get out of your old stuck patterns. I remember one of my brothers taught me that using the word "but" excludes everything that came before it and therefore should not be used. I was grateful for this insight because I was using the word way too much. However, there are times when nothing but a but will do.

How does that feel? Were you able to give yourself *permission*? Did you notice how you were in the flow of *allowing* and then I brought in the last paragraph and I used words like crap and junk and your vibration came plummeting down? That was done on purpose. We wanted you to see how words can raise your frequency and how quickly they can lower the frequency. Yep—I did a science experiment on you. What were the results of the experiment? If you felt no shift at all, then your core is very, very strong. Congratulations! That is fantastic.

If you shifted—that's also great because it shows you how much something less than love can affect you. Use this knowledge to learn from and grow. I love it that we affect each other. Just be aware that we can affect each other both positively and negatively. I love how much it shows us how connected we can be… how connected we ARE. Tiny understandings like this can shift everything. So many are waiting to see how money is going to shift and change as we all live in a higher dimension or reality before they are willing to look at money in a different way. Nope—not how it works. We're waiting for people we care about to become what we want and need them to become before we believe they are acceptable. Nope—not how it works.

Until you are perfect and have no more "things" to work on with yourself, what is out there, or what is someone else's stuff, is none of your business. All the time you waste on how others should be and how certain systems need to change is time you are NOT spending working on changing and improving yourself. What's yours is yours. What's theirs is theirs. All this is true but it isn't true, depending on where you are at in your ascension. Also, there are things that are going to shift your energy because IT IS yours to notice and do something about. This really makes our lives very interesting.

When I look at society with my broadened perspective, I see how most "asleep" humans are spending as much time as possible each day complaining about other people. Telling everyone how right they are and how wrong these other people are. Where is the *allowing* in that, I ask you? Anyone can find fault in another. Let us spend our time instead finding the AMAZINGNESS in another. That is what will shift and change our planet. When you spend your time whining and complaining, you create more conflict. Don't you think this planet has enough conflict already? If you aren't going to help raise the vibration of the planet, then please try to be neutral (actually, neutrality is the goal). If you are lowering the vibration with your thoughts and words, our shift of the ages will take longer. Is that what you want?

The more we *surrender* our old ways of doing things, the more we give ourselves *permission* to be something different. The more we *allow* things to be good instead of bad, right instead of wrong, kind instead of hate-filled, the more we will be able to connect with Spirit on a whole other level. Again, I apologize for all of the duality words. This is such a simple thing and yet it is a game-changer, a life-changing for the better. How have you surrendered your old way of being? How have you given yourself permission to be something different? How have you allowed your way of living to alter? We want change, as long as *we* don't have to change. Nope—not the way it works. We need to BE the change we wish to see in the world, by living as that. If you want peace in the world, you must exist AS peace. Now is the time to use your powerfulness to create our amazing new Gaia.

Celebrate any and all changes, even the ones that seem to take you backward. We need to feel the discomfort when we go backward to help us in our understanding that we are no longer willing to live that way anymore. Spend time noticing if your life choices are feeling more centered and connected to Spirit. Is your floundering happening less and less frequently while your level of trust is becoming more and more prevalent? Yippie! Keep it up. You are excelling so much more than you realize.

We have trained ourselves to see our faults more than our assets. You can test this idea by simply looking in the mirror. What most of us tend to see when we look into a mirror is what we call our defects. Look at that rash, where did that come from? Oh yeah, I ate chocolate yesterday. Why did I do that? I know it's going to make me break out. On and on our self-abuse continues. By the time we step away from the mirror, were we able to see anything we liked about our reflection? It would be beneficial to learn how to look at your reflection and see the perfections rather than the flaws. See how those smile lines are there because you have smiled so much—that's a good thing. Notice how beautiful your eyes are. Smile at yourself, wink at yourself, and see the playfulness within you. Shift your experience of looking in the mirror as something few people experience… see awesomeness and perfection. Then notice how differently you feel about yourself.

As a society, we have so much respect for people who believe in themselves. Believing in ourselves is the way we are meant to be. Another interesting piece is being aware of when we shift from respecting someone to worshiping them and putting them up on a pedestal. If we need to put a person on a pedestal, let it be someone who spreads kindness rather than doubt. Better yet—let's get rid of all the pedestals completely. They serve no one, and they never have. Even Jesus would rather not be on a pedestal. He says it's hard to have a conversation when He is way up there—unreachable. He does have a point. Who do you put up on a pedestal? Are you willing to let them come down off of it? Are you ready to see yourself as deserving the same respect that you were willing to give them? Remember, no one asked you to put them up on that pedestal. You chose to do that. How is it serving you—serving them? *You'll see it when you believe it.*

Keep asking yourself questions, so that you can get some answers. Let's not make life about being good or bad, right or wrong, and simply come to the realization that we are all different. We all have a part in this unfolding that is happening. Are you ready to step up and do your part?

Are you willing to allow yourself to surrender who you believe yourself to be? Can you give yourself permission to be the highest version of yourself that you have ever allowed yourself to be? Only you can give yourself that permission by surrendering all past beliefs and understandings of who you are and allow yourself to be a new expanded version of your amazingness.

Is Going Backwards Really Backwards?

There will be times when we feel like we are living such a magical life. Everything is flowing. People are showing up on our path who are here to assist us, or we get to assist them. Challenges will feel like a far-removed aspect of your life and you are living your spiritual dream. Suddenly, you wake up and something that was effortless yesterday is a struggle today. You wonder what happened as you recenter yourself. Then obstacle number two comes at you and then numbers three and four show up, and they just keep coming one after another. Suddenly confusion is a way of life for you again.

How did this happen? What's going on? This can't be my life. My life is magical—exceptional. Things like obstacles and feeling like I'm back in heaviness and density have not been part of my life for so long now. None of this makes any sense. You notice that now you are judging people. This is crazy! You begin judging yourself for judging others. Holy moly, did you just criticize someone? Was that sarcasm coming from you? DOES ANY OF THIS SOUND FAMILIAR?

Welcome to the opportunities for growth that are on your incredible spiritual path. You may think that I am crazy for saying this, but, I'm so excited for you. You have been given an opportunity to notice how far you have come. Spirit is asking you to take a look at how easy it *would be* to go back to your old way of being. They are asking you, which one do you really want? Which one feels like the TRUE you? Now what are you going to do about it?

If you can, connect to looking at everything from a place of divine neutrality. That means letting go of all your judgments and how you believe things should be, and *allowing them to be exactly as they are.* Connect to your divinity and stay as neutral as possible. Look for the amazing lessons that are present in your experiences and have gratitude for them. We learn and grow so very much from these lessons. What a gift you have just been given. There will be times when you just can't get all of this divine neutrality and gratitude stuff because "your human is showing up too much and is very loud." In these moments when you can't connect to the sacredness, and sometimes you can't even connect to something or someone as being special, it's ok; we've all been there, done that. When it's really challenging, try just using the phrase "how interesting."

Those two words can shift your frequency to a place of curiosity, and wonder—here you are connecting to innocence again. Yep, pretty cool, isn't it? Use your sense of humor also and you will connect to your innocence that way too. Say things like, "How interesting, for a moment there I forgot that we're all doing the best that we can. I can be so silly sometimes." Do you feel how much that can calm down your frequency? "How interesting that I decided to go back to my old way of being again.

It's curious how comfortable it used to be to behave that way and think that way. How very interesting."

All of this assists you in calming down your frequency so that you can recenter yourself. The sooner you do this, the quicker you will process this and move on. The longer you remain stuck in your old doubts and habits, the more likely it is that you will remain there awhile. Then you will simply get to process that again, and that's totally ok. Processing, learning, growing, it's all part of our shift to becoming an ascended being. I also find that saying something like, "You missed the target—try again," reminds me that this is simply a course correction.

Now, because it's ME and MY Guides, we're going to throw in some surprises—because that's what we do. This is called my different perspective. Because of how we are ascending and who will be ascending has changed, we need to understand some things. What I have been told is that originally only a certain "group" of people were going to ascend. These people were the ones who were dedicating their *entire* life to existing as LOVE in any and every way possible. Every breath, thought, word, and deed was living as "Christ consciousness," and as divine love. Everyone was loved by these beings. They saw goodness and promise in everyone.

This is NOT… if they do this or that, I will see them as good. Nope. This is a seeing-goodness-in-a-person's-flaws kind of love. These beings have done such an incredible job of raising the frequency of our planet. They truly are exceptional beings and we are so blessed that because of their willingness, we stand here today experiencing our own ascension.

However, something happened. Spirit asked our souls (our higher selves) if we would like the exalted ones to ascend, or should every soul have an opportunity to ascend. We chose EVERY SOUL. We as a collective asked that every soul be given awakenings and shifts to assist even the most asleep soul in waking up to a new way of being. This was not going to be easy. It would take some time to do all that needs to be done to create this shift of the ages… and here we are, doing it.

We are doing it with every act of KINDNESS that we participate in. We are doing it with every choice we make that creates PEACE. We are doing it as we live from a place of JOY. We are doing it by seeing what is wonderful rather than what is wrong. We are doing it as we live moment by moment, word by word, thought by thought in the highest way possible. Only then will we create LOVE. Love, far beyond our human understanding of love. This is loving all that exists… Even the painful or what could be perceived as negative stuff. All is loved. THIS is living as Christ consciousness or higher consciousness.

Here is another interesting piece (peace) of this. Those of us who are in the first wave of awakening and going through our ascension, have to work harder than the next wave. This is because we had much heavier density to work through. I am *not* speaking of our individual density, but rather the density of the frequency on the planet. To understand this, you must realize that the frequency on the planet is becoming higher and lighter each day, so for the ones that wake up years later, the higher frequency will assist them in having their challenges be less intense. I guess that would be a good way of stating this.

The first wavers agreed to do this more challenging work to assist all of humankind. Why? Because we love all of you so very much and we want each and every one of us to succeed—ascend. We believe that even the people who have created so many challenges are part of our ascension. This is because we first wavers understand how important these challenging people's rolls are. It takes a while to get to this place, but it's true. If you can take a moment and broaden your perspective to see things from divine neutrality (without judgment or agendas), you will see things in a different way.

The ones who are creating "chaos and negativity" are helping people by upsetting them, which is shaking them up and shaking them awake until they realize "being dishonest is no longer acceptable. Being unkind and a bully is no longer ok. Using others by taking advantage of them is not what we will allow anymore." This is how many are being woken up to a new way of being. With this understanding in mind, you can see how eventually we can see the "good" even in the "bad." Because we know all is happening for a reason and all is part of God's divine plan.

Know that your soul chose this. You, along with your other "human becomings" chose to go through so much chaos, confusion and challenges so that ALL may ascend, not just a chosen few. In so choosing, our world will NOT be destroyed. Instead, our world is being transformed into "Heaven on Gaia." Know this… WE ARE ALL THE CHOSEN ONES.

No soul left behind is the goal. However, there are many who don't seem to want to wake up. They are not wanting to let go of the hate and negativity. That is very sad for us to witness, but all have free will and there is time yet. God has not given up on anyone and neither should we.

It has always been difficult for me to understand why so many believe that God just points a bolt of lightning at someone and says, "They must go. They have not fulfilled My expectations." I can't imagine doing that to my own child and I'm not as benevolent and loving as God. Hear this— GOD wants us all to succeed. GOD wants us all to ascend. We all have free will so we have a choice. Know that we have more help from on high and from other "beings" than ever before in our planet's history. Everything is being done to help us succeed in the highest way possible. The part we get to "play" in this, is that we have to PARTICIPATE in our own ascension and we need to ask for help. No one is going to save us or assist us until we begin the process by choosing to be a better human and proving to Spirit that we want to be helpful and kinder to ourselves and others.

Spirit will not override our free will. They will help and assist and do whatever they can *when* we ask. But we MUST ASK! We must PARTICIPATE. Also, understand that there are over a million ways to ascend. The one you choose is precisely that—one way. Allow those 999,999 other ways to ascend unfold also. Do this without judgment so that you don't lower your frequency again.

Those in the first wave of ascension are taking on so much and doing what they can to assist all in the highest way possible. The waves that follow will have a much easier time and that is our desire. We are willing to do all we can so that as many of us as possible will succeed. That is why this book is being channeled for you. We want you to succeed. We want your ascension to be as effortless as possible. This does not mean it is going to be easy—nope, not at all. However, it will be easier than it was for the ones who came before you. I am grateful.

As we experience this "going backward" aspect of the ascension, know it is also a reminder of what those who are still stuck in denseness are still going through. With this reminder, we are better able to assist one another because we get to on some level work through it again ourselves, creating clarity on how to help others. What a sacred gift we have been given. Because of this, we are better able to describe what worked or didn't work for us. We are able to notice the subtle and not-so-subtle shifts that are occurring for us all.

Again, this helps us to take note so that we can assist others. Put on your own mask (as the flight attendant says) before we can assist others. People are better able to understand what is helpful and beneficial when it comes from a teacher who has experience with what they are teaching. So, learn as much as possible. Write down and remember as many of the details as you can so you are better able to assist others in walking through their own incredible and uncomfortable shifts.

I, myself keep forgetting what it was like, so I get to be taken back to the denseness and doubts so that I can remember how to assist others. All so that you get to have an easier time than I did. For this, I am so very grateful. *You will see this when you believe it.*

I remember thinking, hey, if I take longer to get this, the easier it will be for me. Because of that, I'm going to slow myself down. I even remember laughing at how clever I was. Then Spirit stepped in as they always do and said, "Really, Mary Beth? Do you really want to just sit there and do nothing knowing what you know, and knowing who you are? You would be willing to let others do the work that you can do yourself? All so that you could have an easier time?" It took me all of two seconds to say NO, ABSOLUTELY NOT. Know that to write this about myself is embarrassing that I ever even had that thought. However, I want you to understand that I have gone to those silly places, so if you go there—notice the pause and make a higher choice.

I did not come here to sit on the sidelines. I came here to make a difference. I came here to participate. I know for a fact that I see things differently than most others, and I'm very good at it. If I am not willing to step up and do my part, someone else will have to do it for me. That someone wouldn't have my same experiences and understandings. Therefore, their way of looking at all of this is going to be very different. This can be good because we all have something different to offer. However, my different perspective would be missing. My different perspective would not be available to all of you. This is unacceptable to me.

I came here to assist all who want to learn from me. There are some people out there who will resonate with our unique understanding of all that is going on, better than the way others may be teaching it. There will be others who cannot understand at all what we are saying. This is because we are not to be their teacher. However, the interesting part in all this is that our words are light coded, therefore, just by reading our words, they will be changed. Even if they don't understand how or why—they have changed.

You can go to a place of being lazy like I did for two seconds and let others do the bulk of the work that you came here to do, but then why are you here? Why do you need to continue being here? I don't ask these questions because I don't see value in you. Instead, I ask these questions so that you hopefully realize how important your role is in all of us having the ability to ascend.

Before I began writing *The Lie That I Am, a Journey Back to Spirit*, there was that intuitive woman whom I spoke of earlier. She informed me that time was running out for me to write my book. Looking back at the gift that she gave me, I realize that if she hadn't been *willing* to say something to me, all three of my books might not have been written. That would have been a great loss in my opinion. Are you seeing and understanding how if you aren't willing to step up to do and be what you agreed to do and be… so much would be lost? Your piece (peace) of our picture would not be there and our new world would not be complete without you.

We need you. We need ALL of you!

Re-Re-Re Until I Come Back Home

During our times of confusion, going backward can be a beneficial thing for us. What I mean by that is using words that begin with RE. Yep, that's what Spirit told me this morning. When we are lost and confused, rather than push forward into more confusion, it would be better to move backward to re-assess. Look at what has re-vitalized us in the past. See what we can do to re-evaluate our lives. What do you use to re-connect with what makes sense to you when nothing really makes sense?

Know that as you re-connect to the past to gain information, that it's not because you can't handle the present moment or even the future. Instead, see it as you have been holding onto too many things that give you comfort or even discomfort and thus creating a blockage rather than allowing anything new in. Taking the time to re-evaluate your relationships and decide what is working for you and what isn't can be a wonderful place to start. Many people can feel like relationships are heavy baggage that they have to drag around with them. Constantly needing to re-affirm to their loved ones that everything is ok because nothing feels "normal." Are you still willing to re-invest in that relationship? Take some time to re-flect on why you are in a certain relationship. Does it feel like it is time to re-lease this person? Is it time to re-invent the relationship and where it's going? Is it time to re-claim the relationship on a deeper level?

Noticing when a person you spend a lot of time and energy with is re-stricting your growth and who you are working on re-inventing yourself as. Do you find you want to re-move yourself from their presence shortly after you re-connect? Do you need to re-cover after spending time with them? Do they re-charge your energy or re-duce your energy? How much time does it take you to re-pair and re-focus yourself? When you think of a person, do you re-member the way it used to be, or enjoy the present moment?

I have someone in my life who LOVES to live in the past. Every moment is spent re-telling stories from her childhood, AND as an added bonus, it's always the exact same stories. I leave her having learned absolutely *nothing* about her present life. Later, I find out from others that she has moved, she went on some trips, her child experienced some milestones. I hear none of it from her because we only re-capture the past. I'm bored. I notice that I can experience re-sentment because I'm only in her past, I'm not in her present moment. Am I willing to continue a re-lationship where we only re-generate the past? I need to re-flect so I can re-evaluate what I am willing or not willing to do.

As you notice this stuckness in your life, take the time do the RE, RE, REs:

- re-evaluate
- re-asses
- re-organize
- re-search

- re-visualize
- re-invest
- re-move
- re-pair

- re-affirm
- re-negotiate
- re-discover
- re-claim

- re-prioritize   re-flect   re-appraise
- re-formulate   re-consider   re-plenish
- re-view   re-invent   re-charge
- re-lease   re-cover   re-write
- re-start   re-group   re-focus

You can do this with any aspect of your life where you feel stuckness. Your job, where you live, your hobbies, groups you belong to, where you spend your money, books you read, relationships you have, how you spend your time. You get to decide.

When we are willing to re-evaluate all aspects of our lives, we understand what we are ready to let go of. This can be habits, foods, our jobs, what we wear, who we spend our time with… everything. Appreciate all that "it" has done for you, then re-lease "it" from your life with love and *gratitude*. This will free up more of your time, energy, and even your thoughts so that you can pursue new possibilities. Let go of the old baggage that weighs you down so that your new and improved life can show up. *You will see it when you believe it.*

Take the time to notice how freeing all of this can be. Talking about the past and having memories is wonderful. It's a great re-minder of where you came from—where you have been. Don't feel you have to let go of everything, because you don't. I am speaking of the things that KEEP you stuck, KEEP you from moving forward.

To everything there is a time and a purpose. *You will see it, when you believe it.*

Focus on What is Your Focus

In this chapter we are going to learn how to focus our energy with a candle flame or a spot on the wall, and then once we master that, we will use that same focus to start working on healing the physical body, the world, and everything in between. It is best to start small and expand from there. We are going to start so small that we can begin with a candle flame, which many use to learn how to focus; we can also use a dot or even a spot on the wall. With this in mind, let us begin:

- Find the object that will assist you best in staying focused. For me, the more mundane it is the better it works for me.
- Having something dark on a light background or something light on a dark background assists it in standing out.
- Concentrate on whatever it is that you have chosen to focus on.
- Notice and observe—allow the background to blur and eventually fall away. It no longer exists. Your focus is all that matters.

- If you notice your mind wanders, bring it back by saying the words, "Thank you for sharing" to whatever drew your focus away. This is not a time of getting upset or frustrated with yourself.
- Once you have mastered staying focused, you can work on noticing what shows up for you. Are you noticing a certain color coming in? Are the colors changing? Notice and allow whatever shows up to be exactly what you need to experience, know and learn. This is not a time of manipulation. This is a time of focusing and allowing.
- Do you notice a message coming through? What is the message you are being given? What is the meaning of this message for you? Allow more messages to come through.
- As you focus, you open up in a new way, which allows Spirit to show up in a new way. Allow it to be exactly as it is. Allow, Allow, Allow.

When we focus, we allow the "norm" to fall away, and allow something different to show up. We allow our lives to transform into something we didn't even know was a possibility. We allow God to show up. We see the magnificence in whatever way we are willing to allow magnificence to show up.

Focusing helps us to stay on task. There are many times that we need to stay focused so that we can take our experience further. Because of my ability to stay focused, I can stay connected for instance to the tingles in my body. Allowing the tingles to raise my vibration and create healings for several hours. This could not happen if I were not able to stay focused. So focusing keeps you on task. Focusing can assist you in staying with a thought, idea or concept so that you can take it further.

Where we can take this focus depends on your intention as to why you have chosen to focus at this time. If you want to focus on an ailment within your body, or someone else's body? Please ask for permission from the soul of the person you are wanting to focus energy on. It is unacceptable to force your desires on another. ALL focused energy should be for their highest good. Never focus negative energy, for that will only create more negativity within your life and also in the world. We are creating our New Gaia here and now, so all needs to come from love.

Let us look at healing the body now, say for instance you are going to focus on your kidney. Take the time to look at a picture of a healthy kidney ahead of time so that you have a better understanding of what your goal can be. Don't MAKE your own kidney bad or wrong, instead, we are simply showing your kidney its potential.

As you focus, and focus some more, allow yourself to be taken (transported) to wherever it is that you want to focus on in their body, or your own body. Observe all that is around you. Do you see a spot... a stone or a tumor? Are you noticing that things are moving very slowly, or perhaps very fast? While working on certain other parts of the body, you may notice frazzled nerve endings, or is something disconnected or possibly there is a spot of discoloration? Once you are in the body, we *DO NOT JUDGE...* we *OBSERVE*. When we judge, we see something as bad and wrong, which creates more bad and wrong. When we observe, we simply notice all that is. This allows us to be wide open to allow things to shift and change as Spirit comes in and does its magic... its miracles. All of this is done from a place of curiosity and wonder. We need to invite Spirit in to assist in our healings. Follow where Spirit leads you.

Know that manipulation does NOT work here. That was the old way of doing things. If we are here to experience and learn, then that is what we must do. Here you can allow yourself to experience a tumor. Yes, I just said that. Allow yourself to learn why it is here, what it is here to teach you. If you are focusing on a heart, notice what the heart has to say to you. Let it share its pain with you so that it can let go of its pain and heal. If there is plaque which causes hardening of the arteries, ask yourself or them why they felt they needed to harden their heart? How has that served them/you? Are they/you willing to allow the heart to soften instead?

Do you see where Spirit is going here? Do you see what the gift of a question can do? Do you see how important focusing on something can actually help us to see the bigger picture… the truth? When we allow something to be our *focus*, we are saying, "In this moment you are the most important thing in my life. You are all that matters to me right now. How can I serve you?"

Can you feel how this shifts whatever you are experiencing to love and compassion rather than frustration and fear? Can you feel how a dialog is now able to come forth? Remember, a question opens a dialog and a statement can close it. You want to open a dialog with whatever you are wanting to focus on. Why is it present in your life? What is it here to teach you? How can you work as a team? What is the gift in this experience?

As you focus on a part of the body, do you notice light coming in? What color is it? Is the light a strand or stream of light? Does the light instead surround the area you are focusing on? If you are not getting a visual, do you hear a message? Do you have a certain feeling like a heaviness, or a lightness? No matter what you notice and observe, allow it to be exactly what it is. You are the observer—observe. Allow it to do its own thing. Allow it to dance, shift, and change into something else. If it's not ready to shift and change yet, then allow that to be ok, too.

Again, we are not here to judge or manipulate. We are here to notice and allow. Soften and allow ALL to be as it is. Think about when someone tells you that you need to be something that you are NOT. When that happens, you notice a resistance occur. The same is true here. If we force our body or our mind to be something other than what it is, it will resist. However, when someone lovingly allows us to be exactly who we are and to go through what we need to go through, we are able to love ourselves more as we go through it, and from there shift happens.

Why would our body be any different? It isn't? So, allow your body to go through and process all that it needs to process. Allow all to be exactly as it is and that gives it permission to then evolve into something else. Control and manipulation create resistance, while compassion and acceptance create flow and shifting. *You will see this when you believe it.* If you observe the area you are focusing on begin to move or shift, allow that, encourage it and have gratitude for all that you are being given.

Let me give you an example. In May of 2020, I was diagnosed with renal cell carcinoma—kidney cancer. This was my second cancer experience. I had so much compassion for my kidneys. I researched all the amazing processing and functions my kidneys do for my body all day, every day. I was so very impressed by all that I learned, as I now had a greater understanding and respect for all they do for me. I was loving my kidneys and thanking them for a job well done.

The more I focused on how incredible my kidneys were, the more information I was given by Spirit. I witnessed without judgment the truth of my kidneys. I had spent so much of my life *pissed off* at my birth family for not being... kind, accepting, and loving towards me. They never seemed to want to see the real me, or hear what Spirit and I had to share. I had to *hold so much in.* Do you see how the words in italics have to do with my kidneys? Our thoughts and beliefs create our reality. *I'll see it when I believe it.*

As I allowed all that pain and grief to be released from my kidneys, I was given answers and visions. Because of my focus, I was able to witness and observe from a place of Divine Neutrality that all of this was my past, it did not NEED to be my future. Saint Germain showed up as I meditated. He took me into my operating room and showed me the surgery I was about to have. He showed me how he was going to guide everyone who was going to be involved in my surgery and in my healing. He introduced me to my tumor. By the end of my meditation experience, I loved my tumor and I thanked my tumor for all it had taught me. I felt such gratitude for my cancer experience.

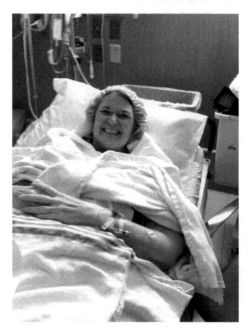

Don't worry, I've got this.

To get the full story on all that happened, please read my book *The Lie That I Am, A Journey Back To Spirit*. I had my surgery. It was fully guided just as Saint Germain had said it would be. Two days after the surgery, I walked two miles. My kidneys and I giggle together all of the time now. We are no longer pissed off. All of this was able to occur because of my willingness to allow all that is unfolding for me to be exactly as it is, as I focus on what I am given.

We are going to totally switch gears here and address other ways that we can focus. Once we learn how to focus with exercises like we did in the beginning of the chapter, we can use our ability to focus on anything and everything. For instance, if we or someone we know is experiencing disharmony in any aspect of our lives, we can *focus* on peace. We can feel peace within us and send it out to others. We can send peace out to the world. We can send peace to parts of the world where conflict is a way of life at this time. AGAIN, it is important to do this without creating more conflict.

This is done by focusing on peace rather than hate and judgment. Hate and Judgment creates more hate and judgment. Remember when someone hates and judges us, it creates more resistance and pain. When others show kindness and compassion, it frees us up to let go of the resistance and allow peace in. When we believe our "enemy" will never change, then that will be our experience. *We will see it when we believe it.* When we believe our "enemy" is not our enemy but instead a lost and confused person that is just trying to figure out who they are, suddenly everything shifts and more light is able to come in, more kindness and possibilities are able to come in.

How often have you, yourself, been lost and confused? What helped you the most during those times? Being hated and judged, or being shown patience and tolerance? Why would we show up as anything less than love if we are wanting to heal anything… especially a conflict. A conflict is two or more different ideas coming together. Bring peace to all of the elements of a conflict. Not just the ones that we agree with. When you can do this, you are a true PEACE KEEPER.

Anyone can bring more love to what they love. The true test comes when you are asked by Spirit to love what you do NOT love. Can you offer peace to your "enemy?" Can you be the peace (piece) that you wish to see and the world to see? Can you be the peace (piece) you came here to be, even when hate, conflict or confusion is all around you?

Focus, focus, focus on your thoughts, focus on what you want to create in the world. Focus on making a difference. Focus on love and kindness. Focus on being the highest version of yourself. Also, learning how to focus so that you can stay connected to whatever you need to connect to, can be so important. For instance, if you are working on connecting to your third eye, focusing is very important. All of this can be a game-changer in your ability to ascend.

Focusing on our ascension is another way to work with this aspect of focusing. Focusing on being a better parent can be your focus. When we are able to focus, we are better able to use this during our sleep state and to remember what happened during our sleep state. Focusing on anything that feels like a priority is what we are doing here. If we don't have the ability to stay focused, we will notice that we are all over the place and nothing really gets done. What is your life focus and why? Do you still want this to be your focus? Are you adding to the light or the shadows? Continue to refocus as your priorities change. Take the time to notice what you choose to focus on today and then do that—be that.

Wow, see how powerful you are!

AvoiDANCE

Once we have been on our spiritual path for awhile and we are living as love and peace most of the time... something happens. We become obsessed with feeling peace-full all of the time. We don't want to place ourselves amongst anything or anyone that could create conflict, or experience anything less than love. From this space, we begin an avoid-dance game. We dance around invitations that include people who tend to lower our frequency. These people can be those who have to always win—always be right. They want to argue their point, OR they could be the type of person who is always complaining about everything and everyone.

From there it is a slippery slope. Once we give ourselves permission to avoid a certain person or group and we notice that our frequency didn't plummet, we begin looking for more people and situations that we want to avoid. In no time at all, you just want to stay in your room. There is no conflict to resolve there. You don't have to defend your spirituality and beliefs. The most important thing is that everything makes sense in your space. I get it. There is a lot of craziness going on out there. It's OK to spend as much time as you can in your safe, spiritual space. Get comfortable with the new you. Reaffirm what you think, believe and know until it's who you are. This is an important element to your growth. However, you must realize that hiding away is not sustainable or practical.

There are people living in caves that are doing incredible work. You need to ask yourself... am I one of them? If the answer is NO, then eventually you are going to have to reemerge and join society again. Take the time to notice if you are making excuses to avoid having to go out. Are you avoiding your old triggers and you haven't even tested if they still trigger you?

All you want is to exist as peace every moment of every day. Conflict, anger, and fear are not comfortable anymore. I get that, but avoidance is not the answer. You can't stand in your truth if you are cowering in the corner. I get wanting to remain in peace, but this is not TRUE peace if it comes at such a high cost. If we hide from what we are seeing and what we are feeling, how is that peace-full? In this case, avoiding conflict can create conflict. Conflict happens when two different ideas struggle to find common ground. Stop struggling, and surrender. How can you be connected if you disconnect and avoid so much of your life? This is NOT peace. This is an illusion; you could even say, a delusion.

When our core is strong and we know what we know, we are not afraid to WALK THROUGH conflict. We own our conflicts, for they are ours. Why would we ever avoid a piece of ourselves and believe the illusion that this is peace? Peace comes once we move through all that we are in conflict with. You shall be peace-full once you experience all that you feel, think, and are from a place of truth—not through avoidance.

When you look at all that you are avoiding with honesty, you will understand yourself better and love yourself more fully. What are you avoiding thinking about? What are you avoiding doing? Who are you avoiding, or wanting to avoid? Why are you wanting to avoid them? What are you afraid of? Can you now understand why peace is so fleeting if this is your experience of it? Know that peace is not the absence of conflict if you are avoiding conflict. Rather, peace is experienced after we walk through what we are avoiding—including conflict. Here there are no casualties. We come to a place of PEACE, with every resolved piece of what we are avoiding. This is because ALL is love and all is loved (not avoided). *You will see it when you believe it.*

Avoiding what pushes your buttons does not create peace. Avoiding members of your family is not peace. Avoiding having honest conversations is not peace. You must connect to your bravery to do this. Look at all that you are avoiding and be present with it. Find the gift in it. From there you will know a new kind of peace, and all you experience will be peace-full. All of this came about because living from a place of peace is who you choose to be.

Let's Experiment

When I notice all the ways that my life is guided, I am filled with such gratitude. So many people say—yeah, well, all of this guidance is easy for you, you have Spirit telling you what to do, where to be, and what to say.

This has not always been my life. I had to ask for almost everything I have been given. Once I asked for a skill or gift such as channeling, I chose to use it to assist others. I choose to help others because it is what I am drawn to. Because of this, Spirit understood that I wanted to make people's lives better in any way and every way that I could. Sometimes I was asked by Spirit to do things that made me feel uncomfortable. Like going up to a stranger and letting them know that their Mom is thinking loving thoughts about them, or whatever Spirit asked of me.

This meant I needed to be the crazy person that many thought— what the heck are you talking about? My favorite part is when clarity comes in once a person truly receives the message that Spirit bestowed upon them. Suddenly, I was no longer crazy, but instead a gift from God. The understanding that something miraculous just happened here crosses their face and I have the honor of giving them peace.

This is why my very favorite thing to do is to step up and be the lifeline when a fellow human being is lost. If not me, then who? Really take those words in… if not me, then who? Every single time that I assist another, I feel a shift in me. I know that something beyond my human understanding just took place. I don't know how to put it into words other than to say that when I help another person, I understand that my reality just shifted and I noticed it rippling out to all humanity. We have a much larger impact on everything and everyone than we can possibly comprehend—until we do.

Recently a neighbor of mine went through such pain and loss as her husband collapsed and wasn't breathing. The fire trucks and ambulance arrived, along with a Flight for Life helicopter landing right on our street. This helicopter just lit up so bright for me and I didn't know why. I assumed it was because it would be the means of saving my neighbor's life. I was wrong. This gentle man who passed away had served in the Vietnam war. A helicopter meant hope and survival to our service members back then. I was able to comfort his wife by sharing with her what I saw as no one else could see this. Scores of these military members from his past along with an Honor Guard stood at attention beside the helicopter waiting for the moment that they would step in and honor this man who they loved and respected.

I saw God cradle this son of His in His arms. I watched Jesus kiss his forehead and place His forehead on my neighbor's forehead. I witnessed Mother Mary holding his hand and radiating so much love and compassion. Then his parents spoke of their love for him and how proud they were of him. Words that he had always wanted to hear were spoken.

While all of this was happening, I saw his body (in my mind) and didn't understand what I was to do? Did I need to pray over the body? A dear friend said, *"No, that wouldn't be appropriate at this time."* Our deceased neighbor's wife began experiencing pain in her back by the shoulder blade. I saw her heart expanding which was causing the discomfort. Suddenly, her deceased husband said, "I have placed myself permanently in your heart. I will never leave you, never abandon you. I love you."

The sheriff stepped forward and asked us to step into the house because the helicopter was going to take off, so the dust and wind was going to pick up. Then I saw it... the military Honor Guard and so many military members took his soul up to Heaven alongside of the helicopter as it took off. Being a military wife, this was quite emotional for me. The next day my neighbor called to thank me for all I had said to bring clarity during such a traumatic time for her. As I spoke about how important the helicopter and his troops were to him, she explained that in the war his job was search and rescue. He jumped out of helicopters into the water and rescued people. Understanding and clarity overwhelmed me. This brave military man had regrets for the ones he couldn't save, and there was some guilt because he lived while others died. That guilt had plagued him all of these years.

That Honor Guard and those troops that had been lost showing up and escorting him to Heaven let him and everyone else know that there was nothing to forgive. All is as it should be. I was so honored to witness all that unfolded and the peace that this information brought his loved ones. Thank you, God.

Know that, as I allow all aspects of my life to continually shift, change and flow—more gifts and opportunities show up in my life. Soon I notice that my WILLINGNESS to make a difference makes all the difference. The more I needed proof, the less proof showed up. The more I trusted my gifts and skills, the more they showed up and so did the proof. Now, I am surprised on the rare occasions when a gift or knowing doesn't show up. These moments tend to be when it is none of my business. This means that I am *not* the one to assist here. This all happens because I did the work. I trusted, trusted, and even in my very dark moments I trusted some more. My experiences are incredible because I believe that Spirit is always going to be there for me and therefore Spirit knows and TRUSTS that I am always going to be there for them. How many of you can say that?

If you CAN'T make such a bold statement, then maybe you now have a better understanding as to why you *do not believe* your life is very guided. It all makes so much sense to me now that I am on this side of my guided life. Back when I doubted everything, especially myself, I had very little showing up that brought me joy. Now I can see joy in all of my experiences. Even my challenges bring me joy, because I get to learn something and have new understandings because of them. What a gift even my challenges can be. I notice also that the more I live in awe and joy, the fewer challenges I encounter. *You will see this when you believe it.*

Recently, my sister Christine and I were asked by Spirit to go to the ocean and put our feet in the water. They then wanted us to send out love and healing light into the water. As we did this, we continually amplified the energy as I watched our frequency touch every continent of our world. Once that happened, I watched as this same frequency went down below the ocean and the land. Going down, down, down into Gaia, intensifying, healing, assisting. BREATHE. Then I witnessed it shoot up into the atmosphere higher and higher until it touched the grid surrounding our beautiful Gaia. I have no words to describe how incredible this experience was. The fact that I was able to do this with one of my favorite humans was priceless.

Christine and I with our feet in the Atlantic Ocean, sending out loving energy to the planet. With so much love, respect, and gratitude.

As Christine and I did this, I laughed because the thing that surprised me the most was how warm the water became. Isn't that crazy? It was sunset and the water had been freezing cold when we started, so I didn't know how long I would be able to hold all of this frequency if I was too cold. Yet, it felt like bathwater within a few minutes.

As a special confirmation, I noticed about eight days later there was something on the internet that on the very day we had done the work, the Earth's Schuman Resonance went kinda crazy with activity for three days. I later found out that there were many light workers that were called on to assist in other ways on that very same day. Christine and I just truly enjoy assisting in any way that we can. If it makes a difference, then we are truly grateful. One thing I know for sure is that if we *didn't step up*, we definitely wouldn't make a difference. This is confirmation that being the crazy, wonderfully guided, loving person can genuinely pay off.

Let's do an experiment. I would like you to perform your own experiment to show yourself how guided your life is. I would like you to start this experiment by greeting everyone you encounter. See how you feel afterward. Notice how most people responded to your greeting. Notice when and how you drop into excuses for both them and yourself… how interesting! Keep this up for days, weeks, months, until it feels very comfortable to you. Like it has become part of who you are. Only after that happens, do I want you to change the experiment.

Now I want you to STOP greeting people. Instead, I want you to notice a person coming toward you and try to notice a vibration *from them* toward you. **ONLY** when you notice an energy exchange do I want you to say something. Here comes the crazy person part… don't greet them. Instead, I want you to notice the words that come to you. They may not always make sense to you, but you are training Spirit and Spirit is training you. *TRUST* that whatever words you are given, are the words that the person you are encountering needs to hear. I'm going to let you know right here and now that the wisdom of your words doesn't always register instantly with the person you are sharing them with. You might even get strange looks. That's perfectly okay. Keep going. Keep trusting. *Remember that you will see it when you believe it.*

Realize that the wisdom, greeting, awakening or whatever it was that you were inspired to impart to this other person, will happen when it is divinely guided to happen. God's will is at play here. It could be a week later before the words you gave them make sense to them. It matters not. At least you are putting yourself out there. At least you are doing your best to make a difference. This is what matters. Be careful that you don't just keep repeating words that worked with one person and use them on another, unless you feel very guided to do so. This experiment is to create a new and "original" way of being. I am trying to teach you how to level up your guided life. This happens when you TRUST the guidance you are being given. You are shifting from quantity (greeting everyone) to quality (only assisting those that Spirit guides you to assist). This was a game-changer for me.

We are training you to look at the individual or group you are encountering. Spirit knows what they need, and *IF YOU ARE TO BE THE PERSON* who is supposed to give them a message. There may be times you get nothing all day. Then you need to say *NOTHING.* YOU ARE SHOWING SPIRIT THAT YOU CAN FOLLOW DIRECTIONS, no matter what those directions are. As you perfect your ability to do this, you will notice who you encounter will change. What topic you will bring up will change. Do *not* assume. Assumptions are not guided. *You will see this when you believe it.*

Do this and you will notice that Spirit will be guiding you more often and in more unique ways. Realize how blessed you are to have these opportunities and the gifts that come with them. Thank Spirit. Live a life of gratitude as your new life unfolds before you.

Anyone can come up with an excuse as to why they CAN'T do this experiment. I challenge you instead to move beyond your fears, beyond your self-imposed limitations and figure out how and why you CAN do this.

Thank you in advance for your willingness to experiment with becoming the answer rather than the problem. This is why Spirit loves working with me. I'm not afraid to approach things from a different perspective and I'm not afraid to look or sound a bit strange. Not if that strange way of "being" assists another in their own shift or awakening. Instead, I am humbly honored. All this comes from being willing to notice what is presented to you. Know that all is in your life for a reason.

Are You Expecting?

When we have expectations and then we have attachments to those expectations—just plan on being disappointed. But where does this disappointment come from? Does it come from the person or situation that we perceive has disappointed us? Does it come from not having the outcome that we desired? Does it come from our disappointment in ourselves that once again we put our trust in someone and THEY disappointed us? All of the above and so much more can be the truth. For when we have expectations, we tend to think of only ourselves and what we desire without allowing the others involved to have their own wishes or desires. We don't even realize that we are doing this most of the time.

The more we expect from our expectations, the more deeply ingrained they are. We begin filling in more and more of the detail of how it is going to be—how it HAS to be. No one can know what they don't know (until they do). We are setting other people up for failure as we do this. We are setting ourselves up for disappointment when we do this. We might ask ourselves why we keep doing this to ourselves.

We learn as children how exciting it is to anticipate something coming up. We are invited to a birthday party, Christmas is coming up, or we have a family vacation. As children, this creates an excitement and a wonderment. As we mature, be become more cynical because of the disappointments that we have experienced. We carry more doubt than we do curiosity. This doubt can shut us down. We lower our expectations of others and begin believing that good stuff only happens to _____ (you fill in the blank with your own beliefs).

What expectations do you have for your parents? I had a girlfriend that was over 40 years old. She still expected her parents to buy her cars and was disappointed when they were used cars. Are those expectations serving her? Well, she got one free car after another her whole life, so maybe yes, maybe no. How is she learning to be responsible? What is she teaching her children? How interesting is this?

What expectations do we have for our children? Some are conscious expectations and some are unconscious. Because of these expectations, how often are your children disappointing you? Can you see the individual that each child is, or do all of your children have to do this and be that? How fascinating is all of this? Now what about your job, your government, your partner. More expectations? More doubts? How are these expectations serving you? How are they raising or lowering your frequency?

Eight years before we bought our brand new, yellow Victorian house, I had a vision of it from Spirit. I was so excited. I visualized and visualized it. I put it up on a pedestal because I focused on it so much. When we purchased the house, it turned out to be a nightmare. I realized over the years we lived in it that I had created expectations. I put it so high on a pedestal that the house was built on a hill. This created challenges in the winter. I also realized once we had moved in that I had never been shown the inside of the house when I had my vision. I had so many expectations of how it was going to be and it wasn't that at all. My vision was correct, however my expectations were not.

I had difficulty finding the good in this house because it didn't fulfill my expectations. The floor plan was weird and all of the rooms were too small. I feel I could have enjoyed it more if my expectations hadn't existed. Expectations that I had fed for eight years as I waited for this house to show up. Having plans for the future is ingrained in us as human beings. Having hopes and desires are important to us. Yet somehow, we keep taking all of this so much further in our heads until it NEEDS to, or HAS TO be a certain way.

Take the time to notice where you have expectations. Now understand that expectations and desires are VERY different things. Expectations are when you *need* a certain outcome. You need "it" to be a certain way. Are these expectations serving you? Are you setting yourself and others up for failure by having these expectations? Ask yourself how having these expectations serves you. Do you notice a parallel between these expectations in your present moment and the disappointments of your past? Do we really want to continue this crazy circle/cycle of old human behavior that did not serve us in the past? *Are you seeing it because you believe it?* Desire means you would like something to happen, yet there is a frequency of ALLOWING "whatever" to unfold rather than NEEDING it to unfold. Do you feel the difference?

Shifts like this happen when we DESIRE great things rather than EXPECT great things. Know that I love you. I'm so proud of your willingness to look at all of this and choose the way that works for you. Your different way makes all the difference, my friend.

The Past is the Past

Think back into the past, to a time when a person disappointed you. How many hundreds of times have you replayed that scene out over and over again? Reliving that pain, reliving that disappointment. Teaching yourself—training yourself—to be a victim of the highest order.

They did this to me. They are bad and horrible. Let me tell everyone I meet how bad and horrible this person was. Let me remind myself repeatedly how "put upon" I was until the greatest definition that I have of myself is being a victim and how others always do bad things to me. Do you see that playing out in your life because you believe that? *You will see it when you believe it.* Whatever disappointing things have happened to you, I want you to know that I am so very sorry that you ever went through something like that. I am so sorry that anyone ever saw you as anything less than magnificent. However, you are the one who has kept the sadness and horror alive all these years by reliving and reliving how bad and wrong they were and how much you were victimized.

Taking responsibility for feeding the hate is so very important in our ability to heal and move on. To be able to let go of the past is vital to our ascension. I do not say this lightly to diminish what you went through—not at all. I myself relived the pain of my past daily—hourly… until I had no present moments at all. How can we enjoy our lives, our present moments, if we spend all of our time living in the past? WE CAN'T. We can't enjoy what is right in front of us if we are always looking backward.

Know this, realize this… if the person or persons who injured you came up to you today and took FULL responsibility for what they did—what they said—how would you feel? Even if they said the exact words you have always wanted them to say, in the exact way you always wanted them to say it… how would you feel? Do you feel the emptiness—the hollowness—around this happening? Almost like you are so stuck in this experience that defines you and don't know how to be—or who to be without this definition of yourself? Yep, that is because you have allowed these past experiences to define you beyond your comprehension. They are your story. They are who you are. IF you forgive this person, can you still define yourself as that? Whatever that is—victim, unloved, abused—it matters not, for YOU gave yourself that definition of yourself.

You believed you were a victim, more than you believed you were powerful. *You will see it because you believe it.* You believed you were less, more that you believed you were more. You believed the old stories and you "re-lived" them all the time. Now is the time to put those stories to rest. Learn what you can from all of the difficulties you have encountered, for these are *your* lessons. What did you learn? Learn it and move on. For if you don't, this label or definition of yourself will be your experience your entire life. Is that what you want? If it is, then you are giving these people who wronged you not only your power but your entire life. The past is the past. It belongs in the past, not the present, not in the future. That is unless we dress it up and take it with us every day of our lives as the definition of who we are.

Here is an important piece: as we forgive others for what happened in our past, it would be beneficial to forgive ourselves also for keeping our tragedies alive for so long. But first, we must recognize and realize that we have played a role in keeping these scary stories forefront in our lives. The people or person who "did this horrible thing" to us has most likely moved on and often they don't even realize that it was ever "a thing." It simply was something that happened and they moved on. It is time for us to do the same.

If you have lived most of your life in the past and used it to define yourself, most likely you are more comfortable with this energy and therefore it would be very natural for you to then resort back to that belief by having expectations that "others" are going to disappoint you in the same way. These are all your old places of comfort, so you know this frequency well. Notice that our places of comfort aren't always comfortable. *You see it because you believe it.*

Ask questions so that you, yourself, will know the true answers for you. The more questions we ask the more answers we receive. Does living in the past make me happy? Am I raising my frequency or lowering it? Question everything you can. Figure out what in your life assists you in moving forward and what assists you in staying stuck. Only you can make the decision to change, and those changes become your present—your future. Yep, you are that powerful and so much more. Are you ready to believe that? Are you ready to live that?

Tell Me Your Story

I can't know what you don't tell me. We all have knowledge. We all have wisdom. We all have had experiences. If you don't share your stories with me, I cannot learn from your wisdom. What I have always been told by Spirit is that your wisdom is what you have taken in and learned from your own experiences. Each encounter carries some wisdom for you. Even the encounters where the other person does not choose to participate. From that experience, you get to witness a person's free will. They chose not to take an interaction further. In doing so, they chose to hoard their wisdom, knowledge, pain, joy, whatever "it" is. There is nothing wrong with that. They may be very busy—it feels uncomfortable to them—or have no interest, it matters not. They have free will and have exerted that.

Can you take a moment to notice this, witness this? There are many people who are choosing to not participate in an interaction because they see it as a waste of time. I KNOW NOT what their piece of our ascension is. Perhaps the world is not ready for their wisdom, their piece. So they must "keep their piece." How fascinating it is to hear those words and then have a different and a greater understanding. So, to go into judgment about another, means that our "ignorance" is showing. We are showing in that moment of judgment that we are choosing ignorance over another way of being, a different way of being.

My YouTube channel and my website are both called Mary Beths Different Perspective BECAUSE I am given the ability to see things differently than most people. It is only through my willingness to see things differently that this can happen, so that I can then share this knowledge, wisdom and understanding with you. In fact, as I wrote the word "because" in this paragraph, I actually saw the words "be the cause." From there Spirit showed me that... *because* of something happening, changing, or shifting, it gets to "be the cause" of our new understanding. Holy moly, this is all so fascinating and fun for me. I know this has taken me off-topic, but it was very interesting to me and therefore I hope that it was interesting to you, also. I live for and get excited by the opportunities I am given to see things from a different perspective even while channeling this book.

Let us return to these beautiful people who do not seem interested in an interaction. I know that when it is time for a person to awaken, they will awaken. Until that time, they get to sleepwalk through their life, as many of us did until we were ready. So, we must allow them to sleepwalk just as others allowed us to sleepwalk. How interesting.

I was absolutely fascinated when a few years ago someone shared an insight they had, which was that for a certain wave of our ascension, a certain group would be woken up through technology. My frequency stood up and took notice. I know not how this will happen, I only know that it carries a piece of truth within it. I don't want to give people a reason or excuse to not get off their devices and participate in humankind. I simply find this interesting.

Many people share their stories through technology and social media. Are you using your time on our devices to complain or to share wisdom? Take the time to notice how you are "spending" your time, and even what you are spending your money on. This will tell you much about where you are on your path and how you can shift and change those choices. Another way to know where you are on your path is when you notice that EVERYTHING is about your connection to Spirit. This is because how we connect, and even *being* connected, is the only thing we want to do or be. Through this experience or understanding, we know that we never want to be "dis-connected" again. *We will see it when we believe it.*

Step out of your place of comfort—share your wisdom when it is asked for. Please don't force your thoughts, beliefs, or wisdom on anyone. This can feel like when a parent lectures their child so that they can spare their child all the pain or trauma that they went through. The child does not listen. They didn't *ask* for this advice. So they close off and disconnect from the parent. They may not be ready to hear this information, or they are not willing to hear it. It matters not. Again, we must be asked—invited in. This one was difficult for me, I must admit. Simply share when you are asked to share. Hoarding is no longer acceptable on any level. And yes, not sharing your wisdom when someone asks from a place of curiosity and wanting to learn and grow… is hoarding. Not sharing your time is a form of hoarding. Not sharing your money or resources can be hoarding. So many aspects carry the same frequency.

The wisdom that we have gained from our experiences are very valuable. When we think about creating oneness, when we think about creating a new planet with new realities, we need to allow all to be available to everyone. Stop believing that you are a nobody and you don't have anything to contribute. For *you will see it when you believe it.* Empower yourself, empower your experiences and know that we all have value. We all have something to share. Share your stories and watch surprise and curiosity show up whenever you do.

Showing Up

How we show up and who we show up as—matters. Really think about what kind of wife, husband, or partner you show up as. Are you demanding? Do you feel that your partner owes you? If so, what is it that you believe they owe you? Do you feel you don't deserve them? Go to the depths with your relationships and your relationships will be transformed. See if you can shift from what another person needs to be or do for you to approve of them. Instead, look at what you can do or be to show up as the highest version of yourself. We cannot change others; we can only change ourselves. My own marriage changed so much when I came to the realization that I believed that it was my hubby's job to make me happy. If I wasn't happy, it must be *his* fault. I realized then and there that I do not give control of my happiness over to anyone. That honor is mine and no one else's.

In your friendships, are you being honest? Are you telling people what you believe they want or need to hear? If you are being honest, is it in a kind, gentle way, or could it be seen as rather harsh? I have had many people in my past who would brag about how they are brutally honest. Since when is being honest and brutal a good combination??? The thing that I love about texting is how I can write something, read it before sending it, and know that I can do better. This was such an incredible tool for me as I learned how to soften my words. Sometimes I would rewrite my text a dozen times before it was soft enough to convey the love and compassion that I choose to *show up as.*

As a person is talking to you, are you spending that time formulating your response rather than really hearing and being present with what they are saying? When we try to figure out a way to one-up the person we are having a conversation with, we turn a conversation into a competition. Compassion is not present. For to show compassion to another, one must first be completely present with that person. Nothing else matters other than this person you care about—feeling heard and knowing that they are loved.

Take a moment to think about showing up as love and compassion. Spirit once told me that we did not come here to be loved—we came here to "BE LOVE." Really think about that. are you being LOVE? To be loved requires another person to be involved. To BE love involves only your willingness.

Think back to a conversation where you felt truly heard. What was different about that conversation that assisted you in feeling that way? I found that it was not so much what the person said, but rather the way a person said it. Like this conversation right here and now was THE most important thing to them in that moment. There is no one that they would rather talk to. There is nothing that they would rather be doing. I have their FULL undivided attention. Wow, I cannot express how huge that was and is for me. To feel that heard—that loved—that important is so all-encompassing for me.

When was the last time you showed up like that for someone? What was going on in their life that you were able to show up in a "higher" way? Do you want to be able to connect in this profound way in all of your interactions? Or is this compassionate presence only for when a person is going through a very dark or heavy time? Unfortunately, this is why so many continue to go through so many difficulties, because only then do they believe people will show up and prove how much they really care about them. How sad. If you are spending time with someone, why would you want to limit the interaction by limiting who you show up as?

When we only show up in such a sincere way when a person is going through a difficult time, they may be drawn to only discussing heavy subjects with you, just so that they can experience this incredible compassion and love from you. Or, maybe you are only really there for them when they are positive and happy. Talk about setting a relationship up for failure. We all need to be allowed to feel what we are feeling when we are feeling it.

I remember being so surprised at how well my husband did when I went through a very sad time with him. I knew how much he enjoyed the fun and silly Mary Beth, but would he still be there with me once he got a glimpse of the sad and insecure Mary Beth? I must admit he was not as comfortable when I was sad, but he truly did the very best he could for being such a quiet, reserved man. I limited him, when *I believed* he only wanted the fun-loving me to show up. Then, when I went through my cancer experiences, I got to fall in love with him in a whole new way. That was when I experienced how much I meant to him on a very different level. Having cancer gave him an opportunity to show up in a new and expansive way. His love and compassion was always there, I just didn't notice it so profoundly. However, during my cancer experience, love and compassion showed up in so many new ways.

My having cancer gave my husband and daughter an opportunity to show up and REALLY be there for me like they had never been before. It somehow gave them permission to be something more. From that experience, I was able to get to know another side of them that I had never noticed or experienced. I was so grateful and blessed by their willingness to be kind, compassionate and vulnerable, during a very challenging time. There is beauty that can be found in even the most difficult times. However, I do not choose to continue experiencing poor health so that I can experience this side of my family. Nope, not at all.

Now, let us look at our relationship with our children or even other people's children. How present are you with your children? How often are you on your devices while in their presence? How would your relationship shift if you were willing to be fully present in your moments with them? I remember when I did home daycare, how some of my parents were frustrated that I didn't text them and send pictures all day. The reason why I didn't was because I spent the entire day experiencing everything with their child. I was in awe of their growth and abilities each day and how much they were continually learning and changing.

Childhood goes by so quickly. Try not to waste the opportunities that you have to make a difference in the life of a child. I would ask my parents at the daycare... what kind of adult would you like your child to be? If you want them to learn how to be kind then you need to be that example to them. If you want them to have a long attention span then you need to have that with them. If you are constantly distracted, they will be distracted. School will be more difficult for them if they need constant distractions.

When our children were born, they were pure innocence. They did not know how to lie—they did not know how to manipulate—they did not know how to hate. Take the time to ask yourself… was I the one that taught them to lie? Am I continuing to do that today? Am I the one who taught them how to manipulate? Either by manipulating them to get what I wanted, or by being the example of a manipulator? Am I the one who taught them to hate? These are questions that we should all ask ourselves periodically as parents or guardians. In my opinion, our children are too important to be treated as anything less than love.

Again, we need to take the time to notice who we are showing up as. We are here to be our children's teachers, not their best buddy pals. Also, they are not our servants; we do not own them. My belief is that we are simply our children's teacher for awhile. What did I teach them today? When you are a responsible adult and they witness that, they are more likely to grow to be a responsible adult. If you do the bare minimum, guess what you will get back from them… the bare minimum. Notice, observe, and learn, and you will never regret the time spent showing up for your children. They are the future of our Gaia—teach them well.

Every interaction we have is an opportunity to show up. This can happen in person, on the phone, in a text, or in an email; they are all opportunities to be the highest, kindest, and softest version of yourself. When you mess up as we do from time to time, please don't be disappointed or frustrated with yourself. Instead, take the time to realize how you can do better next time and then do that—be that.

Allow yourself to continually up your game on who you show up as. When an interaction feels wonderful, take the time to figure out how you can allow this to be who you are more often. We keep thinking we need to be this grandiose thing. I suggest to people to work on being kind. From there, anything and everything is so much easier—lighter. From there it is easier for you to show up as the highest vision, of the highest version of who you are. You show up as kindness itself. And who doesn't want to experience more kindness?

As I show up for others, others will show up for me. *I'll see it, when I believe it.* When we let go of the need for others to PROVE to us how important we are to them, we let go of another layer of our insecurity. Try to remember that this journey of ascension has to do with your growth— your willingness to show up. YOUR journey is not about someone else, it is about YOU and your Soul (Higher Self). As you fulfill your part of the ascension by showing up as a loving, caring human being, you shift the vibration of the planet. Thank you.

All that we do radiates out to create more of that. What are you radiating out? As I have stated before—your piece of our ascension matters. What you put out in the world matters. Who you show up as matters, because YOU MATTER.

When we show up as love—we speak with more loving words. When we show up as kindness—kindness is in everything we do. When we show up AS joy—people walk away from an interaction feeling more joyful than before we met. When we show up AS gratitude—others realize how blessed they are to have you in their lives. When we show up AS compassion— others feel touched by it and share more compassion themselves which radiates out to the world. All because you were willing to show up. We thank you!

The Definition of Who You Are

What defines you? What events happened in your life that stopped you in your tracks and changed your life forever? Do you live continuously through that event? This can be true whether it was a positive event or a negative event. How are you feeding that definition of yourself still today? Are you still reliving your glory days from high school? Are you still living the pain of high school? Think about how much time—how much of your life—you have wasted believing something about yourself that was a lie. What is it that you received from buying into that lie each and every day? Do you still want to continue living as that lie? No matter what lie you took on as your definition, for instance… your family life, your sex, your nationality, where you were born, where you lived, how much you had, whatever it was that kept you from feeling sacred or whole.

I bought into the lie that my life doesn't matter, I have absolutely no value and there is nothing that I could ever do or be that would make me loveable. NOTHING. Now you can better understand why Spirit wants me to learn how to truly love myself. While yes, I have worked through so much of this lie, I still occasionally notice residual effects from the decades of living AS that lie. It has defined me since I was 3 years old. It is my foundation, it's what I have always been able to count on. And yet… it is a lie, a falsehood.

How can I be unlovable when all I want to do is love everyone? How can I be unlovable when my very favorite thing to do is to be kind? Because of this, I had to call out these lies that I used to define myself. I needed to really ask the big questions so that I could begin to start living my life with truths rather than lies. There is nothing about my day that doesn't matter. There is not a single choice that I make that doesn't matter. The choices I make all day long matter—they make a difference. I matter—I make a difference.

This is how we call out the lies that we are living. How we notice what our "lie" is, can be discovered simply by looking at who or what we RESENT. If there is a person or group of people that you judge as bad or wrong in any way, follow the trail that leads you to why you feel that way. What started you on that path of judging them as less than you, or just plain being WRONG. This will tell you so much about where you may have fallen short of being a higher version of yourself. When we resent another, we feel bitterness or indignation towards them. RESENT feels like such a small word compared to HATE, however, it can be ALL CONSUMING! We can resent how people treat us, or how they treat others. We can resent what they represent. There are so many levels to this for you to look at. All are important. Do you still want to judge someone as bad and wrong? Do you still want to live your life "as hate?" When you judge another, that is what you are choosing—I choose hate over love in this moment. How is that harming them and how is it harming you? *You will see it when you believe it.*

Most likely they don't know or even care that you don't like them. They are moving forward just living their lives. Possibly, you aren't even a blip on their screen. However, what it is doing to you is a whole other story. That hate, rage, anger or resentment festers in our minds and creates more hate, anger and resentment. This can turn into disease manifesting in our bodies. Remember the story I told you about having kidney cancer after being "pissed off" for decades. This is what I am speaking of. Disease is you being dis-at-ease.

I want to assist you in looking at who or what you are dis-at-ease with so that you can look at why you are CHOOSING that. How is it serving you? How does it serve in creating Heaven on this planet? Take the time to dismantle your lies so that you can start living your truth. Let go of the hate so that you can live as love.

Take the time to look at what you are allowing to hold you back from experiencing peace. What is creating duality (good/bad) in your life? Do you want duality and separation to be part of who you are? When you define yourself, notice what labels you give yourself so that you can dismantle them. Dismantle anything less than love. Allow yourself to feel compassion for yourself as you gently receive clarity about these lies that you bought into in order to make sense of something that makes no sense.

When I continually say all is love and all is loved, I speak this from Spirit, know that we are speaking of YOU. You ARE Love. So why would you choose to show up as hate? No wonder why you feel so lost and confused. Hate is simply disconnection from love. Do you want to remain disconnected from love? Again, how is that serving you? How has it EVER served you?

Understand that blaming others for anything that is showing up in your life is simply you giving your power, your life and your choices away to someone else. Try to instead reconnect to the powerful, enlightened being that you are. Do what you need to do to heal your past and then leave it in the past. It has no place in the present or the future. It is called your past for a reason.

I find asking questions helps me to get answers about my life. You may want to question yourself. Why do I feel so much resentment when I think about _____? Why do I allow my frequency to drop just thinking about them? They don't even need to do or say anything and I watch everything about me shrivel to something less. How can I change that? Do I want to change that? Am I willing to even admit I want to change? Is this anger, hate, or resentment worth creating disease? Do I value my life, my soul, my evolution enough to let it go? Keep asking yourself questions as you journal all of this, and you will learn so much about yourself. I certainly have and it has made such a difference.

Here is a very different part of how we define ourselves. I have met so, so many people that had a very sacred spiritual experience in their younger years. Because of that, they live off of or from that experience the rest of their lives. While yes, it was an important moment, and yes, Spirit was definitely showing you who you are or who you have the potential to become, know that if you are not stepping up and living as that potential, you have missed the target and it would be beneficial for you to reconnect and live as that now and in the future.

In fact, I will even be so bold as to say because of that sacred moment, if you are NOT stepping up, it's even more disappointing. I can't believe they had me write that. This not the norm. However, for those who have never had such a profound spiritual experience, you can understand their lack of participation and why they are living from a place of ignorance. IF you were given such a profound knowing and don't continue to expand it for all humankind, well—that is truly a waste. I feel such sadness for us all.

Think about what you have done since that gift was given to you. How have YOU expanded it, and not from a place of Spiritual ego. "Look at how special I am, I had this experience when I was five." Yay! And yet I ask you, what have you done with it since then? If you want to blame Spirit, know that they probably stopped showing up because ego does not attract them. Ego is the false self. That experience was 30–40–50 years ago. What have you done since then? You are not this "exalted being" because of that experience. You are an exalted being because you exist. *You will see this when you believe it.*

Know that after you do all of this work to help you become a better person rather than a bitter person, I ask you to then let go of all the definitions you used to get to this place. When we *need* to define ourselves, we limit ourselves. We move into a box that cannot contain us. For we are not here to be contained. We are here to expand beyond all that we have *allowed* ourselves to be.

Allow yourself out of the boxes you have put yourself in and the labels you have given yourself, by believing so many lies about yourself. Lies like—I'm stupid, I'm alone, I'm unlovable, I have no talent, I don't matter, I'll never amount to anything, or even… I'm better than everyone else. These lies and so many more are what are holding you back from allowing yourself to be more.

We are enlightened beings. We are here to "lighten" the energy and frequency of Gaia. When we judge even ourselves, we create "heaviness," which is the opposite of "light." When we let go of judgment and realize someone is different, rather than bad or wrong, we lighten the energy. This is what a light worker does. They work with lightening energy, making it less heavy, less dense, filled with light. Filled with possibilities and creativity, rather that judgments such as wrong, bad, or negative.

If we want to create the new Gaia filled with light, all of those dense thoughts, words, and feelings need to leave. Especially about ourselves—for they are lies. We do that by simply lightening our thoughts and our words by saying, they are different, I am different. We are supposed to be different from each other. So, I choose to be the example, by being the light, and seeing both them and myself as simply different.

You did not come here to live your life as a lie. You came here to be a seeker of the truth. Now go out and do that—be that.

And so it is!

Finger Pointing

We love pointing a finger at someone else. We want everyone to notice what they are doing wrong and how bad and awful they are. Everyone nods and agrees as they give examples as to why this person or group of people are the worst. We do this as a collective to help point out someone else's misdeeds so no one notices our own. As long as people are busy finding fault with others, they feel a sense of pride at how much better they are because they didn't do that.

So often I find myself asking, "What are you doing to help change the world and increase the love?" Condemning another creates more hate. Asking others to join you in hating means you increase the hate on the planet that much more. How is this helping us to create a new planet filled with love and kindness? If the same amount of energy went towards creating love rather than hate, what a wonderful world we would become instantaneously.

Whenever we put down another or find fault, we become less. This is because our frequency lowers. We are very powerful "beings." What we do affects others. Try letting others know of something incredible or fun that you or someone else is participating in where you create more joy, smiles and kindness. Take the time to notice which person you are in this moment and which person you choose to be in the future. All is a choice. Love or hate. Both are very powerful.

An act of kindness ripples out into the world, far beyond our understanding. My husband and I do a lot for the homeless because that is what Spirit is currently asking of us. When a tent, sleeping bag, or even a hat lights up for me, I choose to purchase it. Sometimes I am even shown the person who will receive it and how it will assist them or how grateful they are for it. While buying sleeping bags last year, my friend also purchased one to donate. I saw her bag going to a gentleman in his 50s. Every night before getting in his sleeping bag, he asks God to bless the person who brought this warm bed to him. Doesn't that feel more wonderful than pointing a finger?

This is what it looks like when Spirit guides you to a sale for the homeless.

Feel the love that is being given to this sleeping bag.
Talk about being blessed!

I don't really need to know who any of these items are going to, however, this is Spirit's way of thanking me. I am humbly stepping up and doing what is asked of me, for this is my greatest joy. How did you step up today? How did you step up yesterday and the day before that? If you didn't bother making a difference, did you at least do no harm? I remember as a child hearing about the Hippocratic Oath where doctors must swear to do no harm. Those words echoed and vibrated through my body at that time. How fantastic would our lives be if we did no harm. No harm to ourselves, no harm to others, no harm to our planet.

Can we make that pledge today? Can you go forth and do no harm? Condemn no one? Find fault with no one? Once you accomplish that, your frequency shifts and you find the amazingness in yourself and others all of the time. Once that shift happens for you, you realize how uncomfortable judging another feels now.

Pointing your finger only gives you a tired finger and creates disharmony. Creating disharmony goes against everything that you are now. When you witness another creating disharmony, you feel a guidance as to how you want to respond. Never by condemning. However, there are times that you are given words to assist another to see the harm that they are causing so that they can awaken and shift when they are ready. You will know when it is time for you to stand up for what you believe and what you are guided to do about it. Other times you walk away because you are guided in the knowing that this is none of your business. It is not what you came here to do.

I am not asking you to walk away and do nothing when an injustice is occurring. I am asking you to wait for guidance and then respond according to the guidance you are given.

Being Kindness Itself

As we take on any thought, concept, or idea as TRUTH—total and complete truth—we need to then integrate it. Only after we completely integrate it does it become part of who we are. When that happens, we no longer need to work on it, develop it, or focus on it. It is now an aspect of who we are. After a while, we forget that we worked and worked on having that "understanding" until it became a permanent part of who we are, because it is now completely second nature to us. I'll start with an easy one—being kind.

You cannot ascend without being kind—end of statement. But, as I have said before, we have to take on the thought, concept and idea of being kind as our truth. Then we need to LIVE that truth. We need to have it encompass all aspects of our lives consistently. In other words, we have to be kind to everyone including ourselves. We need to finally let go of enough hurt and pain so that we can even be kind to the people who have "wronged" us, OR at least have kind or compassionate thoughts towards them. This comes from looking at where another person may have taken on the hate or lack of compassion it took for them to have "wronged" you. This happens by looking at the big picture with a broadened perspective.

From a broadened perspective we are better able to understand how a person's past may have affected them to the point that they would or could behave in the way that they did. Suddenly, it is no longer personal. I know that until you live from the ability to see things with a broadened perspective you cannot truly understand this. However, *you will see it show up in your life when you believe it.*

As you are able to look at any past hurt and pain with divine neutrality—where it is no longer personal—you will see and understand so much with the ability to feel compassion. Again, this must be something that you are *willing* to take on as truth for yourself. That willingness to forgive, let go of, or just see things differently, presents to us the ability to move forward with this greater understanding. This is when it becomes a truth for us, where we gain incredible WISDOM. From there everything changes and we can experience kindness and compassion even for those that we "perceived" as our enemies.

The *peace* we experience in that moment when this *piece* falls into place for us and becomes a piece of the puzzle that is called our life can be profound. That picture cannot be complete without each and every piece of our experiences coming into place to form who we are completely in this moment. This is a Peace that takes away pain and heartache on a whole new level. So from a spiritual understanding, peace and piece can be seen as the same thing in this moment.

This is how completely a person must take on something like "being kind" for it to become a complete aspect of who we are. Living from the wisdom gained by all you went through to understand that you want to be kind so thoroughly that nothing can remain untouched by the kindness of who you now are.

If you are able to be kind (or even have a kind thought) for your "enemy," they are no longer your enemy. They now can be seen as a person struggling with their human experience just as you have done repeatedly in your own lifetime. This is where compassion is integrated into who you are. This does not mean you need to continue to have this person in your life… you have choices. We cannot release someone as our "enemy" without experiencing compassion on a very high level. A level so high that it is now part of who you are. You have now integrated compassion as another piece of the puzzle that creates the picture of who you are and again in so doing you are repaid for all your hard work by experiencing— PEACE. I know that all of this got very uncomfortable and heavy. This is where we switch back to light and fun.

Whenever someone lets me know that they are struggling trying to figure out what they came here to be, I always tell them that is easy… they came here to be kind. Now you see how all-encompassing being kind can be. Notice how as you live from a higher frequency you use kind words when you speak. Notice how you continually show up as the kindest version of yourself. Participate in conversations about kindness that you have witnessed and watch others as they want to join in. In so doing, witness how much healing can happen. All from choosing to be kind and making it part of who you are on every level and in every aspect of who you are. *You'll see it when you believe it.*

An important part of being kind is being kind to YOURSELF. You cannot be kind to yourself and still continue to find fault with yourself and belittle yourself. None of that old pattern has anything to do with kindness. Why do we treat strangers better than the one person that we know best… ourselves. Play with this. Have fun with this. Have a be kind to *(state your name)* day. Spend the entire day finding new and different ways to be kind to yourself. In so doing, you will find new and different things to love about yourself. This will be proof positive that all this very intense hard work that you have done was so worth it.

When we notice how much we enjoy being kind to ourselves and how much joy we have experienced, we want to create more joy. We do this by experimenting with being kind to people we love, in new and expansive ways. Doing things in the old way is not enough anymore. Wanting to do things differently, and think about things differently, feels like the only path we want to be on now. How creative can you get? Are you noticing that you are coming from this new connection to your innocence? Are you noticing how curious you are about where you can take this?

Keep going. Keep trying to one-up yourself on how kind you were yesterday and see where that will take you. Notice how I just gave you permission to be competitive? Because everything is true, but it isn't true. Being competitive is something we no longer experience as ascended beings, and then we bring it back to show ourselves that we can have it be part of who we are as long as we no longer experience someone as "the loser." In this example, we see that everyone wins because when I compete with improving on yesterday, I can create a better today. In this understanding, we see how we turn everything upside down and sideways during our evolution of being more.

It is only in our willingness to go as deep as we can, that we will become a higher version of ourselves. I feel giggly just thinking about my higher version of being joyful (JOY FULL). I Love, love, LOVE JOY. So being JOY FULL is where I choose to live from. The path I choose to get there or achieve that is through being kind.

Challenge yourself. Compete with yourself on how you can be kinder and kinder. As I taught my child at a very young age—a smile is the same in any language. I have given my husband so many smile lines because of the joy I have bestowed on him, and it is written all over his face. Again, I am taking something he saw as a negative and showing him the positive.

What are you going to do today to assist in making our world a better place because you are in it? What kindnesses are you willing to bestow on the people that you are blessed to encounter? Is their life better—richer—because of their encounter with you? Is your life better and richer because of your encounter with them? Live from your curious innocence and see where being kind is going to take you. Try not to push any agenda on anyone today and just flow with joy. How did THAT shift your day? Does it assist you in wanting to let go of pushing agendas?

Do you see how easily we can shift our light, carefree frequency just by including words like push and agenda? That is because flow is our way of life now, not pushing. Having an agenda is too constricting and limiting now that we understand that flow allows more possibilities and opportunities than any agenda ever could. So don't put it on your agenda to be kind… flow with being kind and your entire existence will become…

I don't want to limit what it will become by using human-limited words. Instead, I give you permission to redefine what your new existence will become so that you can even let that definition go and become limitless. Wheeee.

You'll see it when you believe it.

Notice Everything & How You React to It

Noticing everything may either seem daunting because that is A LOT to have to do, or it can seem insignificant because it's too general. Well, let me tell you that noticing everything is beyond significant. It's essential! As you begin to notice things, you will go to a place of wonder. For instance, you wonder why you started biting your nails a couple of years ago. As you begin wondering about anything and everything, Spirit shows up in the most interesting ways with the answers to your queries. You will suddenly remember how nervous you had become about the stability of your future a couple of years ago. As you stay in a place of wonder you can ask yourself and Spirit questions like… am I still nervous about my future stability? Connect to the truth of your answer. Not just your truth, but divine truth. Allow yourself to continue to take your understanding further by asking more questions.

For example, I'm not as nervous as I used to be, however I am still concerned. Ask what is it specifically that you are concerned about. When you get your answer, go ahead and ask what you can do to eliminate that concern. Continue until you notice your questions have all been answered. From there you can move forward with a tangible plan that feels right for you in a healthier and more secure way. Suddenly, the nail-biting stops because the reason for it no longer exists. When we do this with everything that shows up in our life, or exists in our life, we move into a place of creating our life, rather than reacting to our life. As a creator, you empower yourself and what you will allow or no longer allow to be part of your life. *You will see it when you believe it.*

I will be honest with you… most likely you will end up letting go of people who are not healthy to the new way you are choosing to live your life. You will notice that there will be people who don't want you to change and grow. They want you to continue whining and complaining about everything and everyone because that's what victims do—they complain together.

People who live from the belief of being a victim, spend so much of their lives looking at who did what to them and how wrong and bad that person is. They waste their precious moments looking for proof of the next time they will be put upon. Or they will continually relive how everyone did this or that to them. So much time spent in the past while creating more pain and disempowerment for themselves and our planet. When they allow their life to be something else, something more, their whole life changes in the most expansive and beneficial ways. *You see it because you believe it.*

The next step is noticing our reaction to what is happening in our lives. How are we reacting when someone says something that we don't agree with? What you CHOOSE to say and what you CHOOSE to do, shows yourself, others, and Spirit who you are showing up as. Are you showing up as a victim? Are you showing up as a dictator? Are you showing up as a bully? Are you showing up as love and tolerance? Are you showing your superpowers?

Notice your reaction by looking at all you are doing. When you put down your phone and realize that you just "wasted" 45 minutes trolling information on the internet to confirm how "right" you are and how "wrong" others are, how do you feel? Do you feel superior? Do you now have more "value" than your fellow humans? As you read these words, what is your reaction? How do you feel when I use words like trolling or talk about you wasting time? If I'm pushing your buttons, you may want to notice that there is an aspect of you that agrees with those words and it is making you uncomfortable. *That* is a reaction.

Discomfort is a very important reaction because it's like a warning sign that this doesn't really feel like you anymore, or rather, it feels awkward compared to who you now choose to be. What in your life is "making" you feel uncomfortable? The way you react to this discomfort will give you clues to assist you in deciding—choosing who you are READY to be. This can only happen if you are ready to change, and if you are willing to step into who you were brought here to be. Until you are willing to change, none of this will matter. You can notice and notice things, but unless you are willing to do something about what you are noticing, nothing will change. YOU won't change.

You don't change by noticing all that you are thinking, feeling, and doing. Your noticing everything is the catalyst to show you new possibilities and potential. It is your WILLINGNESS to change that takes you to the next level. What are you willing to change in yourself to assist you in your evolution to being something "more?"

Celebrate your reaction when you see or experience something very touching and emotional. Are you allowing yourself to embrace those emotions? I love going to the depth of my emotions. When I do this, I feel more ALIVE than at any other time. This is because we connect to Spirit in such exulted ways through our emotions. With this in mind, it would make sense that feeling things—having a reaction to what is going on around us—would assist in "making" us feel more alive, more connected… because we are!

Let us explore our "good" reactions a little more. Notice when a child is showing (sharing) their innocence—their purity—what is your reaction? How does it "make" you feel? Does it connect you to your own innocence? Does it create emotions within you? Do you see how witnessing such simplicity and purity raises your frequency? I truly enjoy watching people's reaction when a mistake happens and I say, "Oopsie poopsie." I get to witness their surprise and then usually joy. In that moment a mistake went from being bad to being a bumaroo, and they let it go and move on. Can you see how our reactions create a pause, where we can take a moment and raise our experience even higher if we so choose? I never thought of it that way before, but I can see and feel how having a reaction really does create a pause.

Now remember, a pause will create a moment when Spirit can come in and assist us in taking our experience and knowledge even further than ever before. This is why we want to react to what we are noticing and wake up from our sleepwalking. From there we notice how a pause assisted in creating a new way of looking at or even experiencing something. This is when our lives move into grace and ease. This is when we understand what an ascended life truly is. *You will see it when you believe it.*

Notice what you are reacting to and why. This will help you to better understand who you are and more importantly, who you are becoming. Our reactions are also connected to our free will. This is because there are some experiences that are on our life path because we came here to experience them. However, our reaction to those experiences can change the experiences so very much. How are you choosing to use your free will as you react to what is happening around you? Eventually, you will notice that you are reacting less and simply observing more, no longer needing to react. When this happens, know that I am here doing my happy dance in celebration of your ability to move beyond the human experience and into your ascended mastery.

No More Excuses

Do you make statements like, "I'm 80 years old and I don't care what anyone else thinks," or "I tell it like it is, and if you don't like it, too bad?" How about, "I've had a bad day and I just don't have it in me to be nice anymore." All of these statements are excuses we use to NOT have to be a better person. In those moments, you choose to be a bitter person instead. There are many people who give themselves permission to be less more often than they realize. Know that NOTHING is a good excuse to be a bully. Realize that when you are mean, YOU CHOOSE to be mean. Be honest about it, realize it, and then be willing to change it to something softer, something kinder.

I had a month yesterday. What that means for me is… I had a month's worth of obstacles and issues all in one day. When I called the plumber today and said to the person on the phone, "I had a month today," she asked what that meant. I told her that "I had a month's worth of issues come up in one day." She said, "I'm so sorry that happened to you." I thanked her for being so compassionate towards someone she didn't even know. Then I said, "This is perfect. Now the next 29 days should be clear sailing." Do you see how I shifted that? I no longer chose to live as a whiner, and so I looked for the positive while being honest. And my sweetie pie husband said, "I guess we get to do one of your favorite things for the next 10 days… we get to go out to eat a lot." This is because the sink we ordered had arrived warped and the plumber is leaving on vacation. All of this is inconvenient, but that is all. No one was hurt, no permanent damage was done—let it go and move on. Now realize that this was just one aspect of my day, but I continually saw opportunities in my obstacles.

Do you see how different being an optimist is versus choosing to be a pessimist? Are you one of those people who when someone asks you how you are, you list all your ailments and all of your family's issues? To start with, I want to thank you for speaking the truth, and I'm sorry you are going through all of that. Speaking the truth is important. However, I notice how some people REALLY enjoy having stuff to complain about, though just remember that like attracts like. That means that they will continually get to experience things to complain about, because they complain about everything in their life. *They will experience what they believe.*

Many people enjoy the attention they get when they complain. Just look at how many people complain about their food at a restaurant hoping that then they will get it for free. Yes, if something isn't the way it should be, go ahead and speak up. The difference here is *why* you are speaking up. Was what you experienced truly unacceptable? Were your goals or wishes for perfection unrealistic? Or were you just wanting your food for free because dishonesty is your life choice? I tend to feel that I can expect perfection from others when I know that I myself am perfect.

This is why when we have that perfect experience, we savor it. And really, once your spirituality becomes your priority, you realize that everything is unfolding for you in a divinely perfect way. You don't need to have things show up a certain way. You know that what shows up is yours, and you are grateful. I know that if obstacles are on my path, they are there for a reason.

Please *stop* making excuses to NOT be kind. An excuse uses a truth to justify a lie. Really think about that. When we make excuse after excuse as to why we can't do or be something, we LIMIT ourselves. We use a truth like "I'm really tired." Then we add the lie… for instance, "…so I can't do that for you." When the *truth* of that *lie* would be… "…I can't be bothered to make you my priority." Right after that, someone else can ask something of us that we have always wanted to do and we notice that somehow we are not too tired.

The honest way in my opinion is to speak your truth. "I am really tired right now, could we do that at another time?" Or if the truth is that you really just aren't interested, then just say that. Once you stop making excuses and start speaking the truth in a kind way, you will feel another shift happen within you. You are no longer living a lie. Spirit puts it much more "out there." They say, "YOU ARE NO LONGER A LIE." Spirit tends to put things like that because it can startle us into understanding what we are doing when we continually limit ourselves by *BEING* an excuse. Can you see that? Can you feel that? *You will see it when you believe it.* Stop telling yourself why you can't, and realize that you can.

Know that if you want to live as an "Enlightened Being," you will need to change your words to reflect who you are and who you choose to be. Your words are always filled with both light and truth. You show up as kindness itself. There's no room for excuses here. Excuses lower our frequency and we don't do that anymore. We don't play such lower-density games as that. We show up in every moment as the highest version of ourselves.

Another aspect of excuses is when we feel we need to make an excuse for something we just really like. For instance, getting manicures, pedicures and even haircuts, we sometimes feel we need to make excuses so we can give ourselves permission to do these things for ourselves. Saying something like, "My nails are constantly splitting, so I NEED to continually get manicures. I have horrible calluses so I NEED to get pedicures to take care of this. My hair has gotten so long, I can't do anything with it, so I NEED to get a haircut."

While all of these things may be true, realize that you are creating an excuse when you can instead give yourself permission to do these things because you enjoy getting manicures or pedicures. You like having your hair a certain length—period. You don't need to justify anything. Just speak the truth. I'm hungry, so I'm going to get something to eat is enough. We don't need to justify this by saying, "I haven't eaten since 8:00 this morning." Who are you trying to convince that it is okay for you to eat? This is especially a habit we get into when we have extra pounds on us. We feel like we have to justify everything we put in our mouths, when the truth is… I like ice cream and I want some.

I remember telling Spirit what I would do with the money if I won the lottery. If I have a "good enough" excuse, maybe they will let me win. That is silly. I want to play the lottery because I enjoy playing with the idea of all I would do if I won. I enjoy being part of someone else's dream if I don't win. I simply enjoy it. I don't need to justify it.

When we make excuses like… I need to get away for awhile because this happened and that happened, and we make a whole list of excuses, this can even be seen as manipulation. Instead, why can't we just say—I'd like to get away for a while. No excuses, no guilt trip, no manipulation, just honesty. Again, this isn't bad and horrible, however, why do we feel we need to make excuses to give ourselves permission. This is interesting, isn't it? We do this without even realizing we are doing it. Are we ready to stop creating stuff in our lives so we have an excuse to do something we simply want to do? Can we? Because that is what we end up doing—we create obstacles so we have an excuse to do what we enjoy doing.

What are you noticing that you are avoiding or making excuses for in your life? Now, what are you going to do about it? When you notice a slight pause before you make an excuse, understand that Spirit is asking you if you really want to continue being a liar. Because remember—an excuse uses a truth to justify a lie, so that means there is a lie in there somewhere. Spirit has taught me that a lie, is a lie, is a lie. It matters not why you chose to lie and what excuse you give. We live from a place of honesty here, and nothing less is acceptable.

Spirit just said, "Think about how you would feel if God made excuses with you. Eventually, you wouldn't trust what you were told. Eventually, you would go elsewhere to find trust. That is what others feel about you when you lie to them with excuses." Know that you are also lying to yourself when you make excuses. And the worst part is that you believe those lies after a while. It's your place of comfort. Is that really what you want to be comfortable with?

Be honest with yourself and others and you will notice enormous shifts happen in your life. Be the person you want God to see you as. You've got this. All of this.

I Can or Can't Believe It

Do you believe the can'ts more than you believe the cans in your life? How often are you telling yourself—reminding yourself—what you can't do?

- I can't bend over and touch my toes
- I can't stand being alone
- I can't remember the last time I…
- I can't run a mile
- I can't understand…
- I can't believe they said that
- I can't get how…
- I can't allow…
- I can't stand it when…

We have no idea how many times a day we let Spirit, ourselves and others know all the things that we can't… do, be, think, imagine—you name it. As we do this, we limit ourselves considerably. I remember how surprised I was as I was beginning to live my life more consciously. I noticed how many times a day I was limiting myself with all of my limited thoughts, beliefs and ideas. This is what we are doing with our "I can't" moments—we are limiting ourselves.

When we make our "I can't" statements, I see it almost like a prayer we are sending out to the universe. We are saying, "This is who I see myself as, and I would like you to send me proof of this so I can take it on even deeper as my truth. So please don't ever let me _____, because I CAN'T." Yep—that is what I witness as a person I am with makes an I can't statement.

To help get my point across regarding "I can't," I'm going to share a story about a teenager in my life. At the time she was 15 or 16, and we were there in her hometown visiting. We hadn't been there for a couple years, so I wanted my daughter and I to have some one-on-one time with her. I offered to take her shopping and I would pay for one item that she really, really wanted. As we arrived at the mall, she informs us that she HATES people who like pink and who wear pink.

I was shocked by this statement. Yes, I have experienced a lot of judgmental people, but this was beyond crazy for me. To hate another because of a color they like moves "I can't" to a whole different place. With a statement like that, she BELIEVES so strongly that she is right, that righteousness takes a front seat.

In that moment, I felt God's hand on my shoulder as I parked the car. I let this very naive soul understand what her bigotry meant on a very personal level. Yes, she was a teenager and we all say and do silly things as we figure out who we are and what we stand for. But, this young woman was wearing a button that said COEXIST. She talked all the time about how important it is to accept people the way that they are. In that moment, I let her know that she was being a hypocrite. You can't coexist and hate people for a color they wear. Anything that creates a separation of good and bad, right and wrong… has nothing to do with coexisting.

I informed her that we need to take her home. "I don't want you to be contaminated by being in my presence and my daughter's presence. I LOVE pink and my daughter likes it, but not as much as me." I told her how joyful I feel when I wear my favorite pink sweatshirt and my beautiful pink sweaters. I wish I could find more pink clothes for adults, but they're mostly made for kids. I could tell from the shock on her face that she expected me to agree with her. Nope—not going to happen. I'm a teacher. She needs to understand that her ignorance is showing.

She began to cry when I told her how harmful using blanket statements like that can be. I asked her how she would like it if I said that same thing about people who wear black (her favorite color). I let her know that HATE is a very strong and powerful word. "I thought you wanted the world to be a better place, not a worse place because you are in it. The choice is yours. Who are you going to choose to be?"

Let's shift gears here. In the last few years, Spirit has put so many people in my life who are much older than I am. I have greatly enjoyed learning from their wisdom. At the same time, I don't enjoy noticing how much they are limiting their lives and their expansion by continually saying "I can't" statements. Every time they do this, I watch another aspect of themselves shut down and give up. I actually mourn for that aspect as I watch it shrivel and die. All because their human states that they "can't" more than they "can." I *do* understand that medical things happen, but are you USING a number on a calendar as your excuse? Are you even trying to work beyond this limitation you just gave yourself?

Now I know that this is true, but it is also not true. I'm just trying to push buttons as I get my point across. During our COVID-19 shutdowns, my 75-year-old sister was working out more than most 30- or 40-year-olds. Her daughter and son-in-law would meet her out in the backyard and they would challenge each other. The progress that they made discovering what they each *could do* and seldom accepting what they *couldn't do* was eye-opening for me. *You'll see it when you believe it.*

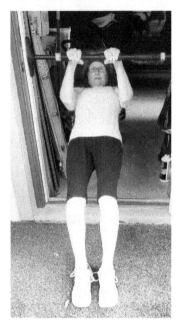

Who we decide to be at 75 years old is our decision. Go, Christine, GO!

With the incredibly broadened perspective I have been given (because I trust it and believe it), I honestly, truly see a physical reaction happen inside a person as they tell me what they "can't." I recently told a friend of mine that I saw the hand of God on a politician's shoulder as they were guided to change policy in a certain way. I watched as sparks flew and circuits blew in my friend's heart and mind as she heard those words from me. She let me know that there was no way that God would be guiding *that* politician. In that moment, her belief was that God was on her side, and this politician is the enemy. I watched and witnessed so much hate and judgment come forth and the fortification that came in to supplement her belief. Since then, I have noticed that Spirit doesn't show up for me to channel for her as often as they used to. Not because they love her less, but because in that moment she shut down the connection of her and my spiritual trust and belief to a mere trickle. She lowered her frequency. She believed the "can't" more than the "can." She has free will and Spirit is honoring that.

Now, here is an interesting part of all of this. I don't like to talk politics with anyone. We all hold so much attachment to being right that we can't see what we refuse to see. However, I personally FEEL COMFORTED knowing that Spirit is guiding someone—anyone. To feel dis-"comfort" from someone being guided makes absolutely no sense to me. Don't we want our government officials to be guided from on high by beings that can see the big picture?? My answer to that would be, YES, but she has her own choices to make.

I noticed as I wrote about politics that I was shifting my own frequency to a place of, see… this is why I don't *allow* myself to talk about politics. I watched a part of me start to connect to righteousness, and then as I watched my broadened perspective come in, I was able to back off from it and allow all to be exactly as it is.

Are you seeing and connecting to the point I am making here about what we *believe* we can't do is exactly that… something we *can't* do? Again— *you will see it when you believe it.*

Are you ready to turn all of that around by looking at what you CAN do? You can remember that your age is just a number. Yes, our physical bodies change as we grow older, but some of this is because we are buying into what society is selling us. Yes, I feel age changes in my own physical body. I also know that I don't work on changing my thoughts and beliefs about aging as much as I could. I guess I am not making it a priority… yet. Who knows where I will take it in the future. I do know that I am not interested in limiting my verbiage and beliefs surrounding the thought of being old and I "can't."

With every "I can" that we utter, we create more realities for ourselves. For instance, I believe I will be given more gifts all the time and that is my reality. I notice many people around me don't believe they can or will receive those same gifts and so they don't. I watch the frequency as this happens. Both the trust I have and the doubt they have are manifested because, as I said, what we believe is what we will experience. *We will see it when we believe it.*

It has been fascinating for me to witness how many people are asking for change on the planet and then with the next breath wishing things would return to the good old days, or having the belief that "everyone else needs to change but not me." Know that the past needs to remain in the past. Learning from our past and being grateful for our past is important. Yet, it has no place in our present moment or our future. We are creating a *new* Gaia, a *new* way of being by bringing in new ways of thinking, understanding and existing.

As we create our NEW EVERYTHING, it will come from our "I can" moments, NOT from our "I can't" moments. Now, here is another little twist for you simply because I can (giggle, giggle). There are some things that you "can't" because it is not for you. Take that statement in for a moment. What that means is perhaps I "can't" figure out all the special features on my smartphone because it is not supposed to be the focus of my life. Note that it's not ok to take this as permission or an excuse to not have to step up in some way that you don't want to bother stepping up in. This is very different.

There are simply some things that are *not* your thing. That doesn't make it bad or wrong, not at all. It is meant for someone else, *that is all.* I have never been a good runner. I stumble, I trip, I get tired easily and I don't enjoy it. Does that mean I can't learn to be a good runner? Of course, I can. I notice as I check in within myself, am I here to be a good runner…? I get a no. So now I don't need to focus on something that I am not drawn to, or interested in. Because of this, I can really appreciate how wonderful it is for those who that is an important focus for them. We are all here to be our own unique selves.

Some of our "can'ts" really are going to be things that we are not here to focus on. Realize that and move on. Please don't take it to a competition or judgment, it is exactly as it is. Nothing more, nothing less.

What is it that you can do?

- I can be kind
- I can share my knowledge with people who want to learn it
- I can make a difference
- I can touch lives
- I can be the best Mary Beth that I can be
- I can be the example of Love
- I can be the example of tolerance
- I can change the world

Take the time to make your own list, and as you do, maybe you will connect to your superpower. To me, my superpower is something that is very strong within me. It is such a huge part of who I am. I believe my superpower is to touch lives. It really is my favorite thing to do and I truly enjoy witnessing the results from it.

What is your superpower? What have you learned about yourself after reading this chapter? How are you willing to change because of what you have learned? Please don't rush off to the next chapter. Give yourself time to take all of this in and digest the information. You have an opportunity right here and now to change some of those old beliefs and patterns. Another option is to go back to what you are used to doing or believing… what is comfortable for you. Who you are and what you choose, makes such a difference. Are you ready to make a difference? Or does playing it safe feel better to you?

I love you no matter which choice you make.

Ascension Symptoms

Forgetfulness is important as an ascension symptom because it's training us to stay in our present moment. If we can't remember the past, we won't stay stuck there. We can't remember the grocery list because as you arrive at the grocery store, your needs may have changed. You can't remember your old patterns and routines because if you do, you'll be stuck in them. If you don't remember, you'll allow something new to come in. This all seems crazy, but it can be the absolute truth. Just recently I had forgotten my list and I was given a picture of my list in my head. My list was transported to me. Spirit says it is because of my willingness to allow things to shift to a new reality without reservations. Awesome. Another aspect of forgetfulness is that our Higher Mind is becoming activated. Our Higher Mind is not ego-driven. It is not centered on the self alone. It is supplying you with source-connected information. I'll take this over remembering my shopping list ANY DAY!

I am not a medical professional. If you have medical concerns about your ascension symptoms, please see a doctor. I have seen my doctor many times just to be sure.

Pressure in your head is expected as your higher mind comes online as old thoughts and beliefs are released, and new neurons can also begin firing. When this happens, ask your Higher Self to assist you in bringing in this new energy without resistance. This also creates higher thoughts to come in. The more you ask and engage with your Higher Self and Higher Mind, the sooner you exist within the 5th dimension and higher. Take note that the 5th dimension is just the beginning of our ascension, it's not the end. Allow yourself to also exist in the 6th-7th-8th-9th and etc. If you limit yourself to the 5th, you have just limited your ascension. Is that truly what you want? I hope not.

Your attitude toward what you need to accomplish feels less burdensome. You just want to keep moving forward, moving forward. You can get so much done here. You do everything with purpose because you have a more purposeful life.

Itchy eyes and tones in your ears are incredibly encouraging to experience. You will notice your eyesight getting worse and better and worse and better continuously. Sometimes fuzzy, sometimes sparkly, other times so clear that you notice colors you've never seen before. There will be times you can see multiple dimensions at the same time where part of what you view will be dull, and the other part will be sparkly, multi-dimensional, and moving, shimmering before your eyes. This is where we remember the saying, "See with new eyes and hear with new ears."

These tones can be a "type" of language used on the other side of the veils. They also carry frequencies that are congruent with every aspect of yourself that is ready to be elevated and activated. These tones can literally raise your frequency. Your tones are also used to activate neurons in your brain that have remained dormant... until now. These new neurons activating will now allow you access to the divine in ways that you have never had access to before. Also, tones are very healing. Hearing certain tones can also bring calm in, it almost feels like your soul is home.

If you are ready to move into being a healer, you will notice extreme tingling in your fingers. Once that happens, it is up to you to encourage it, to increase the frequency and assist it in becoming more. You do this by noticing: as you notice the tingles in your fingers, please allow your mind to encourage them to increase. Once that is accomplished, focus on the tingles, connect to the tingles, and then encourage the tingles to travel up your arms and travel throughout your body. Notice where you are drawn to linger for a while. Notice and allow all to be divinely guided. As a healer, you are learning how to *notice* something within the body and then *notice* what you are being asked to do with this information.

Our next symptom is neck pain or even back pain. I am not a doctor or medical professional, so please don't hesitate to see one if you feel drawn to do so. The back and especially neck pain again has a couple of layers of meanings. One is that your nervous system is constantly, constantly upgrading. This is why many are experiencing anxiety at this time. The nervous system stems out from the spine. Softening and allowing will assist you with this. When we *soften*, which takes us further than relaxing, we let go of all resistance. When we *allow* all the tension to unravel, this is when the shifting and healing can come in. Take your time with all of this and be patient.

Another reason for neck and back pain is that we are connecting the higher heart and the higher mind to work in unison creating abilities you have never had access to before. The higher mind is Spirit-connected, whereas the normal human mind or brain is very ego and linear-driven. This is leveling up beyond comprehension… until you are able to comprehend it.

The next symptom is hot flashes. This can last mere seconds or a few minutes usually. This is your body burning off the old denseness to bring in more light. Again, please encourage this as much as you can. When we let go of the resistance or manipulation and allow all to unfold, our journey is so much easier. At first, there may be confusion and resistance, however, with the information you are being given here, that should *not* be your experience for long. We are here to help, not only Mary Beth, but ALL who reside on the planet and are willing to allow their lives to transcend the old to bring in the new.

What about dizziness and lightheadedness? Yep—this one happens continuously also. As we move from one dimension to another or one reality to another, we need to reacclimate to a new way of existing. The physical body takes much longer to do this than the emotional body, mental body, or the spiritual body. Large solar flares can affect us by also creating dizziness. Be patient with yourself as you ascend and even descend as you buy into the old human way again, rather than this new spiritual way. It is normal to descend once in a while, just try not to stay there. Soon you will notice your frequency ascend again because of doing higher frequency activities and thinking higher frequency thoughts. Just keep allowing yourself to be a higher version of you. A kinder, more patient and trusting you. This needs to be towards yourself and all you encounter on your path. Only *you* decide where to focus your energy. You are very powerful.

Now we move to acid reflux, taste buds changing and certain foods not working for you anymore. Gee, as I look at this list of symptoms, I can't help but laugh. With so much happening to our physical bodies, it is impressive that we are even able to get out of bed each day. However, having this knowledge gets us excited about not only getting out of bed but also moving forward in our transformation to becoming our Higher Self.

It also helps that we don't go through all of these symptoms at the same time. It continually comes and goes—shifting and changing. None of these symptoms should linger very long. Again, if it persists, please see a doctor.

With acid reflux and certain foods not working for you anymore, again, if you are paying attention, you will notice the subtle and not-so-subtle changes in this area. There will be times when you can't even bring the fork toward your mouth. Your body, mind, and spirit are saying NOPE— no more. Listening to your guidance and responding in the highest way will increase the amount of guidance you are given, so encourage new *everything* to show up as you show up as the new and evolved you.

Notice what you are drawn to, whether is it a certain teacher, a modality, an environment. Follow through on whatever it is you are drawn to, whether it makes sense or not. This shows Spirit you are noticing the subtleties that are showing up in your life. Once Spirit sees this consistently in you, they will show up more frequently. All of this assists us in noticing that we are changing on a physical level, not just a spiritual level.

The reason why noticing subtleties is important, in fact I would say vital, is because there will be times when you will have many distractions going on all around you. If you do not know how to notice the subtleties, an experience could be lost. Do you see that? *You will see it when you believe it.* So again, I reiterate how vitally important it is to notice all of the subtleties, in all aspects of your life.

Because of the need to be honest with you, I want to mention something called compassion fatigue, which can be a symptom of ascension. We experience this because it can be exhausting at times holding the compassion for so many people because they are not yet ready to awaken. Be patient and kind to yourself during your compassion fatigue moments. Do some self-soothing. I enjoy a long soak in the tub or sometimes I need movement so I go for a walk or start dancing. You do you. Whatever helps to soothe you so you can move forward and be a higher version of yourself again.

Floating about 6–12 inches above the floor is a wonderful and fun symptom I get to experience. This can happen for a few moments or a few minutes. Talk about confirmation that you have "elevated" your frequency. No one has witnessed this happen to me—yet, but that is not what is important… I notice it.

Transporting people into what I am speaking of is becoming more and more common for me recently. They witness what I am describing and the shock they experience is profound. Another part of this is I am transported to what I am thinking about. Just this morning I had a pan of water on the stove. I had some head congestion and wanted to use the steam to help clear it out. As I waited on the couch, I thought about the pan and there I was—transported to the pan. As I watched the bubbles and steam rise, I was able to take the steam into my sinuses and lungs without leaving the couch. Spirit says this will continue to include more and more aspects of my life because I enjoy it so much.

Sometimes I feel like "The Princess and the Pea." I can have something so very small show up, like for instance a hang nail. It can be all-consuming because it carries for me an "off balance" frequency and I cannot move past it until I "handle" it. In other words, things can feel or seem exaggerated. This helps me to stay focused on it so I can do what needs to be done and move on. Again, this teaches me to stay connected to my present moment.

Feeling and experiencing synchronicities is so incredibly fun. The last couple of days, every time I talk about my daughter, she calls within seconds. She has no idea why she suddenly needs to share an anecdote with me, but she does and I get a wonderful giggle because of the synchronicities.

I can have books fall off shelves as I wonder, "Now where did I see..." I can think, "I wonder when so-and-so's birthday is," and I will have pictures texted to me an hour later of them out having their birthday dinner. This happens so often for me that I forget that there are many out there that this is not their experience. Bummaroo.

Seeing flashes of light on the edge of your vision, but when you turn to look at them, there is nothing there, yep, that's a thing too. Seeing orbs is another part of this. Take your camera and aim it towards the sun. Once you capture an orb in your viewfinder, you can follow it. I call them to me and enjoy showing my hubby how far away from the sun and into the shadows I can bring them. Notice the color of the orbs you attract and how many. This is all so very fun for me.

Here's a strange one—I burn out light bulbs when we make the decision to move. Once the decision is made to move, for the next 30 days light bulbs just pop and stop working. Spirit says the house is not happy with our decision. I have the house's frequency so elevated that the knowing that I am not going to continue to be there holding this higher energy just makes the house react. We can lose between 12–20 bulbs in one move. I now bless the house and thank it before we leave.

Telepathy is very common. Know that we are not getting word-for-word telepathy *usually*. However, it does happen that way sometimes. This started with someone saying one thing to me and I have the truth they are thinking coming in telepathically at the same time. For instance, someone will say to me, "I love how you cut your hair." As they speak those words, I hear telepathically, "Why would you do such a ridiculous haircut." When this first happened, I didn't know which one to respond to. Needless to say, I had some awkward moments until I figured what all this meant. So many tell us what we want to hear rather than the truth. As an ascended being, you don't live that way anymore. There are many other ways telepathy shows up, I just wanted to mention some here.

Another way of being transported is if, for instance, I wonder what day of the week it is, I am shown something that will assist me with that information. For instance, a favorite show of mine comes out on Sundays… and I'm shown a picture of that show. Instantly I go—cool, it's Sunday. I think, "I wonder how my daughter is doing," and I'm shown her sleeping with her head on her desk—ok, she's tired.

There is so much to this being transported, and I am just getting started. We are moving into territories that we can't even imagine and I am so excited. How about you?

My favorite ascension symptoms are living from a more peaceful place. Noticing that people and situations don't push my buttons and upset me like they used to. Seeing the good in others no matter what. Patience for myself as I change and grow. Yes, there are so very many changes you experience on your path of ascension and life just keeps getting better.

When you notice and experience the ascension symptom by living every moment with peace, love, calmness, and no judgment at all—that is when you know you have ascended to a new you. The TRUE YOU!

When we allow ourselves to be more, we become more. All of this is happening FOR US as it happens TO US. *We will see it when we believe it.*

It's Your RESPONS-ability

When we experience anything, we have an opportunity to take it further. We do this by learning from what we just experienced. Did I walk away from an interaction with the feeling…

- I'm glad that's over with
- I'm so bored
- I did my very best
- That could have gone better
- I never want to do that again
- What a magical experience
- I'm so blessed
- I love my guided life

Every interaction, every experience can be seen in a multitude of ways. When you notice your reaction to the experience, you can then take respons-ability (my ability to respond in a different way) as to how you can make it even better, or perhaps how you would like to change, so next time you will have a higher outcome.

Taking responsibility for how something went is the key to shifting. When you notice your pattern of blaming others or making excuses, you disempower yourself. You unconsciously are saying, "I am willing to give others both the blame and the responsibility for my life." Can you see that? Now, this is important... when we take responsibility and something doesn't go according to plan, we must not get frustrated with ourselves. Instead, take it to a softened place by saying something like... "Well, that went differently than I thought it would. However, I learned a lot of valuable lessons from it and that makes my experience priceless." Sometimes my response is, "Well, that was interesting," while at other times it can be, "Oopsie poopsie." Then again, it can also be, "That was awesome. So much better than I thought it would be." All of these responses calm me and assist in making me smile.

Here is another crucial piece of this... really look at what you learned and what you could have done to create a different outcome. If we don't learn and learn some more from our experiences, we get to repeat them. Why do you think people keep dating the exact same type of person and expect different results? Why do we keep working for the same type of employers and expect this time to be different? Why do we end up having similar experiences no matter where we move to? It's because we didn't realize all the lessons available to us with each person we dated, job we had or place we lived.

We "assume" we moved on, but if we learned nothing, how can we really move on. We get to do it again, sometimes repeatedly. I loved it when I heard the saying, "The definition of insanity is doing the same thing again and again and expecting different results." When I heard that for the first time, I noticed a very long "pause." I instantly went to things in my life that I did repeatedly and saw how, sure enough, I kept getting the same results. Every Sunday night, my Mom and I had the exact same conversation. When I went hiking, I felt the same way each time.

When I changed up what I expected and let go of the expectations and agendas altogether, that allowed a new possibility to be the outcome, and that's exactly what I got. Now, some of these new outcomes were still not the best, but it was a start, and at least things were shifting and changing. From my experimenting with agendas and outcomes, I learned more about myself and what raises and lowers my frequency. One of the things I learned is that I really like to be in control. Boy, have I gone through the wringer learning that one. When my daughter was 15 months old, I hurt my back and was in bed for over 10 months consistently and then 18 more months on and off. I had to allow others to help me. I had to allow my 15-month-old to take care of me. I felt worthless.

Because of lying in bed or on the couch all day, I had time to work on my spirituality. Because of this, I connected to Spirit as I had never connected before. My daughter has more patience and tolerance than almost anyone I know (except when dealing with people choosing to be selfish and mean). This happened because she spent her day on the bed assisting me, until we figured out this was going to take a lot longer than we thought and put her into daycare. I also learned from being in bed for so long that I don't have to be responsible for everything. I can even ask for help. Can you see how much I learned from my experience? Eventually, I was healed and was able to move on.

My 18-month-old helping to take care of mommy who has a hurt back.

When I suffered from anxiety a decade ago, again I had to surrender my need to control everything. I had to ask for help. What I resisted learning, kept being part of my experience. During that time, I let go of my agendas, what I believed about myself, all of the things that I needed to be a certain way, it all went out the window. I surrendered and I flowed until I didn't recognize myself. I allowed myself to be reinvented and I am so grateful I did, I really like this new Mary Beth. A beautiful piece of what assisted me in releasing my anxiety was a letter my daughter wrote to me. It opened my eyes and showed me what I was allowing and what I was doing. I want to include that letter here. It shows such clarity and wisdom that I feel it could really help others:

I want you to think about why you are so afraid lately. You and dad are happy, you love where you live, you don't have to work, you are seen, you have friends who actually like you and whom you like, you are at a good place with your mom, you and Christine are doing well, I'm doing well. What is there to be anxious about? I feel that a lot of it is you aren't fully willing to embrace that this is your life, you keep waiting for the other shoe to drop for something to go wrong so that your life long belief that you don't deserve to be happy or that your life cannot be this perfect will come true. But you know that doesn't have to be your truth anymore. You are so anxious because part of you is waiting for reality to come crashing in any moment and take it all away. You live a guided life, you are divinely loved, stop questioning that. There is no reason to be afraid or worried, everything works out and you are always protected. Why do you want them to have to keep proving this to you? They have never let you down before and they never will. Have faith. Release that white-knuckled grip you have. You do not always have to be in complete control. Stop worrying and embrace the knowledge that no matter what happens everything is going to be okay and that good comes from every perceived bad if you let it.

Wow, am I blessed or what. Thank you, my sacred daughter, for bringing in clarity when I wasn't able to.

Can you see how my willingness to learn from my experiences and take respons-ability for what I am experiencing and how I react to those experiences has shifted so much in me? The doctors said the paralysis I experienced from my hurt back would eventually become permanent. And yet I am walking and moving freely now. I was told I would need to be on medication for the rest of my life to deal with my anxiety. Nope, no meds at all. I'm not saying I learned everything that I needed to learn and moved on. And I am not saying that you are bad and wrong for taking medication—I am simply doing what I feel drawn to do. I still want to be in control, but I find I enjoy flowing even more than I enjoy control. After all, I am a work in progress and I am progressing beautifully.

Hopefully, my examples helped you to understand that taking responsibility for your life and how you respond to what shows up in your life is… life-changing. *You will see it, when you believe it.*

Another major step in taking respons-ability for your life and how you are responding to what shows up in your life, is integrating what you learn. When you integrate, you take the lesson in on such a deep level, that it becomes part of who you are. It's now part of your core. Your core belief of who you are. Your understanding of the world changes when you integrate a new way of existing. Who you show up as is more consistent than ever before. All of this happens because of your willingness to take your lessons as deep as you possibly can and then integrate what you learned, until it IS who you are. Once this happens, you will no longer need to focus on this aspect of yourself for it is second nature to you now, that is unless you revert back to your old beliefs again.

The old way of doing this, you may have needed 20 interactions or lessons to teach you what you can now comprehend in one interaction. This integration and shift happens when a person takes the time to understand what just happened. Why it happened. What shifted for them and what shifted for the other person. Notice how you are different now and where you can take it from here. Always noticing. This is because you are becoming very perceptive. Always willing to learn, shift, and take RESPONS-ability for whatever shows up in your life. This is what we came here to do… to LEARN, to EXPERIENCE.

Believe in You

There are many things that I witness in life that confuse me so much. I really don't want to admit I have had this thought, and yet Jesus came through tonight and asked me to please write about it. He said, "If you have had this thought, know that there are others who wonder the same thing. You are being asked to please help *ALL* have clarity. This is why all must be allowed here—even your confusion." Let us begin.

How can people believe in such magnificent things such as God and Spirit, and yet they *don't* believe in themselves? They don't believe that they can or do make a difference. I do not understand this at this time. It is mind-boggling to me. And yet this is where I used to live from all of the time. Now I am so far removed from it that I cannot comprehend it. Isn't this crazy to even think about?

Because my birth family hated—I mean absolutely hated—hearing my stories, I stopped telling them. My stories are not a brief synopsis. I take people on a journey. Just today, as I told a multitude of stories, a young woman said, "I could see it. I actually saw this young man, I saw his dog, I saw it all." And there was my confirmation, that when I am *allowed* to tell my stories I can actually transport my listeners right into the story. Spirit is telling me this is similar to what "beings" in the heavenly realm experience. They get to witness our joy, and our pain, as they watch or observe our lives unfolding. We take all of them along on our journeys. Spirit gets to participate *through us.*

I am being told that this is why I have a team of so many Angels, Spirits and Ascended Masters around me. I am creating so many experiences that few are ready, or willing to experience. Because of this, many Spirits like to join me on my exceptional encounters. They say that I am a pioneer of sorts. Wow, thank you so very much for that. I am both honored and grateful!

As I told my stories even as early as when I was in my 20's, I noticed something shifting in my listeners as I spoke. It was like they were participating in, or witnessing a miracle happening. They were learning how life-changing our lives can be IF we are looking to change our lives. And so, I was watching people wake up to new possibilities even way back then.

I had no idea what this all meant because I wasn't channeling consistently back then, therefore I had no one to explain what was happening. However, something was shifting for people. I noticed that it was my stories that were assisting in causing this shift. I now know that this can only happen when and if a person is willing to shift or change. My unique way of looking at things, my willingness to change, and of course the miracles that are my life, created the perfect combination for this to take place. Except for one thing... I didn't believe I mattered. If I don't matter, how can I make a difference? I can't... and yet I did.

I witness encounter after encounter where a crack or opening happens in a person's heart and I begin seeing a light in their heart center as I am talking to them (the heart center is the space in the center of their chest, though I sometimes see the opening in their mind). The more I trust and believe this, the more it shows up in my interactions, to the point that I am surprised when it doesn't happen, more than I am surprised when it does happen. This is because—*I will see it when I believe it.*

This opening, which looks different in each person, can be just a pinprick, a huge gaping hole, or anything in between. When I witness this, I know with every fiber of my being that we (Spirit and I) just created an awakening—an opening where Spirit is now given permission to go inside and assist with their life-changing-for-the-better magic. During this experience, the person who is opening to a new thought or possibility is continually PAUSING. It is during each pause that there is a new awareness that comes in as they say, "I never heard this explained in such a way before. I want more." Spirit and I are always willing to continue supplying heart-opening and mind-opening thoughts, ideas and concepts through our stories. When I notice someone leaning forward, I know that their soul is engaged.

In other cultures, the storytellers were highly respected. The elders understood the value of having someone take their people on a journey so that they could learn a lesson. That is what I am still doing today. I know that I have this ability because I trust it. It is in all that I am. *I see it because I believe it.* Because of that, this gift is enhanced with every exchange I have and I am so very grateful and blessed.

This is why I feel so confused that so many can believe in a higher power and yet they don't believe in themselves—in their own power. Remember—you are an aspect of God. Are you living your life as an aspect of God? You can't make a difference sitting at home doing nothing. You can, however, make a difference if you are brave enough to get out there and touch a life, say a prayer, or do something positive. Allow the difference that you make to keep growing and changing, as you grow and change.

The more we do this, the faster our evolution will happen. So again, your free will is showing up. Are you going to answer the door?

Are you willing to believe in yourself as much as you believe in someone else? Once you get comfortable with that, are you ready to believe in yourself *more* than you believe in others? What do you need to think or believe in order to create this possibility in your life? Know that everyone has such incredible potential. Can you see it, even when they can't? By knowing and trusting that miracles are your way of life rather than an oddity. Knowing that when we show up AS LOVE—LOVE will be our experience. *You'll see it when you believe it.*

I see amazing potential in you. Do you see the same in yourself? Do you WANT to see the amazingness and potential in yourself? If you do, then you have to actually do something about it. Are you ready to get uncomfortable by doing something different? By "being" something different? Here's a clue… you are different. Now go out and be YOUR different. Whatever that is and however that looks. No one, not one single other person can be YOUR way of being different. Own it. Be it. Show up as it.

Thank you for your willingness.

Are You Being Transported?

When a storyteller with any form of media (book, TV, radio, movies) can transport us into their story or narrative, we have just been given a gift. In that moment we are able to have clarity about something that is not necessarily ours. We are taken into another person's life experience and we feel what they feel, we know what they know. I remember as a teenager struggling with depression and suicidal thoughts. One day I went to a movie called "Ordinary People." That movie changed my life. I saw I was not alone. I felt hope seep into me. I wasn't the only one with an uncaring mother who loved another child more. Unfortunately, within a few hours of seeing it, I was back in my old reality again. Perhaps this is why I went to see this movie ten times. Hoping—praying this time it would stick permanently. This is what being transported can look like or feel like for someone.

Now because of the paradigm (reality) shifts that are happening at this time, we can experience this transportation without having words or video presented to us. Rather, we can experience it simply by being wide open while being in another person's presence. Another possibility is experiencing this during meditation. This carries similar frequency to telepathy, and yet it is very different.

To begin working on accessing this ability that is now available to all of us because of our raised frequency, one needs to be aware of it. This happens by starting to notice as you watch a movie, TV show, or reading a book, that you were living the character's experience rather than through the filters of your own experiences. When you begin to take it in as a realization and have gratitude for it, you create a shift. When you do this again and again you begin to train Spirit and your Higher Self that you are willing to be transported into another person's experience or reality.

In doing this we create a greater connectiveness between ourselves and the other person. This in turn expands out to create a connectiveness to all that is. I have noticed that when I am willing to expand my experiences beyond the lower density expectations, new abilities such as being transported are present in my life. It is so important to realize that if we are not in awe of this, or excited about it, our chances of experiencing it are less likely. *We will see it when we believe it.* Our lives shift and expand exponentially when we are curious and in awe.

Letting your childish wonder show up in all that you do and are, will shift our lives and what shows up in our lives, more than any other way that I know of. The exception to this would be living as love in every moment. However, if you broaden your perspective, you will notice that living in wonder and awe... is living as love. The further on this journey that you go, the more you realize that so many higher aspects carry the same frequency... they are one and the same.

This means that we will no longer need to define everything, and examine everything by picking it apart. Instead, we know that all is exactly as it is. Nothing more, and nothing less. No more need to find what is wrong with it. We simply notice, observe and are grateful. Once you live your life from this knowing, you won't need to get clarity from other's knowings… you are CLARITY incarnated.

Realize that "transported" means that their moment becomes your moment. You are taken into their experience yourself. Usually, this means you witness or watch what they saw or witnessed when it actually happened. However, there have been times where I am transported into a person's moment to FEEL all that they felt during their experience, rather than "see" their experience. This is because Spirit wants me to understand them and their experience on a deeper level.

To help you better understand what it FEELS like to be transported, I am going to share one of my own life stories with you. *Allow* yourself to be transported to what I am experiencing and also into the way this patient in the hospital is experiencing what unfolds in this story. Remember you are trying to create a connectiveness and notice new possibilities. Let me start by giving you some background.

This story takes place in my 30s. I was working at a hospital in a very small town in Nevada. My husband was going to be retiring from the Navy after serving 20 years. We had just come back from living overseas where I felt I had no rights. I had spent the last three years as a DW (dependent wife). This meant I was dependent on my active-duty husband for everything. If I wanted to take an aqua aerobics class, I needed a permission slip from him. If I wanted to take a book out of the library, I needed another permission slip. This is because in the military, he is responsible for my actions. It was a very bizarre culture to experience.

Being back in the U.S.A. was helping me to readapt myself to being an individual person again. I was trying to figure out who this new me was going to be. This gave me permission, in a way, to re-define myself. Because of this, I was really open to new experiences and noticing how differently I was handling my experiences. I'm explaining all of this to you so that you can understand how important my willingness was, in order to allow something different to show up. Do you feel that?

This miracle took place while working in radiology at this small hospital. It was one of those days when we were shorthanded, so they asked me, their receptionist, to transport a patient from their room out to our annex CT space. No problem, something new to learn and experience. When I arrived at the patient's room, I introduced myself and proceeded to explain to the patient why I was there and what we needed to do. I could both see and feel that it took a lot of effort for him to understand what I was saying, so I slowed everything down. I actually felt time itself slow down, my words slowed down. My sentences were shorter. My words became more simple to understand, but not in a condescending way. I could feel that I was coming from a more compassionate place. As I did this, I could feel the frequency in the room change.

As I was focusing and flowing with what I was experiencing, the roommate of this patient began laughing at me. He said, "Don't you get it? He's had a stroke. He doesn't understand anything that you are saying." I was surprised by his words. They made no sense to me. His words took me out of my connected space and back into the old limited reality. I needed to reconnect to the elevated frequency and thoughts. I did this by knowing and understanding that just because someone has difficulty speaking, that does not mean that they can't comprehend what is being said to them. I leaned towards the patient and whispered to him, "Boy, he really doesn't get it, does he? I know that you hear and understand everything that I am saying." I was looking straight into his eyes as I said this. I didn't understand this on a conscious level at that time, but by looking deeply into his eyes I was connecting to his soul.

I assisted him in getting onto the gurney and out of his room. As we started down the hallway, this gentleman was trying to say something to me. I pulled over to the side of the hallway and again I looked into his eyes. I could feel our souls connect, and I said, "I'm so sorry, I missed what you said." He tried again. I got part of it, but not all. I repeated what I had heard back to him and said, "I want to hear and understand everything that you want to share with me. So take your time and tell me again what you want to share with me, if you don't mind." His posture changed. His presence and focus changed. Even the features of his face shifted and changed. They became softer and kinder, with more expression.

He spoke again, but this time his words were almost perfect. Suddenly there was clarity and we both smiled at each other. The facial paralysis was gone, that far-away look was gone. What a dramatic change I was witnessing in this sacred man. In no time at all he was laughing and talking the way I imagine that he used to before his stroke. No pausing, no stuttering. He told me jokes and stories as we continued down the hall. I was sharing stories and insights with him also. I asked him if he felt like in the movies where the patient is being transported to surgery as the lights whizz by overhead? We both laughed as we connected to that image.

The further down the hallways we went, the more we both understood that something truly sacred and miraculous was happening as we were connected to the joy that we were experiencing with each other in that moment. In those magical moments, nothing else mattered, nothing less existed. We were two happy-go-lucky people enjoying each other's company.

When we arrived at the CT annex, I saw who the tech was. Unfortunately, she was the least compassionate of our staff. Dang, how do

I hold this energy? I didn't know how to do it, this was all brand new to me. As soon as the tech began barking commands, my new friend retreated and the "stroke victim" he had been, reappeared. I tried to look in his eyes, but the connection was gone. The vibrant, funny man I had been blessed to experience… had receded.

Every day until he was discharged, I went to visit him. Unfortunately, nothing I did ever recreated the connection of the experience we had received in that hallway. I now see how during those visits I was feeling desperate rather than curious. Afterward, as I would reflect on this extraordinary experience, I always felt that I had been given this precious gift to greater understanding that when we connect to another with true compassion and *no agenda* at all… clarity and healing happens. To me, this is the way our interactions are meant to be.

How do you feel after reading that story? Were you transported to the hallway at the hospital? Did you feel the utter and complete joy this man and I experienced? Were you then plummeted to such disappointment when the transformation wasn't permanent? Every time I think of that experience, I hear his joy-filled chuckle. In that moment, it felt so normal and natural for him to be "normal" and healed. Anything less than that would have felt off and bizarre.

Since this experience, I have noticed that when I am in a stroke "victim's" presence, I want to sit at their feet. I want to absorb and learn all that they are willing to teach me about what they have learned from their experience. This is often done without words. What WISDOM have they gained? For nothing can be lost without something else being gained. I notice myself softening along with my expectations. In return, the stroke "victim" softens their agenda and their frustrations, and some clarity and understanding can come through. I am so honored to be in their presence.

They could have passed on, but they didn't. What is it that they have to teach us—to teach me? What is it that they still desire to learn and experience? Are they willing to allow that learning in? Are they willing to let go of all resentment? Willingness is the key to so much.

This was a very short story. A place to get started from. Starting to think a different way. Allowing another possibility to be your experience. Are you doing that? Are you allowing miracles or other possibilities to be your experience, or are you holding on to the way you have always done something—refusing to be different—refusing to change? Allow yourself to be transported to the new you. What does this new you look like, and more importantly, feel like? How are they different from the you that you were before you began reading this book?

Your willingness to BE and experience something different really does make all of the difference. Are you ready to BE IT? Are you ready to DO this? *You will see it, when you believe it.*

How interesting is it that this chapter is about being transported, and the story Spirit chose to share with you was a story about me transporting a patient from one place to another. There are so many subtle meanings and synchronicities in our writings that have no "real" significance until we allow them to be significant. All of these synchronistic meanings take me to a place of giggles because they remind me of how fun this whole journey is and that everything is significant... especially you!

Here's a fun way to consciously allow yourself to undrestand being transported. When you think of a word or an object, you can notice it transports you somewhere. Let's play with this. When I say the word

Father—where are you transported to? Some may go to a religious Father, others may be transported to their biological father, or perhaps a step-father or grandfather. Do you see how by thinking of a word or object we can be transported? Let's try another one… Park. Where does park transport you to? Do you go to your favorite park as a kid? Do you think of a national park you have been to? Are you transported to the park in your neighborhood that you were at recently?

Do you see how significant being transported can be? Because of all that we have experienced, learned or read about, we can be transported to where our *BELIEFS* take us. Our experiences and our beliefs can be very limiting in this way. Can we allow our expanded consciousness to transport us to someplace more limitless rather than limited? This is done when we allow our thoughts and beliefs to expand to something we never thought or realized before.

To really latch onto this, make a whole list of words. Notice where each word transports you, and then see how you can expand and expand in the most playful way that you can. Use words from your past such as:

doll	asronaut	create
space	Christmas	vacation
joy	time	grown-up
milk	teacher	ocean
clown	mentor	shopping
flying	injury	adventure
TV	friend	bicycle

Now try the same thing with expansive words:

trust	empath	consciousness
oneness	meditation	connectiveness
love	peace	expansion
Spirit	focus	intuition

Notice how the more you allow yourself to be transported, the more interested and interesting it is observing the choices you made. Notice how your beliefs can limit what you are transported to. This is why we keep trying to teach you new ways of letting go and expanding. Allow yourself to believe something different. Keep playing with this and you will notice how much you are being transported with every thought that you have. How very interesting. *You will see it when you believe it.*

Being transported encompasses so much more of our lives than we realize. When we think about "something," we are transported to what that "something" means to us. Once we are connected to that concept, information or proof of what we are connected to begins playing in our head. We see one scenario after another play out in our heads to support what it is that we believe. How interesting is it that we have programmed our computers and cellphones to do the exact same thing. They transport us to what we believe.

We continually encourage what we believe to show up in our lives. If I believe in righteousness, I will spend so much of my day in my head confirming—confirming all that I am right about and all that THEY are wrong about. We don't even need to power up our devices to do this, for we have the most powerful tool of all that runs 24 hours a day confirming all that we believe… our minds. The only way to get this device to power down, is to get out of our head for a while and let it all go. This is called meditation.

When we "power up" again (come out of our meditation), do we choose to go back to the programs that we were running before we took a break? Do we turn the old programs on and crank up the volume? This is why meditation can be one of the most imortant tools we have. It's really the only time that we stop transporting ourselves to our old beliefs and allow in the stillness. The chatter stops. The patterns stop. Peace comes in. New possibilities come in as we are transported to a place where there are no agendas.

Here is where we are given messages from other realms and connect to other realities. We suspend the way things have always been. This is a "pause" beyond what we can experience in our non-meditative space. Our higher wisdom is transported in and calm is our experience. We are letting Spirit know that we are willing to allow something beyond the human norm to come in and this is where we experience such expansive shifts. What happens during our sleep is done for us. What happens during our meditations is what we are participating in. We are choosing to let go of all that we believed, so that we can expand beyond those old beliefs, and instead create new beliefs and understandings.

As we ascend and our frequency is elevated, we become multi-dimensional beings. We can exist in more than one reality at the same time. This is so much fun and oh, so confusing at the same time. We are transported in and out of this way of existing to assist us in getting used to this new… everything. We are less able to connect to limited thoughts and beliefs here. When you are experiencing multiple dimensions at the same time, you understand that you truly get to pick and choose which reality is the one that is compatible with who you choose to be in this moment.

The air itself feels charged with expansiveness when you experience multi-dimensionality. You realize how limited your existence has been. You take responsibility in understanding that you could not have the human experience without living a limited life. Here you move beyond that. You ask yourself—what is it that I want to create? And then you focus on that to bring it forward. Transporting you to all that you need to do to create this—to be this.

So much has to do with transporting. The right people will show up for you. The situations that are necessary to get you where you need to go will show up for you. The support that you experience in this more expansive existence is all that you hoped it would be and so much more. When this fades and you move back into a single reality or dimension, it feels like you have been put on life support and the machine is breathing for you. You feel so robotic and limited compared to where you have been and where you would rather be.

In your expanded state, the air is sparkly and alive. There is a fogginess as you decide which aspects of this reality work and which ones don't work. This is not because they aren't elevated choices, no, not at all. Rather, that frequency is not the direction that you choose in this moment. You have so many choices that you choose several realities because expansion is who you are and what you choose to exist as. I know this can sound very strange, maybe even impossible, however, it becomes normal the further you ascend.

When your frequency is more elevated, you notice so much. For instance, one of the things you will notice is that when you close your eyes and prepare to fall asleep is a very powerful time. What do you do with it? Do you notice that you are reliving your day? If you do, please take the time to notice:

- Am I reliving or being transorted to (ego) my shortcomings from the day? The things that I messed up on or just didn't make the highest decisions about.
- Am I reliving or being transported to other people's sortcomings? How other people messed up and how it affected my life, or how it affected someone else's life.
- Do I notice myself being transported to a place of resentment toward another as I fall asleep? Is it from something in the past or the present?
- Am I transported to a place of free form where new thoughts and ideas are allowed to come in and present new possibilities to me?
- Am I avoiding being transported anywhere? Do I either take substances to avoid thinking or feeling anything, or possibly have I trained myself to fall asleep as soon as I hit the pillow?

How is a person transported? And why are they transported? Where are they transported to? Every thought you have had—every decision you made led you to that moment you were transported to. The breadcrumbs of your life led you there. This is WHY—having conscious thought matters SO very much. If you are consciously choosing to be more loving, then that is where you will be transported to. When we are transported to something more filled with negativity or doubt, we pause and almost shake our heads like, woah… where did that come from.

We pause, because it doesn't feel congruent with who we have *chosen* to be for a long time. We have been choosing thoughts filled with light and this is not a "filled with light" thought—where did it come from? Think of it as a test. Here's one of your old thoughts... what are you going to do with it? Are you going to go back down that "old" path, or are you going to choose the light-filled path again, and again, and again? Which space are you going to choose as you start going down that old path of, for instance, judgment? Are you going to choose the higher or the lower vibrational choice?

This is why consciousness is so very important during our ascension. We *need to* consciously choose who we are in every single moment. If we don't, the choice may be made for us and we end up going back to our old way of existing, and then we are transported to those old lower-level choices that we used to make. Back we go into the denseness and negativity all over again. This is why every choice we make transports us to what it is that we are consciously choosing. *We see it because we believe it.*

I'll Do It Tomorrow

How many times a day do you put things off? Take the time to notice this and you will understand why you feel like you are not accomplishing all that you REALLY want or need to get done throughout your day. You are getting some things done, but there is so much that you are procrastinating on. When this is your truth, you will notice that "I'll do it tomorrow" can feel like your theme song. Notice how you empower a *future moment* more than *your present moment*. Are you ready to shift that?

The moment you think of something that you NEED to do... DO IT. Don't wait until tomorrow. If there is any way that you can do it now... then do it. When we do this one simple change, we notice such a shift in ourselves. I always say, "I'll get up and exercise first thing tomorrow." Then I realize there is no time like the present. I stop limiting myself and then I see so many aspects of my life moving forward.

When Spirit notices my intention and my willingness to follow through, it's like the floodgates open up. I have more energy, I have more ideas, and surprisingly, I actually have more time to do whatever "needs" to be done. This is because my "I can do it" energy just came online for me and it is such a powerful force for my highest good. Why do you think so many people are drawn to the words, "Just do it." We like the thought and idea of it so much that we wear clothes that have it written across our chests. A constant reminder to stop making excuses why you can't and just move forward and do it. Now, take the time to understand that just because you wear the words, does not mean that you are living that as your truth. Maybe it is a reminder—are you ready to stop procrastinating and just do it?

Spirit has been asking me to clear out every inch of my home. Every shelf, drawer, cabinet, closet, wall space, basement, garage and bin gets an overhaul. Do I need it? Does it still feel like me? Does it serve me or do I serve it (that's an interesting question, don't you think)? One-quarter of my basement was my old daycare stuff. Recently I have gone through and released 90 percent of it. Some I'm not ready to let go of... yet. I see new potential and possibilities with my basement now and that excites me. I'm so grateful that a baby will get to play with this toy again rather than it sitting in a box in the basement. Toys were meant to be played with. Doing all of this work was exhausting both physically and emotionally (I loved doing daycare), and yet I'm grateful on so many levels. Interesting side note: once I was willing to let go of the old daycare stuff, an opportunity to take care of a baby presented itself and I will be taking care of a baby a couple days a week. When you let something go and it comes back to you, it's yours.

What are you putting off until tomorrow, next week, until the weekend, the first of the month? Notice what time frame you use as your excuse. Now call out the lie of it. I found that I was constantly saying that I'll wait and do this during the next new moon. New moons are a wonderful time of new beginnings and I used it to give myself an excuse to procrastinate. That is until I noticed my pattern and broke it. This moment right here is new, and I can make it into whatever I want it to be.

My hubby Marsh recently retired and he is getting stuff done around the house non-stop. He motivates me to keep going. All of the things Spirit asks of me are not going to get done by themselves. A new procrastination that I have noticed is that my mom always put things on the steps that she wanted us to take upstairs. Now I am doing the same thing. Is it helping by saving me some steps, or creating more clutter? Continually look at your patterns and excuses; are they serving you, or are you serving them?

Take the time to write down all the "jobs" you're avoiding and what your excuse is. Is your excuse the truth or is it a lie? Remember—an excuse uses a truth to justify a lie. Call out your lies. Don't allow your lies to dictate your life anymore. When something comes to your mind, why not jump up and handle it right away? How does waiting, avoiding, or procrastinating assist you in moving forward with your life? Do you notice that the "tomorrow" that you planned on getting all of this stuff done never comes? If a thought or idea shows up in your head, it's yours to handle or ignore. What "type" of person are you showing up as? What "type" of person do you want to show up as?

You can start small—give yourself one hour. Spend that hour doing the things that you have been avoiding. When that hour is complete, how do you feel? How do you feel about all that you were able to accomplish once you got out of your own way? Is this something that you would like to continue doing and being? Are you ready to be an "accomplished" person?

Here's another way of thinking about this... what if when a thought pops into your head, it is Spirit asking something of you, or they are sending you inspiration? Do you REALLY want to ignore an inspiration from Spirit? There are many who think that Spirit only asks us to do magical and life-changing things. This is NOT the truth. Once Spirit is continually involved in your life, they inspire you to clean out your closet and make phone calls and a thousand other mundane yet necessary things. Are they all magical? They can be. Are they for your highest good? Yes. Allow Spirit into all aspects of your life and all aspects of your life will be transformed. Do you really want to wait until tomorrow to transform your Life?

The next time you hear the words "I'll do it tomorrow" in your head, I want you to jump up and say, "Nope. I am no longer avoiding living my incredibly guided life. My time starts NOW!" Then get up and do whatever it is that you were going to put off until a later time. Notice how empowered you feel. Notice how free you feel from the burden of that "to-do" list called your life. Know this... your life is not a "to-do" list or even a "to don't" list. Your life is a moment-to-moment incredible experience. Turn the "pause" button off and allow yourself to exist in "Play" mode. Take the time to think about that. Take it in on a deeper level. I'm living my life in Play mode. When your "being" has a greater understanding that you *really mean it*, that is when jumping up and handling something will become such a joy. Try to do this with a bounce in your step because remember... you are going out to play. Your life is fun. Doing tasks is now an absolute blast!

You will see this and experience this when you believe it.

Obstacles Are Our Teachers

Knowing and understanding the role that obstacles have in our lives is so much more significant than we understand. Notice also how quickly and easily we see that as truth for others, yet when it happens within our own life, we make excuses. These excuses let everyone know that, yes, you need to stop and notice all that is happening for you because of these obstacles, but my situation is different. Well, we are calling you out on that one right here and now. Yes, all of our own situations *are* different, because we are all different. However, if an obstacle is showing up in your life... *it's YOURS*.

When we own our obstacles and even embrace our obstacles, we transcend so much. Obstacles appear when we need to be guided or nudged in a certain direction or learn a certain lesson and we are NOT wanting to play. Spirit steps in and shows us what we need to learn or understand. If we still refuse, we get another obstacle and another one. An obstacle can be anything from an inconvenience to being diagnosed with an ailment and anything and everything in between. We get frustrated when these obstacles keep showing up nonstop when instead we should be grateful.

Grateful because Spirit is not giving up on us. Spirit is showing up again and again because our growth and what we let them know that we wanted to learn in this lifetime is a priority to them. We ARE a priority to them.

Spirit loves us so much that they will continue to put obstacles on our path to *assist* us in the highest way possible. Sprit will continue to show up in your life (even as an obstacle) until you wake up enough to learn the truth of why that obstacle is here. Usually, an obstacle nudges us in a direction that we are refusing to go. It can also teach us that we are stronger and more powerful than we realize. That which doesn't break us shall make us stronger. It can show us WHAT we are no longer willing to tolerate (until we do). It can show us WHO we are no longer willing to tolerate (until we do). It can force us to change jobs, move, leave, give up, surrender and so much more. Not all obstacles are so big and dramatic as all of that, but they can be.

I would like to share some examples with you. This first story is quite dramatic in that it saved my life and my kidney. In 2018, I had a radical hysterectomy because I had stage 2 endometrial cancer. After the surgery, I experienced an uncomfortable tugging and pulling in my abdomen. When I brought it up to my gynecological oncologist again 18 months later, she said, "Let's get a CT just to make sure that everything is ok." From that CT, they found a very small tumor in one of my kidneys. It was cancerous. I was able to have an incredible surgery robotically that removed less than 10 percent of my kidney.

Do you see how if I hadn't had this uncomfortable tugging and pulling, which I felt was a bother (an obstacle), I would not have had that CT. Kidney cancer can go undetected for a very long time—if it is even caught in time. So, what a gift this tugging and pulling was to me. That whole experience was so incredible and guided. The detailed story about my cancer experience is in my book *The Lie That I Am, A Journey Back to Spirit.*

Another example is that I have experienced off-balance episodes for several years now. Initially, it could last anywhere from a few minutes to a few days. However, lately, it seemed to become more intense and was lasting several months. I went to see several doctors and ended up doing physical therapy. I found myself getting frustrated as I was being taught how to walk. I know how to walk, how ridiculous that they assume I don't know how to walk correctly? I felt so uncomfortable with this frustration. Where was this coming from?

I realized that I wasn't willing to embrace what was showing up for me and so this wasn't leaving. Oh my gosh, I laughed at myself and the choices I was making. As I did this, the clarity came in. You were resisting this time, Mary Beth, so we kept the off-balance experience until you got it. Remember, being off balance can be an ascension symptom. However, this was lasting too long for that. When I went back for my second PT appointment, it was so different. I walked sideways, backwards, moving with my eyes closed, nothing was throwing me off. I was living from a place of knowing and because of that, my experience shifted to AWE-someness. My therapist said her work here was done, and I moved on. What we resist, persists.

A little over a year ago, I fractured my foot in 6–8 places, tore ligaments and had a lot of swelling. I followed my guidance and all unfolded so magnificently. Because it can take a while to get in to see the doctor, and it takes time to get an MRI, and time to have it read and then see the doctor again, I was a month in before the decision to have surgery was given. Spirit had requested my daughter go to this appointment. She stated that so much healing had already happened because it was four weeks since the fracture. She used several medical terms which caused the doctor to pause. The doctor agreed, and said let's wait two more weeks and take another x-ray. When they did, my foot looked perfect.

I mean it was perfect. I was walking better than I ever had. These fractures and ligaments ended up creating a shift in my foot that better aligned my foot because of this injury. Talk about an obstacle being a blessing. My foot no longer turns way out to the side as I walk.

When an obstacle shows up, it is an opportunity for growth. How did you USE IT? How did you use it to catapult yourself forward to becoming something different? When I fractured my foot, I right away asked myself, "What is so scary about the next step in my life that I needed this pause to observe it and learn from it?" From that question, I noticed a multitude of answers came to me. I saw how I was putting so many things off for a later time. Well, guess what—you have got so much time when you are lying around with your foot elevated for weeks on end. Because of my willingness to look at the "WHY" of this obstacle happening to me, I accomplished and learned so much from that experience.

I was able to move forward more efficiently than ever before because of this obstacle. I was also able to take the time to handle all of the things that I had been avoiding. What a beautiful gift this obstacle turned out to be. I am truly grateful—thank you, thank you, thank you. I love learning, growing, and clarity so much!

Clarity is something that happens when we have woken up enough that we understand what is really going on here. Doubt is removed, and we no longer make excuses because… we know what we know. When an obstacle shows up on your path, it is clarity that assists you in what is needed to bring in the highest outcome.

I hope that these examples helped you to see and understand how very different these obstacles were for me and yet they all assisted in my wellbeing, my willingness and my ability to shift, change and move on. I found the blessings in my obstacles, and I am so very grateful for their presence in my life.

I am witnessing during most conversations I have been having, how often people mention obstacles that are present in their own lives or in the lives of their loved ones.

This is good because this means people are sharing their present moments with me. It is not the past, but what is occurring for them and concerning them right now. For this I am truly grateful.

We are of course shifting and changing during these times and some of this can be very uncomfortable for us… especially in the beginning. After a while we stop resisting and just flow. But even in our flow, we may not be paying attention and so we receive an obstacle to assist in making us aware of something. Again, this is a gift. ALL of this is a gift! One of our major shifts happen WHEN we realize that ANYTHING AND EVERYTHING THAT SHOWS UP IN OUR LIFE IS A GIFT.

Once you embrace this understanding, you will notice as soon as an obstacle shows up that you will feel like a kid at Christmas. Oh… what is this going to be about? What direction is this going to take me? How am I going to be transformed because of this?

This is because learning, transforming and transcending is what we love so very much, once we have elevated our frequency enough to see the benefits of the guided life that we exist as. Growth and Change is in our every breath, every exchange, every obstacle. We cannot be MORE without it. We shall remain LESS without it. This is why we get excited when obstacles show up. They are our guidance—our guides showing up and taking us in a New direction. *You will see it when you believe it.*

Throw away your compass, go barefoot as you skip through the obstacles that present themselves on your path. The other option is to dread every opportunity that is presented to you. Whine and complain about all that is happening to you. Then notice how everyone around you whines and complains. This is because we attract to us what we put out to the universe. Now that Spirit has taught you about the significance of obstacles, are you looking forward to your next obstacle or dreading it? Are you curious about where it is going to take you and how it is going to assist in shifting you?

Are you finally ready to embrace your magnificently beautiful life? ALL OF IT? Even the obstacles?

Losing Track of Time

Losing track of time is part of the ascension process because we are no longer thinking in linear terms such as past, present, or future. The only thing that exists is NOW. I have been experiencing this non-stop lately, and when I ask why I can't figure this time thing out, I am told that it is to teach us ALL that *now* is the only moment that matters. I say, oh my goodness, that's wonderful, thank you so much. A few weeks later I ask again, why can't I figure out this time thing right now? They very patiently re-explain to me that time as we understand it is fading away. All that matters is your present moment. I get a flicker of, oh yeah, I now remember you saying something about this before, thank you so much.

This all has been feeling rather strange and bizarre for me. I'm being told that the more that we just surrender to time being abstract and allow it to be exactly what it is, the sooner we will experience our new reality where time will look and feel so very different.

Don't worry, I'm asking the question that all of us want to know. "What does that mean?" I am told that "It means that time dictates our lives right now. Most humans are not ready to eliminate time yet and begin living as time exists in the heavenly realm, for there time does not exist. However, we are beginning to experience and understand that we are ready to stop ALLOWING time to rule both our lives and our reality."

As I ask how this new reality will be experienced, I am told that "This truly depends on where we are individually in our own ascension and where the planet is on its own ascension path as you read these words. For some could be reading these words many years from now and our planet will be very different." When I ask how, they say, "Let's not get too far ahead of the topic here. This is to be about time and how it is shifting. The more we allow time to "slip away" and barely even notice that it exists, the quicker this shift will happen.

If we choose to resist having our experience of time shift, then more confusion will be our experience. This will happen until we are so confused that our time reality shift happens *FOR US*, because we literally can't hold onto time. Only then will our lives totally reprioritize to taking the time for one another rather than what the clock says we should be doing. Suddenly we will have plenty of time to make a difference because making a difference is the priority rather than the clock. You will notice that being of service will be the priority rather than our agendas."

I can really see this and feel it, can you? And of course, they are saying, "*You shall see it, feel it, notice it, and live it, when you believe it.*" I must admit that during my "how may I serve you" moments I never look at the clock, and because of that I am able to be more present with my experience.

When my sister Christine and I did our "walkabouts" while I was visiting her, I had no idea if we had left in the morning or afternoon. I also cannot tell you if we were gone 1 hour, 6 hours, or anytime in between. We were being totally present with our experiences and therefore time didn't exist because time was not our priority. This makes so much more sense to me now. These time-warping experiences began feeling so off to me because it was time for me to notice and shift my understanding of time.

Spending time with my sister Christine is something to be treasured beyond measure.

I have noticed that I am able to accomplish so much in a short amount of time when I don't look at the clock, or allow time to dictate how much I *can* accomplish. In other words, I would have said I only have an hour before I have to leave, so I'll do this one job. Now I say what feels like the next wonderful thing for me to work on. An hour later, I notice that I have accomplished two hours' worth of work. I don't allow time to limit me. I'm getting so much more done when I do it from my happy place. I love all of this shifting.

Here is another interesting aspect of this. Notice how when you do have to do linear things… as in you have to "deal with" time, how frustrated you can become. Notice if you experience more delays along with your frustrations. This is because you are not enjoying going back into making time your priority and you are resenting both time and the experiences. Oh my gosh, this has been my truth so often lately. I have been startled by my level of frustration, because this is no longer "my norm." Because of that, having frustration show up feels bizarre. I am so ready and willing to shift this as my experience. *I will see it because I now understand it and I believe it.*

I hope my talking out my question and answer process with Spirit didn't confuse you too much. Spirit wanted you to have a greater understanding of what my life and my processing of all that I am given from Spirit is like sometimes. There are other times I just get downloads and don't participate as much. I enjoy both ways, however, Spirit knows how much I love the gift of a question because I am actively participating in shifting my life, and my reality. Are you embracing the gift of a question too? Are you asking more questions and therefore getting more answers because of your willingness to ask the questions? *You will see it and experience it, when you believe it.*

Meeting God

If God walked up to you right here, right now, what would you say? What would you do? I really want you to think about that because as the veils thin and our connection or access to the other side (the heavenly realm) becomes more accessible, the possibility becomes more real with every loving choice you make. For when you make choices that raise your frequency, your frequency is more congruent with those residing in the heavenly realm. Thinking about who you would like to speak to on the other side and what you would like to learn from them is an important step. This creates a link, bond or connection to that person (or being).

Having that connection or link can shift so much more than many realize. Many years ago, I was having a therapy session when Jesus showed up. My therapist was used to Spirit showing up and changing the trajectory of our sessions. However, this was different. We were talking about how I didn't feel that I matter and that my existence is not important. Then Jesus shows up with a large wooden bowl of warm water. He kneels at my feet. My therapist says something and I put my hand up like the signal to stop. He knows that this means Spirit is giving me a message and he must wait until I speak. I don't want to miss a single message from my team of Guides and Angels.

Suddenly I am bent over crying, "No, no… I'm not worthy. I'm not worthy." There are so may tears as I weep, begging Jesus to stop as he places my feet in his basin of water and begins washing my feet. I just sob as he does this. I keep repeating, "I'm not worthy." Jesus asks me, "If you are not worthy, then who is?" I said, "Anyone and everyone but me." He says, "I don't agree, for I kneel before thee humbly." I don't remember the rest of his words, but they had to do with my not understanding all that I am and all that I came here to do. My life matters. My existence is of importance. It is vital. I wept through all of it. As he dried my feet and left, I was bent over. I didn't move for a while. I was taking in all that had just happened.

When I finally sat up and opened my eyes, my therapist said, "Wow, I can't wait to hear about what just happened." As I told him, he wiped a tear. We were both so moved by what I had just experienced. Needless to say, I felt a lot better about my existence. I have noticed that Spirit came through a lot during my therapy sessions because in that space I want to (and am willing to) grow, learn, and change. After my session, my therapist spent the next hour going for a jog and reliving what he had just witnessed. Jesus had given him a message too, however, I have no idea what it was because it wasn't my message. Even though he only observed me, he felt and knew something immense had occurred, and he was transported into my experience on some level.

As he jogged past an alleyway, he noticed a figure with a multi-colored aura. It was Jesus. He stared at this figure of the person he most wanted to meet, as he took in the enormity of his own experience with Jesus. When I arrived for my next session a week later, he told me about his encounter. He showed me a picture he had drawn of Jesus and the order of the colors that radiated out from Jesus' body. He felt I would understand this color order—I didn't. Auras are not something I usually see. I have seen them a few times, but it felt more like they were there to capture my attention.

Of course, the first thing out of my mouth was a question. I asked him what he said to Jesus. He just looked at me in shock. He said, "I didn't say anything." My response was—"Bumaroo. You had an opportunity to have a 'real' conversation with Jesus and you didn't go up and talk to him?" I didn't mean to take this sacred moment that he had experienced to belittle him. I was simply curious what he would ask Jesus. In my head, I was quite sad that he didn't realize that he COULD talk to Jesus.

So really think about who you would like to meet. Start to create a dialogue with them in your head. Ask the questions that you have always wondered about. I have been told repeatedly by Spirit that it is my curiosity that opens me up to experience so many different "beings," Spirits and Guides. When I believed that I couldn't do this, then that was my experience. *I didn't see it because I didn't believe it.* Now that I no longer believe I can't, I get to experience a multitude of different beings showing up and sharing their wisdom with me. As a bonus, we get to take our conversations even further because with every answer or statement that they give me, I'm ready with another question. So, by the end of the conversation, my curiosity is sated. We train Spirit on whether we are ok with a simple answer, or whether we want to keep the conversation going so that we can receive even more knowledge. *This will be your experience when you believe you are ready for it and that you deserve it.* Are you ready to believe that you are worthy?

Last year, one of my nieces called me and told me that her son told her he dreamed about meeting Jesus at a skate park. She asked him what Jesus looked like. He replied that Jesus looked like a normal person. I remarked that I would have asked him what Jesus said. I'm sorry if I made her feel like she had messed up, because there are no mistakes. I just want to prepare her for next time. If you don't take advantage of that first moment, then you might not get a second moment. She has an opportunity to teach her child that he can have conversations with Jesus. This empowers our children to move beyond our human limitations.

Start your own dialogue now with Spirit. Notice if you get an answer in your head. Trust it. Ask another question. If you don't get an answer right away, let Spirit know that you will be patient as you wait for them to respond. Desperation will shut down our connection. Relaxing (or softening) and just allowing our experience to be what it is, opens us up to new opportunities.

Spirit says that I am so good at this and staying connected to my curiosity and innocence, that they can show up in a variety of ways for me. I am able to see, hear and feel so much from all these "beings" that show up to give me greater clarity about all that I am so curious about. All these "beings" are part of my "team" that have come together to help me have greater clarity so that I can share that clarity with all of you. Working as a team is important to accomplish all that they have planned for us.

Try multiple ways of connecting to your team. Ask questions in your head during the time when you are quiet and connected. Now try asking questions out loud. Next try writing your questions out. Notice if you begin to write the answers out too. I have even made up songs to Spirit. Again, I'm connected to my joy and my innocence. Play with it. Have fun with this. Let go of the agendas—the shoulds and the have tos.

I promise you that the more playful you are, the clearer your connection will be. Notice how children believe in so much more than we adults do. They don't have all the limitations that we put on ourselves as we become cynical and judgmental. Kids show up and make friends so much easier than adults because they live in the flow of life. What shows up is what they play with next!!

Are you ready to start living your life in that same way? Where there is an abundance of flow, trust, and of course gratitude? When we are grateful for what we have, more shows up. When we doubt, the flow stops or at least slows down to a trickle. *You will see this when you believe it.*

Watch out, I think your curiosity is showing!

God's Will IS My Will

As we connect to God-Source-All That Is, there is a need and desire to continue connecting to and having a relationship of this caliber. When we are not actively connected to the One Source, we look to connect to anything that can connect us to something that gives us that similar feeling of a bond. So we learn to connect to one another. Some do this through their religions, some through doing good for others and making a difference. When we do this, we feel a draw—a pull happens within us. This is the beginning of our connection to oneness.

When we begin to connect to oneness is when we notice that we are more similar rather than dissimilar. We notice commonalities. When we see others making "mistakes," rather than judging them, we chuckle inside as we remember how we too continue to make "mistakes." We also know how vitally important it is to make those "mistakes," because without them we would not be able to learn from them. We have compassion for all that they are going through and will continue to go through.

As I write all of this, it reminds me of a story from when my daughter was in preschool in Japan. The whole class was working on a project, and my daughter was yelling very excitedly. "I made a mistake, I made a mistake!" Her teacher came over to console her and to reassure her that, "It's okay, we all make mistakes." However, this teacher did not understand who my daughter was and how differently she had been raised. Megan looked at her like she was a crazy person and said, "If I don't make mistakes, I can't learn from them and then I can't get smarter."

Megan exploring and immersing herself in the Japanese culture.

When we lived in Japan, our daughter called everyone who lived there her Japanese friends. If you were from the USA but were living in Japan—you were still a Japanese friend. I never corrected her because I saw the truth of her words. My daughter just wanted to get along with and love everyone. Religion, skin color, nationality, she just doesn't see them... only love.

As we learn and grow from our "mistakes," we become a higher version of ourselves. We evolve. We came here to this planet to learn and experience. What did you learn today? What did you experience today? How were you able to evolve into a higher version of yourself? How did your being on this planet make a difference?

Know that as long as you find fault with others and judge others as bad and wrong, you will not be able to connect to oneness. You may think you are, but that is an illusion. You can connect to some pretty amazing frequencies, however they are NOT oneness. When we are connected to oneness... another's pain is our pain. Another's joy is our joy. When they succeed, we KNOW that everyone has succeeded. For TRULY *all* is one, *all* is connected. There is *absolutely* no separation. This is Ascension.

Until that time, you are a student in this planetary school of learning, taking one class after another trying to learn how to experience that feeling of connectedness that we experience when we are one with God-Source-All That Is. As we learn how to experience this more consistently, we don't ever want the connection to be severed. However, as in anytime that we are a student learning a lesson, we must take it in multiple directions to grow.

Some directions take us to something even greater than our past experiences. Some will take us down dead-ends. Others will take us in ways that feel very off and uncomfortable. This is all good, for no matter which of these is our experience, we are learning. We are learning what works for us and what doesn't. Both are important, for they teach us to trust ourselves—trust our "gut" instincts. When we don't trust ourselves, we flounder and feel lost. This is important also, for if we are never lost, we cannot be found.

Emotions help us to immerse ourselves into what we are experiencing. DO NOT shy away from feeling anything and everything to the depths of your soul. For this truly is our soul connection.

I remember telling Jesus, wow, you sure have a lot of people who believe in you. His response was—"Because I believe in them." Another confirmation of what we resonate with is what we create more of. Another way of saying this is... *I'll see it when I believe it.* Like attracts like.

Do you remember those moments when you found a new concept or idea that made so much sense to you that every cell in your body reacted with excitement? The realization that you just had, took you to a "higher level" of knowing. Of understanding... both yourself and your world. These are the AHA moments that we are all searching for. For when we experience them, we know that something important and life-changing-for-the-better just happened. We know that our frequency has risen to a new level as we connected to something that we want every single person to understand and experience. This too is oneness. For your growth is my growth. You just raised the frequency of the entire planet. For we are all one and there is no separation.

When we reach this level of faith in ourselves and all that is unfolding around us, we notice a shift that is beyond amazing. We realize that we are living "God's Will." We have a new understanding. It is no longer "God's will is more important than my will." We now KNOW... GOD's WILL *IS* MY WILL. This IS ONENESS. *You will see it, feel it, know it, and live it—when you believe it and trust it.* The desire God has for us is understood on a different level. We can connect to and understand what God's will is, because God resides in every thought, word and deed that we experience. We see everything from God's perspective... in that we get a bigger picture of what is happening while living from a place of divine neutrality. God doesn't judge, God observes. Once we ascend, we don't judge, we observe. We allow others to have free will just as God allows us to have free will. We no longer need anyone to think, feel and believe as we do because the greatest need is to allow all to be exactly as it is. All is love and all IS LOVED.

When we connect in this way, God, Spirit, you and I are all one and the same. Now that is something to work towards and achieve on a whole new sacred level. Talk about leveling up. Yes, this is my wish... my desire for all of us. For when you succeed, I succeed. As I evolve, you evolve. Your JOY is my JOY, and I love feeling JOY-FULL!

The Importance of Touch

When we touch, we create a connection to another person. This is why a touch can create a healing. Recently I have been experiencing a greater understanding of the importance of having our face touched.

When a friend touches our life, we become a better version of ourself.
Thank you, Kathleen, for being my friend.

This has opened me up in a new and interesting way of being present with someone. I am now touching my own face more. I notice how quickly and effortlessly it calms me down and soothes me. I am noticing how as I talk to people I will have a finger on my chin, cheek, or even my ear. Spirit said that these are energy points that allow me to take myself somewhere energetically. For instance, as I touch my chin, my curiosity opens up. As I touch my cheek, my intellect is activated differently. When I touch my ear, I am self-soothing. How fascinating is that?

This all started about a year ago when I was at someone's home and they were doing a deep dive into the end of the world and Satan's work. Suddenly Jesus was in front of me holding my face. As his hands caressed my face, he said, "Look at me, Mary Beth, listen to my voice. I don't want you to listen to what is being said for it is not for you." I said, "You know that I know the truth of all that is unfolding. I'm not about to buy into these lies." He said, "And yet I am here asking you to look at me and listen to my voice, not hers. Stay focused on me and how much I love you. We need you to stay pure."

As my friend and I left this person's home, she asked me what was being said to me while this woman was speaking of hell and damnation. I asked how she knew. She said, "You had a strange, faraway look in your eyes and your expression was off and didn't change much." I told her how Jesus was holding my face and asking me to focus on him and his voice. I could tell that my friend was a bit envious and yet happy that I get to experience such things.

After that, I noticed that when I needed someone to really focus on the words I was being given for them, I was holding their face just as Jesus had done for me. If we are sitting down, I place a hand on their leg or arm. I saw how when I did this, outside distractions were gone. My words went to a different place within them and they received the message they were being given in a higher, more divine way.

If you are up to it, do a little experiment of your own. When you need to give an important, *loving* message to someone, try doing it while caressing their face. Notice how much eye contact there is between the two of you. Notice that this eye contact is creating a soul connection. Now realize that this should only be done with a LOVING message. *You will see it when you believe it.* If it is a negative message, there will be confusion and they will experience a sense of lostness. This is because they are receiving mixed messages. We shut down somewhat when we get mixed messages. The hands are saying love, but the words say hate or disappointment. Can you see the truth of this?

What touches create a healthy, positive response in you? Are you able to communicate with your partner and loved ones for instance how much you feel heard by them when they hold or stroke your hand when they are sharing compassion with you? I love it when my hubby holds my hand as we walk from the car into a building. I walk in feeling more joyful and cared for when he does that. When my sister strokes my hand as she talks to me, I feel such love and compassion from her and from her words.

Remember the story I told you about when Jesus stepped into me. My body was totally encapsulated by His. As this happened, I was given everything He had ever experienced. His thoughts were my thoughts. His every experience I had access to. It's strange to say this, but it actually felt kind of normal to me. I felt such immense love during this experience. No words were spoken until He stepped outside of me again. He said this is the way we are on the other side. We have no need to hide any of ourselves from another.

Can you imagine sharing everything about yourself with everyone you encounter? Well, get ready because here it comes. Maybe not in the same way that I had experienced it with Jesus. However, we are becoming more telepathic each time our frequency raises. This can really freak people out because the idea of others knowing their lower-frequency moments could change how they are seen. What helped me was the knowing that we have all made mistakes. It's what we came here to do. Why would we judge someone for not being perfect? When you are an Ascended "Being," you wouldn't. No judgment, only love. And All are Loved.

So get out there and touch lives. Touch hearts. I encourage you to touch your own heart. This is your lifetime to do all of this. What are you doing with your time AND your lifetime? What you do with your time matters. How you touch lives matters. Everything MATTERS!

Question Yourself

I would like to ask you some questions to assist you in seeing who you are showing up as and how others may be experiencing you. For the first question, when you greet someone and they inform you that they are going through cancer treatments, how do you notice that you react to this information? Rather than continue reading, I would like you to get a pen and paper and write down (in as much detail as you are willing to) how you have responded to this type of situation and the others that I am going to ask you.

Please don't give me the "correct answer" or the "spiritual answer" but rather the absolute truth. It is time to stop lying to yourself so you can feel/believe better about yourself. Lying doesn't serve you, and it doesn't serve the person you are interacting with. Lying is disrespectful and not on the path of ascension. Lying even in your head is still lying, and trains you to continue lying. Lying lowers your frequency and will feel *very* uncomfortable the further on your path of ascension that you are. Know that no one is going to read your responses to these questions unless you ask them to. This is for your own growth.

- 2nd question: someone tells you that they are going to have surgery next week, how do you respond?
- 3rd question: a person has lost over 100 pounds since the last time you had seen them. How would you react to this transformation?
- 4th question: we have a woman very far along in her pregnancy, what would you say to her?
- 5th question: how about a young couple buying their first house?
- 6th question: someone telling you about how much they love their exercise class?
- 7th question: a person confides in you about their traumatic childhood—how would you respond?
- 8th question: someone you haven't seen in years lets you know that they have been living overseas—what would you say?

Please write your honest responses. When you are complete, please continue to read on so you can have a better understanding of who you are showing up as.

As your frequency raises, you become more present when you interact with another person. When a person is telling you something about their life, you will notice when you shift from being present with them to instead formulating your response in your head about how you can "top" their story with your own story. Please try to be present with them as they speak. When you do, you hear everything that they have to say and you ask questions because you want to learn more. This is a part of being mindful; there are so many books and videos out there that can teach you more about being mindful, but I just wanted to bring it up so you are aware of the existence of mindfulness.

All right, let us go through your answers to my questions. My first question about how you would respond to someone informing you that they are going through cancer treatments was very surprising for me. Most people, when they hear this, start listing everyone they know who has gone through cancer. They tell the cancer patient about who died, who lived, and how horrible they looked during their treatments. They include details like how much weight they lost and if they lost their hair. In other words, they stopped showing compassion and turned it into a narrative about themselves. A one-upmanship.

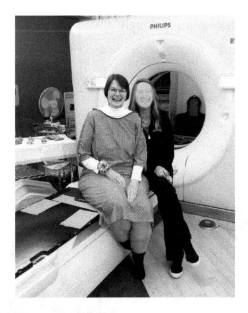

Mary Beth before her first internal radiation treatment.

Rather than experiencing compassion from another, this cancer patient is given more fear and hopelessness. That may not have been your intention, but that is the result. Because of human beings wanting and needing to "one-up" each other, an opportunity to show up as a higher version of yourself may have been lost. This is why many cancer patients don't tell anyone about what they are going through. Many cancer patients know that from the moment another knows of their diagnosis— that person sees them "AS CANCER." All they want to speak of in your presence is cancer. When the truth is that we want to have a few normal moments where cancer is not our focus. For many who talk to a cancer patient, empathy is put on the back burner and one-upmanship comes to the forefront. Again, this is to help you see and understand who you are showing up as. *You will see it when you believe it.*

On to question #2 about a person having surgery. Do you truly listen to what this person is going through or do you start listing all your past surgeries and all your family member's surgeries? Do you mention people's complications during or after surgery? If you do this, please ask yourself *WHY.* Why would you do this and what did you hope that information would accomplish? Do you really want to instill fear at a time when a person is already going through a very challenging time?

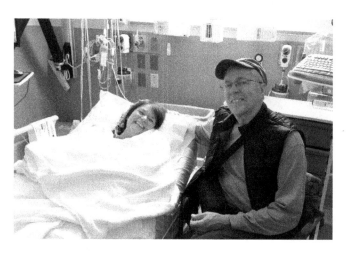

It's so much easier to go through difficult times when you have someone like Marsh at your side (cancer surgery).

I understand most of you have moved beyond all of this. Spirit says that it is a nice reminder of how much you have changed or how much more you will be changing in the future as you become a more spiritual being.

With question #3, notice your reaction. Are you jealous of this person having released so much weight? Are you truly happy for them? Are you asking questions that assist them in feeling great about their accomplishment? Are you giving your *unsolicited* opinion of if you feel they lost too much weight or if they need to lose more? Realize that if you go to that narrative, you are showing your *own insecurities*. If a person asks for your opinion, please give it. If they don't ask and yet you supply your own opinion, ask yourself if you are finding fault so that you can avoid looking at your own life or even your own waistline. Advice is easy. Doing the work is much more challenging. Stop lowering people's vibration because they are in your presence, because that is what you are doing when you make everything about you and what you think.

My daughter and I before and after my weight loss surgery.
We are both inside my old pants in photo #2.

Question #4: our beautiful, pregnant woman. Do you congratulate her, and then let her tell you all about her experience? Do you start telling her how much weight you or someone else gained? Notice if you are bragging or complaining. Do you bring up complications people have had? How many kids people have had? How long your own labor was? Again, I ask you to look at WHY you would want to present information that could instill fear or even failure in another. For even when you inform someone that you were only in labor for 40 minutes, and they end up having 27 hours of labor, perhaps they could feel that somehow they had failed? If they ask, share. If they don't ask, just try to be supportive.

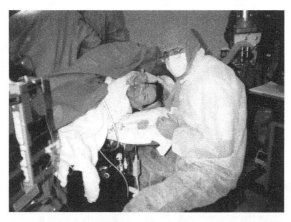

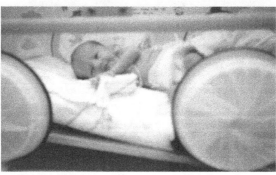

My daughter's challenging birth. Good news—we both lived.

Our 5th question about buying a house—do you list all the pitfalls that you or others experienced? One of my relatives asked me why I would do such a thing as buy a house because now we would have to do our own repairs. If we rented, that expense would all be on the landlord. My disappointment from this response was such a life lesson. I don't share my joyful moments or even my moments of concern with this person very much anymore. They simply cannot be happy for me. When I told them I was pregnant, their response was, "Better you than me." I choose to share my important life moments with people who are more "awake" than this now. That is my choice. What are you choosing? This is a picture of my yellow Victorian house that we bought. I began telling people about it eight years before we moved in. I simply knew that it was coming to me. I just didn't know when. *I'll see it when I believe it.*

My dream home, which ended up being a nightmare.

A small side note about this yellow Victorian house that I knew I was going to live in someday: it turned into a nightmare inside the house.

Allow your visualizations to encompass more, so you don't limit yourself or your experience in any way. I learned a lot from that house and in that house. With my visualization, it would have been beneficial to see inside the house—how it would be paid for, how big the rooms were and what I would be doing while living there. This is not to limit me, but rather to create new possibilities.

When a person mentions something that brings them such joy as in question #6 about exercising, can you be happy for them and leave it at that? Can you ask questions that give the person an opportunity to share their joy on an even greater level? Or, do you notice yourself listing all the reasons why this doesn't work for you? When we can step into making a person's interaction with us joyful and uplifting, we see a shift in how much people are willing to share with us. We have a greater understanding of why they choose to share their stories with us and the difference we just made. *You will see the difference you make when you believe you make a difference.* When a person confides in you, do you realize what an HONOR that is?

As we look at question #7 about sharing childhood traumas, you have an opportunity to assist others in healing their past. Are you willing to step up and do that? The choice is yours. Are you dismissing their trauma by listing all of your own? Be careful in the way you show empathy and compassion. It is so easy to shift it from a "sacred place" to an "all about me" or even a "complaining" place. Spend more time noticing what you are saying to others and why. Who did you used to be, and who are you now? Are you still responding and reacting the way you did as a teenager? Are you ready to be something more?

Not every childhood is magical, nor every child embraced.

In question #8, how do you respond to someone living overseas or doing something like the Peace Corps or joining the military? Just because a person is doing something that you know very little about does not mean you can't contribute to the conversation. When we ask questions, the person we are conversing with notices and understands that you are wanting to learn more. You are interested in having a new understanding or even seeing a different point of view. All of these questions and the curiosity you show assists us in expanding who we are and what we know. When I came back from Japan and was telling one of my brothers some stories, he would constantly look at his wife and do the eye rolling thing. Later in life when they finally traveled, I had an opportunity to do as he had done to me, or I could listen, smile and ask questions. Which do you think that I chose?

Cherry Blossom Festival in Hirosaki, Japan.

Living in Hawaii felt like coming home to me.

Love looks very good on us.

On our path of ascension, we notice all the time how curiosity raises our frequency. *You will see it when you believe it.* Wanting to learn and expand in any way brings in more questions and more curiosity. We felt this chapter was important in helping you see who you are showing up as. We can't change what we don't know. So we give you this information to empower you—not to judge you. If you are already living from this higher place, thank you. If you notice you have surrounded yourself with people who are not assisting you or even listening to you, you might want to have some healthy conversations.

Again, they can't change what they don't realize that they are doing. I absolutely love it when someone's willingness to change and grow is showing. I witness their frequency shift and the world is a little bit brighter because of it. This is because they are letting their light shine. And if they aren't ready, we love them anyway. We do this because we remember ourselves what it felt like to have someone want us to do or be something, but it wasn't the right time for us... yet. Were they patient with us, or did they walk away in frustration?

Patience is who I choose to show up as, how about you? We have so very many choices in every moment. What are you choosing?

My World is Not a Mess

It's Simply Under Construction

Take a moment to really think about the words—My world is not a mess, it's simply under construction. I don't know about you, but those words seem to calm me. It's a reminder that, first of all, things aren't as bad as I'm imagining them to be. Secondly, when something is under construction, you expect things to not be in perfect order. Third, under construction lets you know that things are shifting and changing, however, it also says that this is TEMPORARY. Just knowing that something is temporary will help your mind and your nervous system to calm down.

Let's break it down some more. My world is all that I *involve* myself with. If I were to say my planet isn't a mess, that would create an entirely different picture and feel quite different. When we talk about the planet, we are connecting to the energy of everything and everyone on the entire planet. Spirit chose "my world" instead of "my planet" because we can look at, shift, and change things in our own world more easily than we probably can look at, shift, and change the entire planet, and yet this is happening also. Do you see how Spirit is setting us up for success? They are ALWAYS and in ALL WAYS helping us to succeed—not fail. It is our human beliefs that kick in when things aren't as we would like them to be. We tend to look for someone outside of ourselves to blame for anything less than what WE want.

When we live from an elevated frequency, we don't blame anyone, not even ourselves. Instead, we take responsibility for our lives and what is occurring. We look at what we have been focusing our thoughts on and seeing where we can change our thoughts and actions to create more harmony. Know this—we are Spiritual beings having a human experience. We are not human beings having a spiritual experience. It makes sense that we want to expand our spiritual aspect because that is who we are.

With this in mind, as you look out at both your world and the planet, you may see a lot of discord. There is a lot of wild and crazy stuff going on out there. If you are drawn to it, I would have you ask yourself, "How do I feel drawn to assisting in creating more peace and harmony?" When you ask yourself questions like that, you create a dialog between yourself and your Higher Self or perhaps with Spirit. When we do this, Spirit and/or our Higher Self knows that we want to have a greater connection or relationship with them. Here is a wonderful reminder: a question opens up a dialog, a statement can close it.

Keep the dialog going as you assess what the greatest need is and how you can fulfill your part in it. *Sometimes* the piece you are to contribute is nothing. Absolutely nothing. How egotistical are we if we think that we need to be responsible for everything and everyone? When we do that, we are denying others the opportunity to step up and make a difference. This does not mean that you continually do nothing because you are using the excuse of, "I'm giving others an opportunity to step up and assist." By going within and checking what we can do, we learn a bit more about why we are here.

I am here to be a teacher and a writer. I am given the information that will assist myself or others all the time. It is not uncommon for me to ask Spirit what can I do to assist when devastation has struck a community. They usually respond with, "Please send calming energy, clarity, and light." Then they usually ask me to please continue with my writings, for that is the greatest way that I can assist one and all. Then they inform me that there are many ready to step up and assist these people who are in such great need. Because of this, I understand my role at this time, and I give others an opportunity to step up and assist also. This does not mean that we do nothing and allow others to do what is necessary. No. We listen to our guidance and from there, we know what OUR PART IS.

When the experience that is happening out there in the world that is getting the most attention does not have to do with devastation or loss of life, but rather someone making poor life choices and it is not really affecting others, this is when Spirit usually tells me that it is none of my business. We as a collective are concerning ourselves with so much that truly is "None of our business." This is why sensationalism has become so prevalent. We want to gossip about how awful anything and everything is. This keeps the frequency of chaos and negativity going. Is that the role that you want to participate in during our shift here? What assists me in staying centered and connected is knowing—I mean truly knowing—that all is well.

There is a divine plan. I promise you this. That divine plan is playing out in the exact way that it is supposed to. I know this because once our connection to Spirit is so solid, they ask us "Earth Angels" or "Gaia Angels" to show up at a certain place during this time. They make sure that everything unfolds EXACTLY as it is supposed to. I will give you an example from my own life.

Remember the story of when I was 22 and writing my suicide note, and Spirit intervened? A voice asked me if I really wanted to die. I was taken to the heavenly realm (the Akashic records) where I was shown my future. Afterward, I remembered none of this, for when we return to the earth plain our veils are placed back on us. I did remember that this man was blond-haired, blue-eyed, 6 feet tall, and wore a navy blue uniform. That's it. Everything else was GONE. I met my husband two years later.

To assist you in understanding what had to happen in both my life and my husband's life during that two-year span so that we could meet and fall in love was a very detailed, extravagant plan that involved a lot of people and a lot of territory.

- I needed to be laid off from my job at a hospital in Wisconsin.
- I couldn't find another job because I had made really good money at the hospital.
- A young man who ran a dance studio in Tennessee had to become ill, and it needed to *not* be a quick fix.
- My sister was then asked to move down there and manage the dance studio.
- Her receptionist needed to quit, so my sister asked me to come down and help out.
- My future husband, who was stationed in the middle of the Indian Ocean, needed to be chosen for a school in Tennessee.
- He and his girlfriend needed to break up.
- He needed to have a desire to learn how to dance before he moved to Hawaii.

- He needed to choose to come into the dance studio that I worked at for his lessons.
- The second time he came in for lessons, his teacher needed to be busy signing a contract, so I had to do the warmup dance with Mr. Smith.
- I needed to look into his eyes… and I knew. I knew he was the one God had sent to me—and for me.

Do you see that no matter how I fought it, God was going to get me to Tennessee during the time that Marsh was there because it was part of our divine plan? Obviously, there were many, many more steps to all of this that I didn't include. There were times during this process that I dug myself in and said, "No" and then a calm would come over me and I stopped resisting. One of those times was when my mother told me that I needed to move to Tennessee to take care of my sister. I said, "NO. My sister is 2 ½ years older than me—I shouldn't have to take care of her." Later, I calmed down and felt grace enfold me.

There is so much more divinity going on here on the planet than we can comprehend. Actually, there is no need to comprehend it. Our "job" is to learn to trust it. Trust all of it. Know that if you lose your job, it's because Spirit needs you somewhere else. If a relationship ends, it's because you are supposed to be with someone else, or they are supposed to be with someone else… or both. When we resist, less opportunities show up. When we go, "Well, this is going to be interesting. I wonder what is going to come from this?" we are wide open for new opportunities to happen for us (not to us). This is because you have a divine plan. You chose your divine plan. This is why sometimes a person or place seems familiar even though we have never been there or met them. This is what happened when I met Marsh.

We set markers for ourselves, usually at very boring, casual times when we suddenly experience something familiar. Many call this deja vu. That is a gift you gave yourself, saying… when you experience this, know that you are right on track. You are doing exactly what you're supposed to be doing. Keep it up. You've got this! When these moments happen, notice how long you "pause" to take that moment in.

That was a lot of detail all to show you—prove to you—how divinely guided our lives are. So, as you look out at the reconstruction going on out there, know that we've got this. There are so many Ascended Masters, Angels, Spirits, and even beings from other planets helping us. Every single one of them is encouraging us and reassuring us that we came here to Succeed. We will succeed. It is part of our collective divine plan. Now, all that is left is the need to walk through our divine plan. Sounds pretty easy to me. After all, we've got each other and a lot of help from on high.

Does knowing all of this and understanding all of this help you to worry a little less about the construction work going on both in your own life and on the planet? Can you surrender your fear and move to a place of curiosity? I am so excited about what is going on. What we are doing has never been done before. This is why we have so much help from on high. They love watching us succeed. I want to thank every "being" who is assisting us during our time of reconstruction. Thank YOU for your willingness to be part of all that is unfolding.

It's time to put on your hard hat and get out all the tools that you will need to complete the job. Tools like compassion, understanding, tolerance, willingness and TRUST. Make sure that you are surrounding yourself with the best team possible to get the job done in the right way. Keep yourself well-fed, hydrated, and in the best shape that you can be in, because when you are asked to show up, it needs to be in the highest way that you possibly can.

Make sure your Angels and Guides understand how willing and able you are to do WHATEVER is asked of you. The limits you placed on yourself need to be lifted. Time to do the heavy work of letting go of doubt, lack, hate and fear. There is no place for them here. I sometimes wonder if future generations will even know what those things are. Isn't that a wonderful thought? Our future generations may never experience hate, fear, doubt and lack.

Yes, sign me up for whatever is needed of me so that we can exist in such a beautiful, magical world. It's all waiting for us. The blueprints have been designed. We already have the land. We have billions of people to help do the work. All the resources already exist. What are we waiting for?

We're not waiting anymore!

We'll see it when we believe it!

Being a Light Worker

I know not what the definition is that others give to you about being a light worker. I only know what I have been shown through my own experiences and understandings. When we exist as, and show up as the divine light that we are, that is when we are a light worker. When every interaction we have is filled with light, we are a light worker. When our words carry compassion, love and divine wisdom, we are a light worker. When you hear those words, what do you think? How do you feel? Are you reminded of times when you experienced that? When you were that?

If you have been blessed with past experiences where you felt that you existed as a light worker, you may ask yourself why you are unable to stay in that frequency. Why does it seem so fleeting? The answer lies in the title of this book, *I'll See It When I Believe It*. You must believe, know, understand, and trust with everything that you are. Only then will the truth of what you believe show up in your life. Who you show up as will continue to morph as your beliefs morph.

How stuck are you in your beliefs? I mean really, really stuck. "It HAS TO BE this and nothing else!" type of belief. When you notice this as your belief, that is when you will understand why you are stuck. You are not allowing yourself or anyone else to expand and be something more. You are limiting everything. You limit your experiences, you limit who you allow in your life, you limit your children, you limit your community, and here comes the big one… YOU LIMIT GOD. Yep, you limit God when you believe that God will ONLY allow this and would never allow that.

This is when you play God or even *place yourself above God*. For if you truly have a relationship with God, Source, All That Is, you know that this lifetime is about flowing and evolving rather than restrictions and limitations. God can't wait to see what we are going to do with the lifetime we have been given. This is why we are given free will… to lift those limits and restrictions and allow ALL to be more… or even allows us to be less. You may want to ask yourself why we were given free will, yet *WE* refuse to give anyone else free will. Could it be because you believe you have greater clarity and understanding than God? Wow, Spirit is going all out today in pushing us to realize more about ourselves than ever before.

As light workers, we absolutely know when we are being of the light, we feel the flow, we feel the joy and the lightness in all situations. We also realize when we have just limited ourselves or others. By now, after reading this book, you know what words come from the light, and what thoughts are filled with expansion. You know what is the highest thing to do and be. You know, you know, you know. And yet you may notice how the shadows or even the darkness can pull you in at times. Call yourself out during those moments and remind yourself of how incredible it feels to bring light into our challenging or learning opportunities. Remember how quickly you can notice when your energy or frequency falters and becomes less. YOU become less.

The longer you allow yourself to stay in this shadow energy the more comfortable you become there again. Take the time to remind yourself of how much goodness shows up in your own life when you are creating goodness in the world. Do something special, or even something simple for someone else. Allow that kindness to create a frequency of wanting to perform more acts of kindness. Notice how quickly your focus is on the light again. See how this light feeds you. Being on a "light" diet of feeding yourself and others with "light" words, and "light-filled" deeds will get you back into light worker mode again. From there all things are possible.

Recently, my sister Christine decided to go on a walkabout. She needed to clear her mind and recenter herself. She wanted to go to a certain park, but her body kept leading her towards a different park. There were three women there with signs saying, "Free Hugs." She paused for just a moment. No one was stepping up for a hug, and the frequency was awkward. Then she released all her old limitations, threw open her arms and said, "Really, you're giving free hugs? I'll gladly take you up on that." When Christine finished with her free hugs, there was a line of people behind her.

Can you see how if she hadn't been willing to release her limitations, these three women may have lost their faith that love can make a difference. The people who stepped up afterwards would have missed out on something sacred touching their lives and their hearts. Of course, we can't forget the shift that was able to happen for Christine. We all want to believe we would do the same thing and step up to love, but we need to let go of our limitations and allow love and kindness to be who we are in every interaction.

Are you willing to get out of your place of comfort and be something spectacular? This does not have to cost money, it's just a matter of performing one kindness after another and then yet another until all you are is love, light and kindness. *You will see this repeatedly when you believe it.*

Here's some interesting facts that you may not know about light workers. Simply by being in our presence others tend to make higher choices. This is because the light we send out assists people in "pausing" creating an opportunity to connect to our light and then make a higher choice. This is because just being in our presence can raise a person's frequency. Remember me telling you about showing up at a store near closing time and talking to the clerk, and whatever was said between us and just being in my presence helped that woman to make the higher choice of not stealing. Spirit said that this is absolutely true.

My husband receives frequency upgrades and healings every time we sleep together because I radiate out so much light without even needing to ask for it… for I AM the light. It simply is my experience. There are strangers who walk up to me and ask me questions about their future or what choice they need to make that would be the most beneficial for them. If I didn't radiate out a certain frequency, how would they know they could ask ME—a stranger to them—these kinds of questions.

I once had the woman checking me in for an MRI get all excited because she got to be in my presence. I was so flustered I didn't even know what to say, and that is a real rarity for me. She had the ability to see my light just by being in my presence. In those moments, no words are necessary.

Another aspect of this is those who live in the shadows have a difficult time being in the presence of so much light. They tend to shy away from light workers because we make them feel uncomfortable.

So, get out there and shine your light. Be a beacon of hope for all who get to experience the light that you are.

Our Higher Self Emerges

When we call on our Higher Self, we start to create a relationship with the essence of who we are on the other side (in the heavenly realm). This relationship will start conversations that feel very different from other beings that you may channel or otherwise experience. Your Higher Self feels more comfortable and friendly and yet there is a deeper understanding that exists. This is because this IS you. Your Higher Self makes sense to you. Your Higher Self is going to present things in a way that resonates with you at your deepest core. Again, this happens because this IS YOU.

When this happens, EVERYTHING makes more sense. Things you have struggled with your entire life are finally understood. This is because you have access to more information. You see things from all perspectives, not just your own. You even see things from Spirit's perspective. When this happens, you will truly know on ALL levels that "All IS WELL." When I experience this, it feels like the course we are on and the destination we are heading towards are already known and we simply need to walk through it. The question is… how are you going to walk through it? Are you going to continually say, "I NEVER want to have another human lifetime." This is not higher thinking. Or are you going to be curious and notice everything that is presented to you? After all, to make decisions from a human perspective rather than a Higher Self perspective might not be a "higher" decision. You will know what you know when you know it.

I remember thinking multiple times that I must have an incredible sense of humor to have chosen such a course as my life. I have thought— wow, my Higher Self really has a lot of faith in me to believe I can handle so much in just one lifetime. This assisted me in having more faith in myself. I *HAVE* got this! I just choose to walk through it with my eyes wide open and saying things like—Now that was an interesting choice that they made. Or—Holy cow, I get to really multi-task today, don't I? All of this is because I notice so much from a broadened perspective. I see and understand that everyone is going through so much learning just as I am. This can create such empathy and patience which adds to the light that you are. *You will see it when you believe it.*

I see life without all of the attachments to the outcome and I choose to instead enjoy my moments, my journey. I do this with curiosity about the choices that I'm going to make today. I also have curiosity about the choices others are going to make today. I am curious as to why they made those choices. If they had another opportunity, would they make that same choice again? I am so curious about everything. This curiosity opens me up to so many amazing and interesting possibilities.

For instance… I really enjoy helping the homeless. As the weather becomes cooler in the fall, I start thinking about my annual sleeping bag donations and anything warm that I can provide to make someone who is already going through a very challenging time in their life, a little easier. This year Spirit showed up in such a strong and powerful way, reminding me of how very connected I am.

We were driving by a sporting goods store and Spirit asked me to please go inside and purchase some sleeping bags. As we headed towards the sleeping bags, an employee approached us and asked if there was anything he could help us with. I responded, "Absolutely." I explained that I needed sleeping bags for the homeless for the coldest weather possible at the lowest cost possible, so we could purchase more and therefore help more people.

He said to give him a minute and went into the back. We looked at all of the sleeping bags, and NONE of them were on sale. It's not like Spirit to ask me to do something like this and pay full price. Instead, when they make a request such as this, it usually means we will experience an incredible deal. Not only were the bags full price, but there was only one type of bag that was ok for zero degrees. Colorado winters can be brutal sometimes.

When the employee approached us again, he had good news. He was authorized to give us a huge discount on the zero-degree sleeping bag. We got 60 percent off. I was so excited that I asked him how many they had and how many we could buy. They had three in stock, so that is how many I purchased. I practically skipped all the way to the register. Spirit had me ask if any more items in the store were at a huge markdown that the homeless could use such as hats, gloves, and socks. He looked at his paperwork again and said he could give me these thick, warm hunting-type socks that were $10 a pair for $2 a pair. Again doing my happy dance, I asked him how many can we purchase. He said how many do you want? I didn't want to take all of his stock, so I settled for 20 pairs.

I was practically in tears as we got into our vehicle. I thanked my husband for letting me do this, especially since this is our first Christmas since retiring. Once we started driving away, Spirit asked if I was willing to help out some more. I asked Marsh if it was ok, and he agreed. They gave me the name of another store and off we went to find abundance after abundance to help our homeless friends that we have never met. The store that Spirit sent us to was an outlet-type store, so the price was already reduced. They had an additional 60 percent off winter coats, and we ended up getting seven of them. The original price of these coats was $180 each. We paid $28 after our military discount and a special discount the manager gave us. We got ten pairs of new boots, originally $110 a pair, for $17 a pair. I also got some more socks. Yes, this was one of those magical days when I was in my flow. I want you to think about a homeless person being handed a coat with a price tag of $180. I think it will help them to feel even more special and less like no one cares.

As a little footnote, the gentleman who assisted us in getting the sleeping bags and socks at such incredible savings let us know as we were checking out that he had been homeless for nine months. He truly understands how important these supplies can be for someone who is living on the streets. My heart was deeply touched by both his story and his generosity. Spirit said that it was so important to his growth and his own healing that I was able to show up in this way and assist him. It was important for him to remember how far he had come in such a short amount of time. We are all so blessed.

I have noticed that the more time that I spend on my devices, the less curious I am. My attitude changes and my frequency drops. I find I am filled with more doubt about myself and my fellow human becomings. When I put the devices away, I notice I become curious again. So, that makes me curious as to who is running who? Am I running my devices or are my devices running me? Take the time to notice for yourself what level your frequency is at before you turn on your devices and then evaluate your frequency again as you power off your device. Did your exploration assist your ascension, or did it create a de-scension? You may also want to notice if you make excuses if your frequency dropped. From here, you will know what adjustments you may want to make. That is, if your ascension is your priority. I ask myself, how do I want to spend this *lifetime*? And then I take action and follow through on that choice. It may take me a while to reconnect to my Higher Self, but she is always there waiting patiently as I go through one human evolution and understanding after another.

Just yesterday I woke after three hours of sleep with my Higher Self presenting a question to me. "Why are you not able to allow something to be more or something to be different?" Because it was my Higher Self presenting the question, I felt like I was floating inside the question. I know that sounds strange, but when you experience it, you will understand. When I have conversations with my Higher Self, it feels like there is no right or wrong answer, just innocence and curiosity.

I spent all of 30 seconds before saying, "Of course I am able to allow something to be more or different." The floatyness just disappeared when my righteousness appeared. To reconnect to the floatyness and a realm of allowing the absolute truth to be my truth, I allowed the words to wash over me again, and I saw the wisdom I was gaining from all that I allowed to unfold. Recently, I had been experiencing old family members rejecting me again. They were making their old choices and so I felt I "needed" to make my old choices. This was what my Higher Self was talking about my not allowing my response to be something different—something more. I was given a vision of me lugging around on my shoulders, back and head, one of my brothers and one of my sisters.

When I witnessed this, I realized that I didn't want to carry them around anymore. I realized as I witnessed the old patterns emerge again that I was exhausted carrying around these burdens called my siblings. It's time for me to let them go. They are big boys and girls and they can walk on their own. They don't need me to carry them around anymore. My carrying them does NOT serve me and it does NOT serve them. Suddenly I understood the gift of the question my Higher Self presented me with today.

As I cried with the freedom that I felt, I realized that not only was I *able* to allow them to be something more or different, I was also *willing* to allow that for myself. This was one of those moments when you truly understand and experience the *free will* that we are given. It is through my *willingness* to allow my experiences to be different that *free will* IS my experience. So, I placed my brother and sister back on the ground and allowed them to walk away and my burden was lifted.

Healing old family wounds and relationships can be some of our most challenging. However, when we allow them to be exactly as they are, we give ourselves permission to be exactly who we are—without all the old baggage. What greater gift can we give someone?

I would like you to notice that my Higher Self knows me better than anyone else—because she is me and I am her. Therefore, she knew that NOW was the perfect time to point out the old pattern that I had just walked into. She also knew that I was ready to allow the old dynamics to change into something different. I know that and trust that my Higher Self is always and in all ways working for my highest good. When I succeed— she succeeds. We are one and the same. Our goals, desires and wishes are the same… to learn and experience ALL from the highest place—from love and acceptance. *You will see it when you believe it.*

Start a dialogue with your Higher Self. Ask them to make their presence known to you. Let them know that you would like a more real and connected relationship with them. One where their wisdom is shared with you on a regular and connected basis. Then watch, wait and listen for what is presented to you. I began this when I noticed a sparkly presence when I closed my eyes. I spoke to it as my Higher Self. From there, our dialogue and our relationship became more present, and I am so very grateful. When I hear information in more of a whisper, I know that is my Higher Self talking.

Please give yourself permission to ask the questions that you were never brave enough to ask before. Ask the silly and ridiculous questions. Ask the questions that have always evaded you. Keep asking because that means that your curiosity is showing. When that happens, our innocence shows up and our connection to other realms and realities is unlocked. All we need to do then is to walk through that doorway. A doorway to new possibilities. A doorway to you living AS your Higher Self.

Clear a Space

When I explain how differently I see a person's space that they live in, most people are rather surprised. I'm going to ask you a bunch of questions to get you thinking about the space you live in, in a different way. What room is your giggle room? Take the time to notice what room you tend to laugh in the most. Look at how you can enhance that (if you want more laughter in your home). How I create this is, I have a picture of me bent over because I was laughing so hard. I have pictures of my husband and I smiling, laughing, and being silly. I have pictures of Happy times and things that assist in "making" me feel happy.

My walls are painted baby blue and yellow throughout the house. One creates calm, the other creates joy. What color are your walls painted? If you can't paint your walls because you rent, what do you have on your walls? Do you even bother putting anything on your walls or windows (as in curtains)? Does your energy even exist in your living space? I recently noticed that most of my furniture is the lean-back-and-put-your-feet-up type. When I have a formal visitor, I kinda giggle because they don't quite know how to be formal in my space.

Think back to the first time that you entered your home. What vibes did you get? Now go outside and enter your home like a visitor would. How do you think your home feels through their eyes? Is there a welcomed feeling? Does it feel sterile? Does it feel like no one lives there? Does it feel safe? What would you like people to experience when they enter your home?

Now look at the entrance that you come in from—like the garage or mud room. Is it cluttered? Do you feel all the "shoulds" as soon as you walk in—I should do the laundry; I should get dinner started; I should let the dog out. Try to broaden your perspective and see how you can shift the way the entrance into your home feels and make it into something more welcoming—again, if that's what you want to create. And please do let the dog out.

Think about the room where you do most of your work. If it's important to stay focused there, do you have too many distractions? If that isn't important to you, maybe you can make that space more playful, calming, or inspiring, whatever works for you so that you don't mind being in that space, and also so you will feel creative and inspired there. I remember having a slinky in my space. I used it to defuse the energy when I was getting too tense.

Try thinking about what your priorities are for each and every room and how *you* can connect to those priorities more easily. Ask your partner or roommates these same questions. Will having happy memories from your childhood help? Marsh has a Tin Man windchime in his computer space because *The Wizard of OZ* is his favorite movie. I got him a beautiful painting of a duck because ducks mean a lot to him. He has WW2 planes because he likes to fly virtual missions. Can you see how he has made his space… "his space?" Think about what you want to use a space for, then think about what connects you to that—you can shift so much by doing this. I have been in so many homes that feel like no one lives there. I find that very interesting, how about you?

I love soaking in the tub. Water is so important to me. I am an earth sign. Spirit says that water feeds the earth. My tub is my sanctuary. I have yellow walls because it feels like sunshine, I have crystals that I put in my bath water. I have a very large poster of Marianne Williamson's poem "Our Deepest Fear" so I can read it daily and remind myself that it's time to be powerful beyond measure. I have seashells to connect me to Hawaii where we were married and I delivered our daughter. I have a Pooh Bear sign that says "Be Happy Be You." I really love Pooh Bear's energy... simple and kind.

Look at what you surround yourself with. Is there too much of the past around you? Is it keeping you stuck in the past? Are you doing what is trendy and not what resonates with *you and your family*? Are you going for being neutral, or are you wanting to be more bold? Neither is right or wrong, I simply want you to create a space that supports the *new* you. One that encourages you to keep growing and allowing who you are to shine through.

Think about the colors you surround yourself with. Do they inspire you? Do they calm you? Do they put you to sleep? Do they assist you in feeling joyful? Again, think about what you want to create. Think about who you want to become and then create an environment that supports that.

I have a spiritual room; it looks like a little girl's room. My bedspread is full of color like small stained glass pieces. My walls are golden yellow, which is an ascension color, and my curtains are a sheer purple. I have butterflies draped across my valance. I have a huge metal sign with John Lennon's words "You may say I'm a dreamer, but I'm not the only one. I hope someday you'll join us. And the world will live as one" reminding me to stick with my dream of a new way of being and allowing others to join me in that dream.

I have butterflies and dragonflies all over the place, along with my angels. So much flying and twirling in this space. It's all about connecting to my joy, my innocence, and ascending. The little 3-year-old in me who is beyond amazing comes out to play in this space. Again, what I choose is very different from the norm. I'm allowing myself to embrace my ways of being different.

Now that you have gone through your home and gotten rid of what no longer resonates with you, painted some rooms to change the vibration of it, or maybe chosen to simplify everything, this is your space—this is the new you. Embrace, embrace, EMBRACE who you are, no need to hide it anymore. Now comes the time to bless your home. I do this with a chime. Most people use sage and some use water that has been blessed. I do the basement first, then I bless the main floor and move up to the top floor. This raises the vibration of your home upwards.

In the basement, because it's unfinished, I say things about allowing flow and peace to be a part of this space. Bless our furnace, water heater, pipes, and foundation. I thank them for all they do to make our lives better. I go outside and come in the front door. All who enter here are safe for me and my family, and assist others in feeling safe and welcomed. Allow whatever is needed to help all in the highest way to be a person's experience here. As I go into the living room, I ask that fantastic conversations happen here where hearts and minds are opened up in the most sacred, loving ways. Let there be joy, laughter and love in every moment (our living room is our giggle room).

As I move into the dining area, I ask that all who break bread here feel heard as they share their day and their life experiences with us. May the food bless and nourish our bodies in the highest way possible. As I enter the kitchen, I ask that the pantry always be full. May the food prepared here be filled with light, love, and nutrition which will assist in healing our bodies. Let the joy of creating be a part of each meal. Bring joyful conversations and new ways of looking at food into this incredible space.

Entering each bathroom, I ask that all may feel cleansed and purified here. May they release what they no longer need both down the toilet and down the drain, and allow it all to bless Mother Gaia in the most sacred way. Let all see the magnificence of who they are as they look in the mirror. Assist them in seeing the perfections instead of the perceived flaws. (Normally, I don't include what I don't want to create, but Spirit asked me to make an exception here). Remind yourself of how much flow exists here in the bathroom to encourage more flow in your life.

Each bedroom is blessed for the individual. For our room, I ask that honesty is part of every interaction. Kind and loving touches are who we are in this space. Allow us to connect to and remember how blessed we are to have each other, and to please not take that for granted. Let giggles and dreams of the future be shared here. May we find peace and enlightenment as we sleep. Allow Spirit to come in and inspire us. When we wake, I ask that we feel rested, connected and inspired to be of service in whatever way we can.

In the office, I ask for money to flow in and out of our finances, to remind us that abundance is who we are in all aspects of our lives. Allow what we need to know to show up on our computer screen or at our door. Communication with others comes from the highest place with complete honesty so that every interaction is a win for everyone concerned. All that goes out to the world is exactly what is needed to raise people's vibration in the highest way for all.

As you can see, I word things in a very loving and honest way because that is what I want my home to BE. Keep changing your space as you change and your needs change. Continually bless your space to keep the vibration as elevated as possible. Know that where you meditate and pray is the space with the highest vibration—use that knowledge to assist you in taking your spirituality and your connection to Source further. If you have a visitor that created some chaos or put out negative vibes, clear it out as soon as you can after they leave, by blessing your space with love and releasing the negativity. *You will see it when you believe it.*

Creating a space where you feel love, support, and creativity is so very important. Bless your car each time you drive it. Thank it for running so well and keeping you comfortable and safe wherever you go on your journey. Let your car know how grateful you are that you get to do your journey together with your car. What a wonderful team you make.

Play, explore, and expand any and all of this until you feel so safe, loved, and nurtured in ways you didn't even realize was possible. Bless objects that you bring into your space. Allow this to flow into your clothes also. Does your wardrobe still fit you both in style and in size? Does it show the world who you are at a glance? Does your wardrobe assist in making you invisible? Are you a black cloud? All these things are ok, if that's what you want to create. This is your lifetime. Own it! Take ownership of your space. Assist it in saying, "_____ LIVES HERE!"

All Is Transitioning

Every aspect of every aspect is going through a transition... an evolution. We ARE evolving. When you look out there at the old paradigm collapsing, you can feel overwhelmed. So much anger—so much hate. You may ask yourself, you may ask Spirit... how can this be our ascension? This feels more like our de-scension. There is so much division and separation. Connecting to oneness can feel like an illusion at times.

During these times we must connect to our knowing. Know that the anger and hate is the illusion. The separation is an illusion... or is it? There is a very great need for you to separate from ALL at times during your own evolution. Know that this separation can be very different from the separation and division going on out there. This separation has to do with taking time for yourself and taking care of yourself so that you can stay in your sovereignty rather than buying into the collective chaos that is dismantling the lower vibrational existence at this time. Isn't this interesting how the word "separation" can be a positive and a negative? This is an example of "it is and it isn't." Do you see that? Feel that?

When we experience the questioning and doubt of anything, it can be because we are ready to transition into something else... something more. This is so exciting. This happens when we allow ourselves to separate from others to explore who we have become and who we are becoming. Are you ready to become true Christ Consciousness (higher consciousness), or not quite yet? What does this transition feel like? How is it different from your other transitions? Again—look for the subtleties.

Notice how feeling the disconnection which is necessary for the dismantling of the old, feels like we failed. It can feel like we messed up somehow and lost our connection. This is part of the multitude of lies we buy into for a while. This is an essential part of our transition until you have evolved enough that you no longer fight this process. For how can we release the old and truly celebrate its leaving if we don't reconnect to the old stuff that we are about to transcend? Yes, there are other ways to do this, but if this is what you are experiencing, then this is your way for now. Embrace it. Embrace all that is presenting itself to you as your beautiful, sacred gift.

Eventually—as soon as you acknowledge that you are noticing a shift—it WILL shift. For when you live as Christed Consciousness, all is transcended and shifted so effortlessly. However, we are speaking of the time before this happens. We are speaking of the time of massive doubt and confusion. We are speaking of the questioning of the self. Do you realize on a whole other level that if you don't ask the questions, you do not receive the answers. Know that this is true EVEN when you question yourself and your purpose or existence.

We would like to enlighten you to the knowing that—IT IS ESSENTIAL that you question yourself and your existence. This is where you PARTICIPATE in your transition on a higher level. You WALK

THROUGH your old pain, patterns, beliefs, and understandings. You thank them for all of the lessons and understandings that they bestowed upon you. From there, you experience the gratitude for this new batch of lessons you are ready to experience and then move beyond them and release them as well.

Once you release on this higher level, you can only access this old energy by going into a past record, for it is no longer held within you the way it used to be. So many are pausing and having memory difficulty—this is good. This means that your present moment has become the priority. The past is NO LONGER what you focus on or even have access to sometimes. Reliving past traumas is not a priority anymore. Remembering how wrong others were in your past does not serve you... actually, it never did. We wanted... needed... others to see how wrong and bad they were so that we could keep "our victim" alive and thriving. This also created the separation of "I am so much better than they are." However, that way of "being," lowers your frequency.

Know that there are NO VICTIMS in higher consciousness. None at all. We move beyond such limitedness and move into limitlessness. Here all is love and all is loved. We know, understand and are grateful for all of the lessons we were able to receive from each and every experience. We are grateful to our family unit who supplied us with such a multitude of lessons. It is important to realize family can be our greatest teachers, for we learn so much from them and with them.

We understand the significance of their role in our transition and evolution to experience this moment of now with utter and complete gratitude. You are the amazing and magnificent you, because of the challenges they created for your growth. Are you seeing the experiences with family as learning opportunities, or do you FALL into a place of judgment again? I say "FALL" because we lower our frequency and "fall" into our old ROLE again as a victim, or just less.

The big transition happens when you notice this shift begin to take place and you start laughing. You realize, oh my gosh, I almost ALLOWED myself to buy into that old role again. Wow, I am so silly sometimes. Why would I choose being a victim over being an empowered being? I wouldn't—and I don't. End of statement.

In that moment, you realize how true that statement is, because you are the sum total of your choices. You are choosing a different way... a different role. Your new role as a compassionate, empowered being means that you no longer need to make the other person wrong and bad. They were simply playing their part in teaching you how to stand up for yourself. Think of it as if they were subconsciously asking you, are you going to be a victim today? Are you going to roleplay with me again?

When your answer becomes a NO, you realize what a huge step you have just taken in your own transition during your ascension. We are ALL celebrating with you. Well done!

Now you see why we need to separate ourselves from others to do our own processing, shifting and evolving. When we are ready to reconnect to the outer world, we are a very different person. Our centeredness, our connectiveness, is so strong that nothing "out there" can throw us off, and when this is our truth—our existence—we ARE adding to the light of the world rather than looking for validation. Do you see this? Can you feel this? *You WILL see it when you believe it.*

This is when you step into what you came here to do, on a much higher level. You need not know what it is that you are here to fulfill. For when you are full of light, you will fill others—as light. You walk, talk and exist AS LIGHT! Every encounter is transcending. You are assisting others in their own transcendence simply by being present in their presence. So this big ROLE you came here to be… starts with just being. Being what feels so right within you.

In your moments of being the light, all you want is to be one with all that appears on your path. This is the next transition that you get to participate in. This moment is all that matters. There is no place that you would rather be. There is no one that you would rather be with. This moment is absolute perfection. You are absolute perfection and you see absolute perfection in all that exists before you. This can be a person, nature, a situation… it matters not. All is perfection. *You will see it when you believe it.* You will know it, you will be it, you will see it—you are IT!

All is transitioning, and transitions can be messy. Many are fighting to hang onto the old way of being. They shall not win the fight. For the old way is gone—dead. Their cries of hate, anger and separation are their final battle cry. Show compassion as you watch the dismantling and destruction of the old crumble at their feet. Realize that there will be great loss as we experience great gain. And when more is unfolded for us, the realization is that nothing was really lost, it has simply gone through a transition.

We will witness the crumbling of businesses, families, jobs, schools, governments, money, food, health, climate, water… if you can name it, then you will see that ALL is going through transition. HOW CAN WE ASK FOR CHANGE AND THEN COMPLAIN WHEN CHANGE SHOWS UP? This is God's Divine Plan—not *your* divine plan. And yet, God's Divine Plan IS your Divine Plan. Again, "It is until it isn't." Allow all to unfold. For that is what transition is. Allow all to be as it is, as it goes through its own transition… its own TRANSCENDENCE. When we do, all is allowed to transcend more quickly and effortlessly.

Remember—what we resist, persists. Never have those words carried greater meaning than now. We needed others to allow US to experience our own way of transformation. Why would you *disrespect* another as they go through their own transformation? This is an individual AND a collective transition. Allow yourself to know when to step back and when to step forward. Both are important. Both are ESSENTIAL.

When another asks for help, please step up and help. When they need space to process, please allow that also. For we are here to assist with whatever shows up in our lives. This is to be an organic experience, rather than a manipulation or a push-and-shove experience. Listen to the guidance given to you from beyond the veils and trust it.

Show Spirit that you are very WILLING to do whatever is asked of you… whatever is needed of you. ALLOW it to be what it *is*—not what you *want it to be*. For our roles are not limited to one aspect. Remember we are moving into limitlessness. Know that YOU are the one who is limiting yourself and those who come on your path. That is until you learn, understand, and live as the enlightened being that you are.

I am grateful. We are grateful. All are grateful!

How to Lower Our Frequency

Yes, you heard us correctly, we are actually going to speak to you about lowering your frequency rather than raise it. Once our frequency elevates to the point that there will be things that we can not connect to or resonate with because it exists at such a lower vibration. We don't really even notice such things because they no longer exist in the reality that we participate in. However, if we would like to spend time there, we must lower our frequency. We do this by focusing our energy on whatever it is that we want to connect to and wait as our frequency lowers enough that we can even connect to it.

There are many people who still exist as such lower dimensional beings. They love to create conflict and chaos. They speak of all the things that they hate and hate some more. Some of these beings have barely a flicker of light within them. The distance between where their frequency exists and where my frequency exists can feel like light years away from each other. For me to be able to even concentrate on their words, I must lower my frequency to cover at least half of the distance our frequencies are separated by. If I want to, or am asked by Spirit to assist them in some other way, I must bring my frequency down even lower in order to connect to them, and assist.

When you do this lowering of frequency, know that it is temporary, and know that you may feel dizzy and possibly even nauseous. Being in such a lower vibration is something that we actually have to reacclimate ourselves to. It is a beautiful reminder of how far we have come AND that we no longer choose to exist as this anymore. When you remind every aspect of you that this is temporary, it does ease the side effects, however they may still exist.

Once you are able to hear, see and understand what this person wishes to share with you, you have lowered our frequency enough. If you can not quite understand or hear their words, you must lower your frequency further. This is the gauge you use to know how far you need to go. If you have been willing to lower your frequency to assist this person, then it would be beneficial to do it FULLY. Help in any and every way that you can or are willing to help. Be the light that you came here to be. If you become dizzy again, you either need to complete your time together, or you need to lower your frequency further. Know that this will feel strange and uncomfortable, but it is not impossible. When you are complete, send them off with as much love in your heart as you possibly can.

Again—once you are out of their presence, you may feel very off and dizzy. This is because it took more energy than you realize to hold both yourself and them in this same frequency.

Ready or not, here comes another twist. You know how you can talk to someone and you think that they aren't listening, and you get frustrated with them? Well, this is similar to what we are talking about here. Now yes, it might be true that they are not listening, but it might also be that you are both existing in totally different frequencies. So, they can't really hear you because the gap between you is too great. This can also have to do with the subject matter. If it is so elevated or different from where they are willing to go, they can't hear or understand the words. This happens a lot with husbands and wives, along with parents and children.

I have been experiencing this repeatedly with my stylists. I am on my 6th stylist in less that four years. These stylists practically can't see me sitting in their chair because my energy is so high that it can feel uncomfortable for them. My new stylist is finally a good fit, and we are both so comfortable with each other. Well, that may be a stretch. It takes awhile for anyone to get comfortable with me because I ask them to consider stretching themselves to be a higher version of themselves and many aren't ready... until they are. *They will see it when they are ready to believe it.*

All of this makes so much more sense to me when it is presented to me in this way. I feel tolerance and compassion showing up from this understanding. How about you?

Now it is time to raise our frequency back up. Pull out all the tools you have to assist in raising your vibration... music, meditation, a warm bath, reading, soothing words. Give yourself time to not have to do or be anything for a while. This could take a while in the beginning, but you will figure out what assists you the most. If this becomes too uncomfortable, please have a conversation with Spirit. Let them know that the gap between yourself and these lower dimensional beings has become so extreme and can they assist in raising the other person's vibration more or to stop bringing such lower dimensional beings on your path. Whatever it is that you are feeling, talk to Spirit about it with honesty. Know that it is not just PEOPLE that have this lower vibration—it can be a place or even an object. You must ask if this is for you. Are you the one that is to assist here?

All of this distance between you and another has to do with the separation that is occurring on the planet. Unfortunately, those who are not willing to raise in vibration will fall away. We will not be able to bridge the gap eventually because the gap will be too large. Until that time, we must acclimate to lowering our frequency so we can continue to assist. From there we will be given guidance.

I know that you could tell from the title of this chapter that it was not going to be a fun and uplifting chapter. However, I feel it is a very necessary and important chapter. Because of that, I am going to remind you of another "heavy" but important topic that occurs when we help others in this way… Spiritual fatigue. This comes from holding a higher frequency while others are not willing to do the same. It also happens when you are helping others all of the time and you are not fulfilling your own needs. You need to take time for yourself on a regular basis. Do things that fill you rather than deplete you. Get out and play, be silly and have fun whatever that looks like for you. No one knows you better than you. Remember, we can't assist others if we have nothing left to give. *You will see this when you believe it.*

You ARE Being Guided

Look at—notice—and understand that every single thing that is showing up in your life is teaching you—guiding you. Are you looking for a teacher? Are you willing to be guided? *You will see it when you believe it.* So much... so very much is showing up in your life to take you in a beneficial direction. Do you have your blinders on and your headset on? OR do you have your eyes wide open, ears perked up and heart accessible to ALL you are being given?

Yes, you are being *given* so much each and every day. However, if you are closed off by your unwillingness, beliefs, or even your distractions—all of these teachings and guidance will be lost. Lost to YOU and lost to ALL who you *would have* had the potential to help or assist on your path this day. Lost to stepping up and making a difference. Lost to the knowing of the magnificence of who you TRULY are. When you *know* the magnificence of who you are, you behave in a different way. Not as arrogance or ego— but as an ascended being—maybe even an Ascended MASTER. You have ascended living as ego. You have ascended living even as the self. For you encompass so much more. Constantly stepping up as more. Showing up as so much more than ever before.

Each day feels like a new beginning—a new opportunity to redefine the essence of you. Only to then let go of anything that is so limited as a definition. You are limitless. Your thoughts and understandings allow ALL to show up and guide you on your path of ascension. You will then notice and know that your path of ascension is the ascension of ALL. Again, we do not speak in limitations, so it is not just all people, but all that exists. All that exists is being shifted, transformed and transcended to the highest vibration that cosmic law will allow.

Make note that if we ascend too quickly, we would need to ascend out of body, for our bodies need to shift and then acclimate continually. Our bodies have been made for the shifting and changing of one cell at a time. There are a lot more cells and work that our body must go through to ascend. This work is done TO you and FOR you as your willingness to embrace all that you allow yourself to be.

Know that we humans are the ones limiting ourselves. Those out there in the "cosmos" are encouraging us by guiding us to think in a more in-LIGHTENED way. Exist in a more in-LIGHTENED way. This shows up as patterns and guidance for us. Because of this, noticing patterns in your life gives you clues as to what is showing up and you may want to do something about it by enhancing it or releasing it. We are blind to such things until we open our hearts and our eyes to see the AWE-someness that is unfolding around us. Just yesterday, my hubby Marsh and I arrived in New Mexico to experience an eclipse. I must admit that I had a bit of an agenda mixed with a curiosity about what is going to show up on our path. Thusly, things were not happening as smoothly as I had hoped.

We stopped for gas just inside New Mexico, and had the strangest gas station energy going on around us. As we pulled off the interstate, dozens and dozens of vehicles *followed* us, I kid you not. I had told Marsh that I wasn't comfortable with this first gas pump that we pulled up to. When Marsh got out to pump the gas, the credit card slot on the gas pump had a definite resistance as the card was partially inserted. Once Marsh felt the resistance, he felt off about it too, and got into the vehicle and took us to another gas station across the street.

Inside this new gas station, everything felt off and tilted, too. We used the bathroom and left. Nothing was to be purchased here. All was simply off. Not bad, not wrong, just not congruent with our own energy. Beside the station, there was an enormous fenced-in area with one person shrouded in blankets at a picnic table, as the high winds swirled dust around them and their luggage. I wanted to go read the sign on the fence because of my curiosity, but Spirit let both of us know that the answer was NO. This was none of our business.

We have been noticing and paying attention to the patterns and frequency around us for so long, that we don't question, we simply flow with our guidance. Later, as we entered our hotel in Albuquerque, a housekeeper was walking towards me. I smiled so radiantly at her as I thanked her for making such an important difference. She looked at me with such curiosity and then a smile. I saw an awakening happen within her—new opportunities. Once we got all of our luggage into the hotel, Marsh went to park the car and I checked us in.

I enjoyed my interaction with the woman checking us in. The more I radiated light toward her, the more messages she imparted to me. As I turned to see if Marsh was coming, I saw him outside through the window and he was radiating the energy of an adorable little boy on an adventure, with a huge smile on his face. And then I saw it... the housekeeper I had spoken to earlier was chasing her trashcan as the high winds blew it away from her.

As Marsh caught it, I imagined a superhero cape appear on his shoulders. He was laughing and smiling, and she was too. It was a very minor thing, but that doesn't mean it wasn't significant. I allow a broadened perspective to show up in all the situations that exist in our lives. I saw how if Marsh hadn't bothered to step up and assist, this trashcan could have caused damage to a vehicle. The trash could have gone everywhere because we were experiencing 50 mph winds. This trash could have blown into traffic and caused an accident. So, while it was just Marsh being the kind, observant "being" that he is, he made a difference. He had felt that he needed to move the vehicle right away rather than wait until we were settled in our room. Both of us just follow the slight nudges we are given.

Our very expensive room had a tub with a lot of rust in it. I was sad for about 20 minutes when I saw this. I love to soak in the tub. When I allowed the knowing that I live a guided life to be my experience, I felt the shift in me. I know there is a reason I will be taking a shower for the next three days, and I am grateful. This is not what I prefer, rather it is what is showing up as my experience. When I get out of my own way, so much guidance, so much everything shows up all around me. My guides are willing to assist me and all I encounter in the highest way. I am truly blessed.

Watching the eclipse in New Mexico.

As we were heading home after the eclipse, I saw the name of a town on a road sign light up. I informed Marsh that this is where we need to stop and have lunch. As I took my first bite of my fast food, something felt off. I took a second bite and that was it, I was done. I ended up filling up with French fries because my sandwich was bizarre tasting.

As we drove through the mountains, I became sicker until we finally arrived in a town somewhere in southern Colorado. I was finally able to use the restroom as I lost my lunch. When I came out of the restroom, so many things lit up. Certain crackers in the store lit up to help calm my stomach along with popcorn, a reliable tummy aid for me. I noticed Sprite lit up as what I needed to drink first and then water. Then I noticed the clerk lit up so we had a quick life-altering conversation. Like I said, a lot of things lit up. I paid attention to all of them.

Further down the road, we noticed there was no southbound traffic, and soon our side of the interstate was directed off onto side streets on the edge of a town. We found out later that a railroad bridge had collapsed after a train derailment, spilling cars and coal over all four lanes of traffic and crushing a tractor-trailer. We tried to follow the line of traffic and our

GPS to work our way around whatever was up ahead on the interstate, but the only two side roads paralleling the interstate were blocked by police.

We finally got turned around and headed into town looking for a hotel. We found several on the north edge of town and one lit up for me. I told Marsh that we needed to spend the night here because I was now experiencing diarrhea from my food poisoning. As we settled in at the hotel and watched the news of the crash, Marsh and I both knew with every fiber of our being that this food poisoning was our Guardian Angels keeping us safe. Our guided lives were showing up in such a divine way.

No wonder why we had spent so much time at that gas station. There were so many things that lit up there to get us to spend more time. All of this was done to keep us safe. We just kept looking at each other and shaking our heads in wonder and awe. Thank you, God—thank you.

Have I told you how much I love my divinely guided life? Well, I do! My life is guided because I truly believe in my guidance. *I see it because I believe it.* Our entire trip had been so off and strange almost like we were simply reacting to all of the strangeness that showed up for us. We flowed through it as magnificently as we could because that is who we are and that is what we do.

Start noticing on an even more subtle level what is showing up and unfolding for you. The clues can be so very minute. You barely notice their existence—until you do. *We will see it when we believe it.* When Marsh and I leave home on an outing, we can sometimes turn around and go back home several times before finally getting on our way. This is because we get a feeling and have an understanding, which means we are going to follow through on them. Every time that we do this, we show Spirit that we are paying attention to the clues and information that we are being given. As we do this—more clues and more information show up. In fact, a couple of months ago I had this different type of "feeling lost" show up for me. I was not understanding why this felt so very different to me. Eventually, clarity came in and I had a good laugh. I was experiencing feeling lost because my level of connection to Spirit had increased to the point that I no longer was living as Mary Beth, so much as I was now living more as Spirit. My humanness was fading.

This has happened many times to me in this lifetime as I continue to LEVEL UP and evolve in my ascension. And each time, there is a bit of an adjustment that I go through to integrate this new experience of myself. If I fail to integrate, then I may not necessarily keep this leveling up as a permanent aspect of who I am. It is important to understand this on as deep of a level as you can. For this will assist you from needing to repeat a lesson or learning multiple times before you integrate it and it becomes who you are. *Again—you will see it when you believe it.*

Notice the patterns that are showing up for you, what are they trying to teach you? Are you willing to notice the message that they hold for you? Are you willing to allow yourself to shift and change because of these messages and the guidance they are giving you? Are you willing to be a higher version of yourself? Realize that every obstacle is a guidance. Every challenge is a guidance. Every opportunity is guidance showing up and asking—ARE YOU READY TO BE MORE?

By now you will notice that we continually speak of becoming one with Spirit, being who we are on the other side of the veils, and existing as our Higher Self. This is because these are all one and the same, and this is a very, very important aspect of our ascension. This IS our ascension. Because of this, we want to… need to approach the understanding of this from as many different perspectives as possible. That way you may find the ways to complete this part of your ascension with as much grace and ease as possible.

Spirit is trying to set you up for success here. *You will see it, when you believe it.* They are presenting you with as many tools as possible in this book, along with different approaches so that you will find the ones that feel most congruent with who you are and who you are becoming. We do not repeat what has been said before, to fill pages. NO. We repeat what has been said before to awaken the soul again and again so that you are able to STAY awake rather than fall back asleep. Which is what we continually do as we work (or play) on our path of ascension.

Know that each of you will resonate with DIFFERENT thoughts, words or ideas. So ALL must be presented in multiple ways and from different approaches. This is not because we think that you are dense and cannot get this. Not at all. This is because we love you so very much and we choose to set each and every one of you up for success. For when you succeed, all of humankind succeeds, and our planet succeeds.

What is unfolding on this planet is no small or insignificant thing. This is why so many millions and billions of beings are working on the other side to assist. Always *assisting*—NOT doing it for us. For this is OUR journey. This is OUR evolution. This is OUR ascension. Who better to do this, than OURSELVES? For when one of us is successful in our own ascension, the vibrational frequency increases and we all evolve—we ALL succeed. Hallelujah!

So we do not apologize for repeating ourselves, we are simply explaining why we repeat ourselves. We do it because we love you. We do it because when you evolve, we all evolve, our souls evolve and the universe evolves. Win, win, win, WIN! We all Win.

All is Well

When life feels challenging or even just less than perfect, this is when changing your thoughts, words, and beliefs changes everything. When I notice the obstacles that are keeping me from experiencing peace, all I need to do to shift that, is saying the words—All is well. I then notice that I feel a calm come over me. I have an understanding that everything out there is going to be what it is going to be... I don't have control over that. However, what is happening within my heart and within my mind is what I am encouraging to be—peaceful and calm with the words "All is well."

I ask myself, am I encouraging my thoughts and beliefs to be filled with kindness towards myself and others? Am I encouraging fear or hate? Am I giving others permission to dictate who I am and what I believe? Am I living as love or hate? Joy or fear? Do I BELIEVE I deserve love? Do I BELIEVE I deserve compassion? Do I BELIEVE I deserve abundance? If I DON'T believe I deserve all of these positive and amazing things in my life, why would I be surprised when they don't show up? *I will see it when I believe it.* I am the sum total of all of my parts. If I believe I deserve to have good things happen to me, then I have the answer as to why my life looks and feels the way that it does. Again, *you will see it when you believe it.* How you shift your life to be the highest expression of who you are is by believing that you deserve to be happy. You deserve to surround yourself with people who are kind to you. You deserve abundance in all forms. Abundance of opportunities, abundance of happiness, abundance of money, abundance of JOY.

Until you commit to *the knowing* that you deserve more FROM yourself and FOR yourself as you notice what you allow your life to be, nothing can change. For change comes from within, not from without. Commit to your own happiness and happiness will be who you are. In those moments when happiness evades you, saying a phrase such as "All is well" can re-center you... calm you. This creates a pause, during which time you can find the blessing in your challenge. Can you feel that shift within you?

My three favorite go-to phrases to re-center myself during my questioning times are:

- All is well
- I've got this
- It is what it is

All three of these calm me. I let go of doubt. I let go of the fear. I let go of my agendas. This creates an opportunity to see things from a different perspective. I am able to remember that all the drama out there does not serve me. I serve me. Am I serving myself in the highest way?

I am in charge of my life. I decide what I will allow and what I won't. When I give that power to someone else, I disempower myself. Know that

YOU are the highest authority on you in human form. YOU decide what you believe in, who you believe in and why you believe what you believe.

It is time to let go of the beliefs that do not serve your highest good. It is time to believe that what you *think, feel and are*, matters. It matters so much more than you realize. You Matter. The choices you make matter. Who you choose to be matters. How you show up matters.

Every time something shows up in our life, we have an opportunity to accept it or reject it. That choice is ours. Are you listening to your ego more than your Higher Self? Is your ego giving you one excuse after another as to why you CAN'T—why you WON'T—and why you DON'T? Know that excuses serve the ego—they do not serve the soul. When we show up as our spiritual selves, those excuses diminish and eventually disappear. How many excuses do you make each day?

Our minds think—our Soul feels. How are you feeling? Know that this lifetime was not meant to be easy for any of us. However, the rewards are astronomical!

Are you noticing that you are trying to take the easy route in life rather than the route of the highest integrity? Is that who you want to be? What is your soul learning from the choices you are making? Remember, we came here as a human being so that our soul could experience and learn. Ask yourself, do you think that your soul rejoices when you get away with something and someone else loses out, or even when you take the easy route? Take a moment to ask your Soul what it would like you to understand in this lifetime. My soul said it wants me to understand and experience self-love. Authentic, incredible self-love. Can I do that? Am I willing to do that? What is your soul asking for?

Who are you willing to show up as today—your human or your spiritual self? The choice is yours. No more excuses, no more wavering, no more waiting until everything is in alignment. YOU *ARE* THE ALIGNMENT you are waiting for! The time is NOW. YOU are the answer to your prayer. It matters not what your prayer is… you are the answer.

The answer to all questions is within you. In fact, the only reason why you continue to question anything is because you believe the doubt within you, more than you believe the truth. You believe in something or someone outside of yourself more than you believe in YOU. Please note that questioning something is totally different from asking questions *about* something.

The time to lovingly release any beliefs that lower your frequency is at hand. Allowing is the key here. You already exist as a higher vibrational being on the other side of the veils. As you allow yourself to remember this, the veils fall away. As we allow the old ways of existing to fall away without fear or resistance, more veils are released. As we allow creativity, wonder and awe to be how we see all that is around us, poof, more veils vanish. Soon we are standing in the truth of who we are, and in that moment, NOTHING will ever be the same again. For we are no longer veiled. It is the lies that shield us from the truth.

Eventually, why, why, why doesn't matter. All simply is as it is. We no longer need things to be different. This is because the lies have been exposed about who you doubted you were and you live as the truth of who you are. EVERY single thing is perfect because it aligns with what you believe. *You see it because you believe it.* When you exist as this—All is well because you believe and know that ALL IS WELL.

It Is Done—And So It Is

As we come to the end of this book, I reflect on all I hoped it would be and all that it actually ended up being, and I am grateful. I have learned so much and I hope that you have also. Hopefully, you are a little less concerned about all that is unfolding out there as the old way of existing crumbles. Maybe you see more possibilities and potential rather than fear and doubt. I like to stand back with anything and everything that shows up in my life and ask is this filled with love or fear?

To me, it is that simple—love or fear. When I reflect on all of the things that brought such fear to me in the past, I realize that I have shifted and changed so very much that now all I feel is love and compassion. I have been brave enough to take responsibility for ALL that shows up in my life. No more blaming others. Why would I want to give someone else that power over my life and responsibility to do the right thing with my life? God gave them their life to do as they see fit. I stand here in my sovereignty cheering them on. However, I give my life over to no one. God gave me this lifetime to see what I would do with it. I am grateful for the trust this invokes and I am doing all I can to make a difference in the light.

What I have chosen to do with my life is to show up where I am needed. To say the words that a person needs to hear by following my guidance from Spirit. To be the light in a time of many challenges. To bring hope to the hopeless, joy to the hopeful, and peace to the soul that is ready to try something new, but doesn't know how. Hopefully, this book helped you see what you couldn't see before, understand all that made no sense, and trust that "we've got this."

If one person can make such a huge difference, what can two people do, a hundred people do, a million people do? Perhaps this is the true meaning of one in a million. This planet is so ready to be something very different than what it has been. The question is, are the people on this planet ready to be transformed? Are you ready to transcend the old and begin living a—new? A new way of thinking, a new way of believing, a new way of thriving?

If so, please join me and so many others as we let go of all that we believed ourselves to be. As we step into our new roles as superheroes. It is no accident that superhero movies are so popular. The only problem is that so many are waiting for a superhero to come in and save us, when the truth is that we are the superhero and we are here to save ourselves.

Spirit is standing by. Watching and waiting for you to invite them in to assist you. Are you ready to do that? Are you ready to save yourself from hate and fear, by living in the light? Being the light? Are you ready to step into your new life each day as the highest version of yourself that you can be? Are you ready to let go of being a victim where everyone does stuff TO YOU, and instead realize that all is being done FOR YOU. See how easily it all shifts when you see yourself as brave and strong?

Recently, Spirit was telling me how very brave I was. I thought that they were being so silly. Then they showed me how I was willing to start my own successful daycare business even though I was afraid. That was very brave of me. How I was willing to face cancer when it showed up in my life. I told them I didn't always feel brave during those times. They said, "And yet you were. You showed resilience and strength to the other patients and the staff. You taught them how to laugh and to learn from their own experiences."

They showed me how brave I was to bare my life and my soul in my first book, *The Lie That I Am, A Journey Back to Spirit,* knowing there could be disconnected people who would doubt and criticize. Then I was brave enough to publish book number two, *With a Promise of Ascension,* where I was going to say things that some may not be comfortable with. However, the needs of the many outweigh the discomfort that may arise from those who simply aren't ready to be something different, something more… yet.

Here we go again in this book number three. Taking everything further to help enhance all that has come before. And this is only the beginning. I no longer feel brave writing what is asked of me, I feel honored. I can't imagine doing anything else. Each day I look forward to touching lives— including my own. For without my willingness, I would still be stuck, alone, having a pity party about all that everyone did to me. Yuck! No, thank you.

I, Mary Beth Smith, am an amazing, empowered, loving, compassionate human becoming. I look forward to every moment I get to spend with myself and with others. I love seeing the difference that my choices make. I love noticing the unique way I look at things and approach all that shows up in my life. I love being ME! I am so grateful for this life that I have been given, and the choices I have made along the way.

I thank you for taking the time to read what Spirit wanted to share with you. I hope that their/our words were able to assist you in a multitude of ways. I look forward to hearing about all that has shifted and changed for you because of your own willingness to allow yourself to be something beyond your most fantastic imaginings.

The time is NOW to show the world who you truly are and who you came here to be.

And so it begins.

Remember this,

LOVE is an option

KINDNESS is an option

PEACE is an option

Choosing a different way of BEING

is an option

You shall *BE IT*

When you Believe it

—God, Source, All That Is—

About Mary Beth Smith

I, Mary Beth Smith, am a channeler, intuitive, empath, baby whisperer, author, wife, mom, and a really nice person! Touching lives brings me joy above all things. Spending time with my hubby of more than three decades is sacred to me. Watching my daughter learn and grow from everything she encounters as an adult is fascinating. All is well.

My Favorite activities are going out to dinner, going for walks with joy in my heart, and watching movies that inspire me. I also look forward to Spirit waking me up in the middle of the night with a new chapter for us to write together. What an amazing gift my life is! I hope that you enjoyed this book given to you by my Angels and Guides.

Contact Mary Beth through the following venues:

Website: https://marybethsdifferentperspective.com
YouTube: www.youtube.com/@marybethsdifferentperspective

Other books by this author:

The Lie That I Am, A Journey Back to Spirit

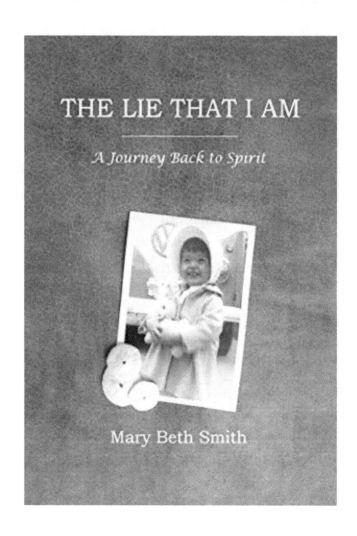

THE LIE THAT I AM

A Journey Back to Spirit

Mary Beth Smith

What if… what we were told as children about ourselves, was a lie?

What if… we then looked around for proof to support these lies?

What if… we took those lies on as our belief of who we are still today?

No matter what lies you may have believed because of the family dynamics you were born into, all those lies that have so deeply impacted your life can be unraveled until you can move beyond them to live instead from a place of peace.

This book takes you on the journey of my life. A life filled with doubt, pain, depression, suicide, sexual abuse, obesity, illness and almost dying. As I learned to connect to Spirit more and more, Spirit connected with me. Together we transcended the lies I believed, into the truths of who I have become.

It's time to stop believing our lies, and start living our truths.

With a PROMISE of ASCENSION

My Angels and Guides will take you through what the experience of Ascension looks and feels like as you evolve to a higher frequency of existence.

Leave behind all the old density and duality as you embark on a journey of becoming more: more connection, more clarity, more gifted abilities, and more of who you came here to be.

NOW is the time to expand your understanding of the world and your place in it. Step up and be the highest version of yourself.

Printed in the USA
CPSIA information can be obtained
at www.ICGtesting.com
JSHW011143300724
67147JS00006B/29